ALSO BY DAVID BROOKS

*Bobos in Paradise: The New Upper Class and How
They Got There*

On Paradise

Simon & Schuster

NEW YORK · LONDON · TORONTO · SYDNEY

Drive

How We Live Now
(And Always Have)
in the Future Tense

David Brooks

SIMON & SCHUSTER
Rockefeller Center
1230 Avenue of the Americas
New York, NY 10020

SIMON & SCHUSTER and colophon are registered trademarks
of Simon & Schuster, Inc.

For information about special discounts for bulk purchases,
please contact Simon & Schuster Special Sales at 1-800-456-6798
or business@simonandschuster.com

Designed by Paul Dippolito

Manufactured in the United States of America

1   3   5   7   9   10   8   6   4   2

Library of Congress Cataloging-in-Publication Data

Brooks, David
On paradise drive: how we live now (and always have)
in the future tense / David Brooks.
p.   cm.
Includes bibliographical references and index.
1. National characteristics, American. 2. United States—Civilization. 3. Social
psychology—United States. I. Title.
E169.1.B79826 2004
305.8'00973—dc22   2004042956

ISBN 0-7432-2738-7

To Joshua, Naomi, and Aaron

Contents

On Paradise Drive

The Great Dispersal

LET'S TAKE A DRIVE.

Let's start downtown in one of those urban bohemian neighborhoods, and then let's drive through the inner-ring suburbs and on to the outer suburbs and the exurbs and the small towns and beyond. Let's take a glimpse at how Americans really live at the start of the twenty-first century in their everyday, ordinary lives.

As we go, we'll find some patterns that are intriguing but probably not that important. For example, did you know that 28 percent of Americans consider themselves attractive (a figure I consider slightly high) but only 11 percent of Americans consider themselves sexy? Did you know that 39 percent of eleven- and twelve-year-olds say that Chinese food is their favorite food, while only 9 percent say American food is? Did you know that a quarter of all women have considered breast-augmentation surgery, which is kind of depressing, and so have 3 percent of all men, which is horrifying.

But we'll find other patterns that are probably more important. For one thing, we are living in the age of the great dispersal. As Witold Rybczynski has observed, the American population continues to decentralize faster than any other society in history. In 1950 only 23 percent of Americans lived in suburbia, but now most do, and today's suburbs are sprawling out faster and faster and farther and farther, so in the past few years, many exurban places have broken free from the gravitational pull of the cities and now float in a new space far beyond them.

Americans are still moving from the Northeast and the Midwest down to the South and the Southwest. But the really interesting movements are outward from cities. The people who were in move out, and the people who were out move farther out, into the suburbs of suburbia. For example, the population of metropolitan Pittsburgh declined by 8 percent over the past two decades, but as people moved away, the amount of developed land in the Pittsburgh area increased by 43 percent. The city of Atlanta saw its population grow by twenty-three thousand over the last decade, but the surrounding suburbs grew by 1.1 million.

The geography of work has been turned upside down. Jobs used to be concentrated downtown, in office buildings, stores, and urban-manufacturing zones. But 90 percent of the office space built in America in the 1990s was built in suburbia, and most of it in far-flung office parks along the interstates. The sprawling suburbs now account for more office space than the inner cities in every metro area in the country except Chicago and New York. In the Bay Area, for example, there are five times more companies headquartered in Santa Clara County than in San Francisco.

That means we have a huge mass of people who not only don't live in the cities, they don't commute to the cities, go to movies in the cities, eat in the cities, or have any significant contact with urban life. They are neither rural, nor urban, nor residents of a bedroom community. They are charting a new way of living.

These new places are huge, and hugely attractive to millions of people. The fastest-growing big counties in America—such as Douglas County, Colorado (between Denver and Colorado Springs), and Loudoun County, Virginia (near Dulles Airport)—are doubling and tripling in size every decade or so. A vast suburb such as Mesa, Arizona, now contains more people than Minneapolis, St. Louis, or Cincinnati and will soon pass Atlanta.

It's as if Zeus came down and started plopping vast towns in the middle of the farmland and the desert overnight. Boom! A master planned community! Boom! A big-box mall! Boom! A rec center, pool, and four thousand soccer fields! The food courts come first, and the people follow. How many times in human history have two-hundred-thousand- or five-hundred-thousand-person communities materialized out of practically nothing in the space of a few years? What sorts of institutions get born there, and what sorts of people emerge?

This suburban supernova subtly affects every place in America. The cities and inner-ring suburbs are affected because only certain kinds of people get left behind. Quite often the people who stay are either the very poor, because they can't afford to move; or the very rich, because they can afford to stay and live well in upscale enclaves. In the exploding exurbs, there are no centers, no recognizable borders and boundaries, and few of the conventional geographic forms—such as towns, villages, and squares—that people in older places take for granted. Up till now in human history, people have lived around some definable place—a tribal ring, an oasis, a river junction, a port, a town square. You could identify a certain personality type with a certain place. There was a New York personality, an L.A. personality. But in exurbia, each individual has his or her own polycentric nodes—the school, the church, the subdevelopment, the office park—and the relationship between those institutions is altered.

People have a different sense of place. They don't perceive where they live as a destination, merely as a dot on the flowing plane of multidirectional movement. Life is different in ways large and small. When the New Jersey Devils won the Stanley Cup championship, they had their victory parade in a parking lot, because no downtown street was home to all the people who love the team.

Virginia Tech demographer Robert Lang compares this new exurban form to the dark matter in the universe: stuff that is very hard to see or define but somehow accounts for more mass than all the planets, stars, and moons put together.

Making Sense of Our Reality

When it comes to suburbia, our imaginations are motionless. Many of us still live with the suburban stereotypes established by the first wave of critics. Yet there are no people so conformist as those who fault the supposed conformity of the suburbs. From *The Organization Man* to *Peyton Place* to *The Stepford Wives* to *American Beauty* to the vast literature on suburban sprawl, generation after generation of American writers and storytellers have paraded out the same clichés of suburban life. Suburbs are either boring and artificial, or else they are superficially boring and artificial but secretly sick and psychotic. If you were to judge by the literature of the past century, nobody is happy in suburbia.

But driving through the suburbs, one sees the most amazing things: lesbian dentists, Iranian McMansions, Korean megachurches, nuclear-free-zone subdevelopments, Orthodox shtetls with Hasidic families walking past strip malls on their way to Saturday-morning shul.

At some point in the past decade, the suburbs went quietly berserk. As if under the influence of some bizarre form of radiation, everything got huge. The cars got huge, so heads don't even spin when a mountainous Hummer comes rolling down the street. The houses got huge. The drinks at 7-Eleven got huge, as did the fry containers at McDonald's. The stores turned into massive, sprawling category-killer megaboxes with their own climatic zones. Suburbia is no longer the land of ticky-tacky boxes on a hillside where everything looks the same. It's the land of the gargantuoids.

One quickly sees that suburbia no longer hews to the stereotypes. We think of suburbs as places where families move to raise kids. But in fact, married couples with children make up only 27 percent of suburban households, according to the 2000 census. Today the suburbs contain more people living alone than families with kids. We think of the suburbs as white, but almost 60 percent of Asians, half of all Hispanics, and 40 percent of African-Americans live in the suburbs. We think of the suburbs as middle-class, but 46 percent of all people living under the poverty line reside in the suburbs.

One sees tremendous economic, technological, and social revolutions. We've already lived through one economic revolution that was largely a suburban phenomenon. According to Joel Kotkin, the author of *The New Geography*, by 1992 only a third of computer-industry employment was in cities, a figure that must have plummeted since. There will be other office-park revolutions—in robotics, biotech, military hardware, nanotechnology, and so on. How do these bland-seeming places produce so much change, and how will they manage it? What happens when people acculturated in these sprawling suburban zones are given the power—through the biotech firms they are now starting amid the Fuddruckers—to remake human nature? What values will guide them then?

For centuries we've read novels about young people who come to the city looking for opportunity and adventure. For centuries we've romanticized and demonized rural and urban life, built mythologies of lonely pioneers and city gangsters. What happens to storytelling when we all realize that suburbia is not just derivative of those two places but actually dominates them? What happens when we realize that suburban culture has quietly deepened over the past few decades and become more dense and more interesting?

This simple fact is that Americans move around more than any other people on earth. In any given year, 16 percent of Americans move, compared with about 4 percent of the Dutch and Germans, 8 percent of the Brits, and about

3 percent of the Thais. According to the Census Bureau's Current Population Survey, only a quarter of American teenagers expect to live in their hometowns as adults, which reflects a truly radical frame of mind. Today, as always, Americans move so much and so feverishly that they change the landscape of reality more quickly than we can adjust our mental categories.

Cultural Zones

When we take this drive, we won't have to go far to see different sorts of people. Human beings are really good at finding others like themselves, so one comes across distinct cultural zones; and the people in one community sometimes know very little about the people in the community just up the road. Despite the recent popularity of aging in place, senior citizens are still moving in large numbers to a certain number of sun-drenched communities around Naples, Florida; Myrtle Beach, South Carolina; Las Vegas; and Las Cruces, New Mexico. Affluent African-Americans are moving to suburbs around cities like Atlanta, Orlando, Norfolk, and Charlotte. Highly educated white Americans are moving to developments around medium-sized cities in the Northeast and Pacific Northwest.

The late U.P.I. columnist James Chapin observed that in the information age, every place becomes more like itself. People are less likely to be tied down because their job requires them to be near certain natural resources—oil or coal deposits, fertile soil or a harbor. Today's economy relies more on human capital, which can be grouped anywhere you can put up an office building. Thus, people's relocation decisions can be based more on cultural affinity than economic necessity. People who conscientiously recycle their brown and green glass herd together in Madison, Wisconsin. They might know more about what happens in Boston or Berkeley than they do about a small Wisconsin town thirty miles up the road. Tractor-pulling people might live in, say, Waynesboro, Pennsylvania. The political joke about Pennsylvania is that it's got Pittsburgh on one end, Philadelphia on the other and Alabama in the middle. People in the more conservative parts of Pennsylvania probably have more in common with small-town folk in Tennessee and Texas than they do with their fellow Pennsylvanians near the big cities.

Far from bringing homogeneity, the age of job mobility and targeted media has brought segmentation. All sorts of perplexities emerge. Why is it that Kansas, Rhode Island, and Tennessee lead the nation in oatmeal consumption? Why is it that the number of married-with-children families declined by 16 percent in West Virginia during the 1990s but increased by 29 percent in Arizona? Why is it that hundreds of thousands of whites flee from Los Angeles and New York every decade, even as the country becomes slightly more racially integrated overall?

After the 2000 election, political analysts became obsessed by the divisions between Red America, the heartland counties that supported Bush; and Blue America, the coastal and Mississippi Valley counties that supported Gore. I came to think of it as the global-warming divide, because if the polar ice caps do melt and flood the places near water, the Democratic Party will be basically wiped out.

But there are many other ways to grapple with the new geography. The demographer William H. Frey argues that there are three Americas. First there is the new sunbelt: the fast-growing suburbs in places such as Nevada, Georgia, and Colorado. This region attracts huge population inflows (only 24 percent of the people who live in Nevada were born there, compared to 78 percent of the people who live in Pennsylvania). It has high percentages of intact two-parent families. There are only ten states that gained such families during the 1990s. Nine of them are in the new sunbelt.

Then, Frey says, there are the melting-pot states, such as California, Texas, Florida, New York, and Illinois. These states are growing because of new immigration. They are home to three-quarters of the nation's Hispanic and Asian populations.

Finally, there is the heartland, consisting of the remaining twenty-eight states, including New England, Pennsylvania, Ohio and Indiana, and the upper Midwest. This is the overwhelmingly white, slow-growing part of the country. Since young people have, by and large, been moving out of these places, aging baby boomers make up an especially large share of their populations.

Meanwhile, market researchers at firms such as Claritas and Yankelovich devise other categories for the new American divides. Claritas breaks Americans down into sixty-two psychodemographic clusters. If you are a member of the Boomtown Single cluster, you are likely to live in towns like Beaverton, Oregon, or Ann Arbor, Michigan; earn about $32,000 a year; enjoy roller-skating and Comedy Central; and drive a Toyota MR2 or a Mazda MX-6. If you are a member of the Shotguns and Pickups demographic, you probably also earn about $32,000 a year, but you live in places like Dallas, Georgia, and Hager City, Wisconsin; you enjoy chewing tobacco, tractor pulls, Diet

Rite cola, and *Family Feud;* and you drive a Dodge or Chevy pickup.

As one thinks about these and the many other categories used to explain the diversity of America, one begins to realize that whatever else has changed about Americans, we have not lost our talent for denominationalism. As early as the eighteenth century, visitors to the New World were dazzled by the explosion of religious denominations, sects, and movements. They quickly sensed that the tendency to split and multiply was made possible by space and wealth. Americans had the room and the money to move away and found new churches and new communities that they felt suited their individual needs. Since everybody was so spread out, no central authority could hope to impose uniformity. That spirit survives today, in both religious and secular ways. America is without question the most religiously diverse nation on earth. In a 1996 study, J. Gordon Melton, director of the Institute for the Study of American Religion, counted 32 Lutheran denominations, 36 Methodist, 37 Episcopal, and 241 Pentecostal—just among the Protestants. And this tendency has replicated itself in the secular spheres of life: Americans go shopping for the neighborhoods, interest groups, and lifestyles that best suit their life missions and dreams.

As we take our drive, it will become obvious you don't have to go far to see radically different sorts of people. How do all these different sorts of people regard one another? Where does each group fit into the social structure, and what sort of social structure can possibly accommodate such a flowering of types? Further: Does it make sense to say that all these individuals with varying values and tastes cohere to form one people? If so, how does being

American shape our personalities, and how will this suburban civilization, with its awesome military and economic power, seek to shape the future of the world?

I will try to do three related things in this book. First, I will describe what life is really like in today's middle- and upper-middle-class suburbs. For the most part, I won't describe what life is like for poor people or rich people (those are fascinating subjects for another day). I'm mostly after the moderately affluent strivers, the people who hover over their children, renovate their homes, climb the ladder toward success, and plan anxiously for their retirement.

Second, I will try to solve the mystery of motivation. I will try to explain why Americans move to new places so avidly and work so feverishly and cram their lives so full once they get there. I will try to explain what it is about being American that drives us so hard to relentlessly move and labor and change.

And third, I'll try to answer the question: Are we as shallow as we look? Americans do not, at first glance, look like the most profound, contemplative, or heroic people on earth. You could look around and get the impression that we are moral mediocrities, concerned only about our narrow concerns and material well-being. But toward the end of this book, I will probe to see if down beneath the surface activities of everyday life, there is a grand, complicated, and deeply American idealism that inspires not only shallow strivings but also noble ones.

In the first part of the book—Chapters 1 and 2—we will take this long-promised drive and sample some of the ways Americans live now. In the second part—Chapters 3 and 4—I will summarize two long-standing views of America. One set of observers has argued that this country, especially its suburban parts, is indeed shallow and materialistic. Another set has argued that deep inside middle Americans is a spiritual impulse that is quite impressive and profound. People who hold this less secular view tend to be unspecific about it, but they sense that Americans, even suburban middle-class Americans, aren't motivated primarily by grubby bourgeois ambitions but by a set of moral yearnings and visionary dreams that they can't explain even to themselves.

With these two competing views in our heads, it will be time to plunge into Chapters 5 through 8: an attempt to describe slices of American life. It's worth repeating that there are large parts of America that will not be covered. But I do offer glimpses of the main activities of middle-American existence: child rearing, learning, shopping, working, settling, and worshipping. In this section, I'll include some statistics to illustrate the emerging patterns of twenty-first-century life. But I will also speak in parables, composites, and archetypes, for the personality of a people, as much as the personality of an individual, is a mysterious, changing thing. One has to feel one's way into the subject, tracing the patterns with your fingertips, developing a responsiveness to how the constituent elements play off one another. That's why many nations have national poets or composers who are thought to express the soul of a people, but few nations have national statisticians or national political scientists. One simply must tolerate imprecision of the poetic if one is to grasp the true and powerful essence of a place or people.

Since I am no poet, I will try to use humor to get at the essence of the way we live, comic sociology. While this book is motivated by love of country, it's not the ardent, humorless teenage form of love. It's more like the love that old companions feel, in which they enjoy jibing each other for their foibles and perhaps love the foibles best of all. If at times the book seems exaggerated, caricatured, impious, or sarcastic, my only excuse is that one of the distinctive traits of Americans is that we have often tried to tell the important truths about ourselves through humor, whether in the tall tales of the nineteenth-century storytellers, the novels of Mark Twain, or the wisecracks of Will Rogers, Mr. Dooley, H. L. Mencken, or Garry Trudeau.

In the final part of the book—Chapter 9—I will present my own opinions on the central questions: What unites Americans? Are we as shallow as we look? What force impels us to behave as energetically as we do, to head out in pursuit as we do, to play such an active and controversial role in the world? And how does this force—how does being American—shape us?

CHAPTER ONE

Out for a Drive

So LET'S GET IN the minivan. We will start downtown in an urban hipster zone; then we'll cross the city boundary and find ourselves in a progressive suburb dominated by urban exiles who consider themselves city folks at heart but moved out to suburbia because they needed more space. Then, cruising along tree-lined avenues, we'll head into the affluent inner-ring suburbs, those established old-line communities with doctors, lawyers, executives, and Brooks Brothers outlets. Then we'll stumble farther out into the semi-residential, semi-industrial zones, home of the immigrants who service all those upper-middle-class doctors, lawyers, and other professionals. Then we'll go into the heart of suburbia, the mid-ring, middle-class split-level and ranch-home suburbs, with their carports, driveway basketball hoops, and seasonal banners over the front doors.

Finally, we'll venture out into the new exurbs, with their big-box malls, their herds of SUVs, and their exit-ramp office parks.

Bike-Messenger Land

We could pick any sort of urban neighborhood to start our trek, but just for interest's sake, let's start at one of those hip bohemian neighborhoods, such as the Lower East Side of Manhattan, the U Street corridor in Washington, Clarksville in Austin, Silverlake in L.A., Little Five Points in Atlanta, Pioneer Square in Seattle, or Wicker Park in Chicago, where the free alternative weeklies are stacked in the entry vestibules of the coffeehouses, galleries, and indie film centers. As you know, the alternative weekly is the most conservative form of American journalism. You can go to just about any big city in the land and be pretty sure that the alternative weekly you find there will look exactly like the alternative weekly in the city you just left. There are the same concentrations of futon ads, enlightened-vibrator-store ads, highly attitudinal film reviewers, scathingly left-wing political opinions, borderline psychotic personals, "News of the Weird" columns, investigative exposés of evil landlords, avant-garde comic strips, and white-on-black rock venue schedules announcing dates by local bands with carefully grating names like Crank Shaft, Gutbucket, Wumpscut, and The Dismemberment Plan.

You look at the pictures of the rockers near the concert reviews, and they have the same slouchy, hands-in-the-jeans pose that Roger Daltrey and Mick Jagger adopted forty years ago, because nothing ever changes in the land of the rebels.

If you walk around the downtown neighborhoods, you're likely to find a stimulating mixture of low sexuality and high social concern. You'll see penis-shaft party cakes in a storefront right next to the holistic antiglobalization cooperative thrift store plastered with "Free Tibet" posters. You'll see vegan whole-grain enthusiasts who smoke Camels, and advertising copywriters on their way to LSAT prep. You'll see transgendered tenants-rights activists with spiky Finnish hairstyles, heading from their Far Eastern aromatherapy sessions to loft-renovation seminars.

In these downtown urban neighborhoods, many people carry big strap-over-the-shoulder satchels; although they may be architectural assistants and audio engineers, they want you to think they are really bike messengers. They congregate at African bistros where El Salvadoran servers wearing Palestinian kaffiyehs serve Virginia Woolf wannabes Slovakian beer.

Many of the people on these blocks have dreadlock envy. Their compensatory follicle statement might be the pubic divot, that little triangular patch of hair some men let grow on their chins, or the Jewfro, the bushy hairstyle that curly-haired Jewish men get when they let their locks grow out. Other people establish their alternative identity with NoLogo brand sportswear, kitschier-than-thou home furnishings, thrift-shop fashionista sundresses, conspicuously articulated po-mo social theories, or ostentatious displays of Martin Amis novels.

The point is to carefully nurture your art-school pretensions while still having a surprising amount of fun and possibly even making a big load of money. It is not easy to do this while remaining hip, because one is likely to find that a friend has gone terminally Lilith (denoting an excessive love of sappy feminist folk music) while others have taken their minimalist retro-modern interior-design concepts to unacceptable extremes, failing to realize that no matter how interesting a statement it makes, nobody wants to lounge around a living room that looks like a Formica gulag.

Downtown urban hipsters tend to have edgy alternative politics, or at least some Bennington College intellectual pretensions, and probably the New Yorker's disease—meaning that anything you might tell them, they already heard two weeks ago. You could walk up and tell them that the Messiah just came down from heaven and tapped you on the shoulder, and they would yawn and say they've been expecting that since last spring. But they are cool, and their neighborhoods are cool, and that counts for a lot.

We sort of take coolness for granted because it is so much around us. However, coolness is one of those pervasive and revolutionary constructs that America exports around the globe. Coolness is a magical state of grace, and as we take our drive through America, we will see that people congregate into communities not so much on the basis of class but on the basis of what ideal state they aspire to, and each ideal state creates its own cultural climate zone.

In the hippoisie cool zone, Charlie Parker, Thelonious Monk, Miles Davis, Lester Young, Billie Holliday, Jack Kerouac, James Dean, the Rat Pack, William Burroughs, Elvis Presley, Otis Redding, Bob Dylan, Andy Warhol, Janis Joplin, Patti Smith, and Lou Reed never go out of style. Coolness is a displayed indifference to traditional measures of success. The cool person pretends not to be striving. He or she seems to be content, ironically detached from the normal status codes, and living on a rebellious plane high above them.

In the cool zone, people go down to move up. It's cooler to be poor and damaged than wealthy and accomplished, which is why rich and beautiful supermodels stand around in bars trying to look like Sylvia Plath and the Methadone Sisters, with their post-hygiene hair, a red-rimmed, teary look around their eyes, their orange, just-escaped-from-the-mental-hospital blouses, and the sort of facial expression that suggests they're about forty-five seconds away from a spectacularly successful suicide attempt.

In the cool zone's nightclubs, you find people dressed and posed like slightly over-the-hill gay porn stars. You find that at the tippy-top of the status ladder, there are no lawyers, professors, or corporate executives but elite personal trainers, cutting-edge hairstylists, and powerful publicists: the aristocracy of the extremely shallow. Late at night in these neighborhoods, you find the Ameritrash, the club-happy, E-popping, pacifier-sucking people who live in a world of gold teeth caps, colorful scarfwear, body-conscious tailoring, ironic clip-on ties, gender-bending neo-vintage Boy George–inspired handbags, and green-apple flirtinis, which are alcoholic beverages so strong they qualify as a form of foreplay. In the cool zone, people are always hugging each other in the super-friendly European manner and talking knowledgeably about Cuban film festivals. People in the cool zone pretend to be unambitious and uninterested in the great uncool mass of middle Americans, but they are well aware of being powerful by example. Drawn by images of coolness, young people in different lands across the globe strive to throw off centuries of rigid convention in order to wear blue jeans.

Highly pierced social critics in downtown neighborhoods lament the spread of McDonald's and Disney and the
threat of American cultural imperialism. But in fact, American countercultural imperialism—the spread of rock and
rap attitudes, tattoos, piercing, and the youth culture—has
always been at least as powerful and destabilizing a force
for other cultures. It vibrates out from these urban-hipster
zones, with their multicultural Caribbean Schawarma
eateries, their all-night dance clubs with big-name DJs, and
their Ian Schrager hotels, which are so Zen that if you turn
on the water in one of the highly hip but shallow bathroom
sinks, it bounces a cascade of water all over the front of
your pants, making you look like you just wet yourself
because you were so awed by your own persona.

Cities, which were once industrial zones and even manufacturing centers, have become specialty regions for the
production of cool. Culture-based industries that require
legions of sophisticated, creative, and stimulated workers—
the sort of people who like to live in cities—have grown and
grown. In hip urban neighborhoods, there are few kids, and
those who are there are generally quite young (when the
kids hit middle school, their families magically disappear).

Surrounding these hip young urban areas are neighborhoods with plenty of kids, but they tend to be dispropor-
tionately populated with poor people and members of
minority and immigrant groups. They carry their own
brand of cool. In fact, they define cool, but with few excep-
tions, they never get to cash in on it. So they are often
trapped in no- or low-income jobs, because it's very hard to
go from being a high school grad to being a senior editor at
Details, no matter how objectively with-it you are, and
most of the other jobs have fled the cities or disappeared.

Cities have made a comeback of late, because the world demands cool products and ideas, but as Joel Kotkin concludes in *The New Geography*, they will not come back and be, as they once were, the main arenas of national life. "Rather than recovering their place as the geographic centers of the entire economy," Kotkin writes, "city centers are readjusting themselves to a more modest but sustainable role based on the same economic and cultural niches that have been performed by the core from the beginning of civilization"—as generation centers of art, design, publishing, entertainment, and cool.

Crunchy Suburbs

From the cool zone, we drive out of town, just across the city line, to the crunchy zone. Here one finds starter suburbs populated by people who regard themselves as countercultural urbanites, but now they have kids, so the energy that once went into sex and raving now goes into salads. They need suburban space so their kids have a place to play, but they still want enough panhandlers and check-cashing places nearby so they can feel urban and gritty.

Dotted around most cities—especially in the northern rim of the country, through Vermont, Massachusetts, Wisconsin, Oregon, and Washington—there are one or two crunchy suburbs that declared themselves nuclear-free zones during the cold war, although some would argue that the military-industrial complex was not overly inconvenienced by being unable to base ICBM launch sites in Takoma Park, Maryland. You can tell you are in a crunchy suburb by the sudden profusion of meat-free food co-ops, the boys with names like Mandela and Milo running around the all-wood playgrounds, the herbal-soapmaking cooperatives, pottery galleries, dance collectives, and middle-aged sandal wearers (people with progressive politics have this strange penchant for toe exhibitionism).

You have to remember that crunchy suburbs are the stoner versions of regular suburbs. All the status codes are reversed. So in a crunchy suburb, all the sports teams are really bad, except those involving Frisbees. The parking spaces are occupied by automobiles in need of psychotherapy because they are filled with self-hatred and wish they were Danish wood-burning stoves. The locals sit around on the weekends listening to Click and Clack, the self-amused NPR car-repair gurus who tell other crunchy-suburb people how to repair a crank shaft on their 1982 Honda Civic—the one with 285,000 miles and a Darwin fish on the bumper, next to the sticker attesting to the driver's tendency to practice random acts of kindness and senseless acts of beauty.

The true sign that you are in a crunchy suburb is when you come across an anti-lawn. Crunchy-suburb people subtly compete to prove that they have the worst lawn in the neighborhood, just to show how fervently they reject the soul-destroying standards of conventional success.

An anti-lawn looks like a regular lawn with an eating disorder. Some are bare patches of compacted brown dirt with sickly stray pieces of green matter poking out, the vegetation version of Yasser Arafat's face. Other anti-lawns burst forth with great symphonies of onion grass, vast spreads of dandelions and crabgrass, expanding waves of depressed ivies and melancholy ferns—such an impressive array of weed life uninterrupted by any trace of actual grass that you can only conclude some progressive agri-business makes a soy-based weed enhancer/grass suppressant, with special discounts for Nader voters.

When you are in these neighborhoods—maybe you've been invited over for a backyard stir-fry—you might want to ask for terrible lawn-care secrets, but you get distracted by the housepaint issue, which is another moral dilemma for crunchy-suburb residents. Painting your house exterior colonial white or production-home beige would, in these areas, be the moral equivalent of putting a National Rifle Association sign in the front yard. So crunchy-suburb residents again fall into two categories, starting with those who choose to paint their house every decade or so, but do so in such bright New Age colors—lavender, cobalt blue, fuchsia, or purple haze—that no one can possibly doubt the Buddhist bona fides of the people who live inside.

The other camp regards exterior housepaint in the same way they regard makeup, as something that was probably developed using animal testing. Centuries go by without any fresh coats, and the run-down drabness of the exteriors is highlighted only by the peace signs made out of Christmas lights that pop up around holiday time. The roofs in these homes tend to undulate in great waves and warps, because the residents either cannot afford roof repair or reject the rigid uniformity of straight lines, unchipped shingles, and the whole symmetry thing. The front porches are rusted and cracked, buried under sedimentary deposits of former lawn furniture picked up from neighborhood thrift shops (crunchy-suburb residents are not really into material things, but strangely, they still can't manage to throw anything away). The settlement in these homes is such that if you put a marble in the middle of a living room here, it would pick up so much speed as it rolled downhill that it would bore into the philosophically named housecat if she happened to be standing in its path.

The nice thing about these crunchy suburbs—aside from the fact that 96 percent of all children's book illustrators live in them—is that their residents are so relaxed. The ethos is almost excessively casual. While these folks might regard it as unusual to show up for a dinner party in anything other than black jeans and Birkenstocks, a suit and tie not made from hemp won't bend them out of shape. In other words, you may not really be part of their culture, but if you come to one of their towns, they will still welcome you. They may have little direct knowledge of anything that happens outside the nonprofit sector, but they tend to be genuinely warm toward new people. Tolerance is practically their profession. The cool zone is built on exclusion and one-upmanship, but the crunchy zone is built on inclusion and open-mindedness.

To their credit, the crunchy zones represent the last bastions of anticommercialism. The world used to be dotted with cultures that rejected the marketplace mentality. There were agrarians, old-family aristocrats, artsy bohemians, southern cavaliers, Marxists, Maoists, monks, and hoboes. But now the marketplace has co-opted or overrun each of those subcultures. Now, if you want to live an anticommercial lifestyle, or even a pseudo-anticommercial lifestyle, crunchiness is just about your only mode.

Amid the organic cauliflower stands and *Moosewood Cookbook*-inspired dinner parties, you'll find people suspicious of technological progress, efficiency, mass culture, and ever-rising affluence. The crunchies don't let their kids watch much TV, they disdain shopping malls, they prefer the small and the local and the particular and the old to the powerful and the modern. In any normal political taxonomy, they would be called conservative; though they are progressive on civil rights and social issues, they shelter the idiosyncratic, ethnic, and traditional institutions from the onrush of technology, homogenization, efficiency, and progress. But in the U.S., political orientations are defined by one's attitude to the free market, and the word "conservative" has been assigned to those who defend the free market, which of course is not a conservative institution. So crunchy towns tend to be associated with the left (though Rod Dreher of *National Review* has emerged as the champion of the Crunchy Cons—the pro-life vegetarian high-church Catholics who can their own preserves, care too much about zucchini, home-school their kids, and read Edmund Burke while wearing Swedish clogs).

Crunchy people also tend not to have a lot of money, and some of them actually don't care about it—they aren't merely *pretending* they don't care. Maybe you wouldn't want to spend your life in towns where half the men look like Allen Ginsberg, where the chief dilemma is whether to send the kids to Antioch or Hampshire College, or where Celtic folk/bluegrass songs intersperse with Phish anthems on the teahouse sound systems, but it is kind of interesting to be in a place in which the holy dollar has lost its divinity.

Professional Zones

As we drive farther, we begin to notice that the houses are getting bigger, the lawns look professionally manicured, and the driveways tend to be filled with Audis, Volvos, and

Saabs. In these upscale neighborhoods, it is apparently socially acceptable to buy a luxury car so long as it comes from a country that is hostile to U.S. foreign policy. Soon you begin to see discount but morally elevated supermarkets such as Trader Joe's. Here you can get your Spinoza Bagels (for people whose lives peaked in graduate school), fennel-flavored myrrh toothpaste from Tom's of Maine, free-range chicken broth, gluten-free challah, spelt-based throat lozenges, and bread from farms with no-tillage soil. (What, does the dirt turn itself over?)

Trader Joe's is for people who wouldn't dream of buying an avocado salad that didn't take a position on offshore drilling or a whey-based protein bar that wasn't fully committed to campaign finance reform. Someday, somebody should build a right-wing Trader Joe's, with faith-based chewing tobacco, rice pilaf grown by school-voucher-funded Mormon agricultural academies, and a meat section that's a bowl of cartridges and a sign reading "Go ahead, kill it yourself." But in the meantime, we will have to make do with the ethos of social concern that prevails at places like Trader Joe's and Whole Foods.

You get the impression that everybody associated with Trader Joe's is excessively good—that every cashier is on temporary furlough from Amnesty International, that the chipotle-pepper hummus was mixed by pluralistic Muslims committed to equal rights for women, that the Irish soda bread was baked by indigenous U2 groupies marching in Belfast for Protestant-Catholic reconciliation, and that the olive spread was prepared by idealistic Athenians who are reaching out to the Turks on the whole matter of Cyprus.

The folks at Trader Joe's also confront higher moral problems, such as snacks. Everyone knows that snack food is morally suspect, since it contributes to the obesity of the American public, but the clientele still seems to want it. So the folks behind this enterprise have managed to come up with globally concerned stomach filler that tastes virtuously like sawdust ground from unendangered wood. For kids who come home from school screaming, "Mom, I want a snack that will prevent colo-rectal cancer," there's Veggie Booty with kale, baked pea-pod chips, roasted plantains, wasabi peas, and flavor-free rice clusters. If you smuggled a bag of Doritos into Trader Joe's, some preservative alarm would go off, and the whole place would have to be fumigated and resanctified.

You usually don't have to wander far from a Trader Joe's before you find yourself in bistroville. These are inner-ring restaurant-packed suburban town centers that have performed the neat trick of being clearly suburban while still making it nearly impossible to park. In these new urbanist zones, highly affluent professionals emerge from their recently renovated lawyer foyers on Friday and Saturday nights, hoping to show off their discerning taste in olive oils. They want sidewalks, stores with overpriced French children's clothes to browse in after dinner, six-dollar-a-cone ice-cream vendors, and plenty of restaurants. They don't want suburban formula restaurants. They want places where they can offer disquisitions on the reliability of the risotto, where the predinner complimentary bread slices look like they were baked by Burgundian monks, and where they can top off their dinner with a self-righteous carrot smoothie.

The rule in these pedestrian-friendly town centers is "Fight a war, gain a restaurant." You'll find Afghan eateries, Vietnamese restaurants, Lebanese diners, Japanese sushi bars alongside dining options from Haiti, Cambodia, India, Mongolia, and Moscow. And this is not to even mention the Cosi-style casual dining spots offering shiitake mushroom panini sandwiches or the gourmet pizzerias serving artichoke, prosciutto, and brie pizzas (which can also come with a black-bean topping). When you stumble across Teriyaki Fajita Salad du Jardin, you realize it is possible to cram so many authentic indigenous cultures together that they've created something totally bogus and artificial.

Ozzie and Harriet would find it odd that their old suburban town center now has a vegan restaurant for feminist reproductive-rights activists and their support circles, but these inner-ring suburbs are sophisticated places. They are the home of the upscale urban exiles—affluent sophisticated types who disapprove of the suburbs in principle but find themselves living in one in practice. Like the crunchy suburbanites, they disapprove of the sterility of suburban life, the split-level subdivisions, the billiard rooms, and the blueberry bagels. But unlike the crunchy suburbanites, these inner-ring people just happen to have landed jobs that earn them a quarter million dollars a year, darn it, and they somehow moved into recently renovated Arts and Crafts mansions with an Olympic-sized Jacuzzi in the master-bathroom spa, the emblem of their great sellout.

The people who live in the inner-ring suburbs are hardcore meritocrats and the chief beneficiaries of the information age. This economy showers money down upon education, so the fine young achievers who went to graduate school and got jobs as litigators and mortgage-company executives can now live in towns that are close to downtown theaters and concert halls but also filled with houses big enough to support a kitchen the size of Arkansas. About

15 percent of American households now earn over
$100,000 a year. There are over seven million households
with a net worth over $1 million. This nation, in other
words, now possesses a mass upper class, and many of these
folks are congregating in the upscale archipelago of such
places as Bethesda, Maryland; Greenwich, Connecticut;
Tarrytown, New York; Villanova, Pennsylvania; Winnetka,
Illinois; San Mateo and Santa Monica, California; Austin,
Texas; Shaker Heights, Ohio; and the Research Triangle
Park of North Carolina. In the mornings, there are so many
blue *New York Times* delivery bags in the driveways of
these towns, they are visible from space.

Back when the old WASP elite dominated these places,
they were rock-ribbed Republican. But the new educated
elite has brought new values and new voting patterns. In
1998 *National Journal* studied the voting patterns of the
richest 261 towns in America and discovered that the
Democratic share of the vote had risen in each of the previous five elections. In 2000 the Democrats went over the
top. A Democratic presidential candidate carried the area
around the Main Line, outside of Philadelphia, for the first
time in history. And the first Democrat ever won the area
around New Trier High School, north of Chicago. Once
Republican strongholds, the inner-ring suburbs have
become Democratic zones, thanks to the influx of the educated and affluent cultural elite, with their graduate
degrees, high incomes, and liberal social values.

These places have their good and bad features. On the
downside, they are strangely insular. Though the people
here are in most ways well informed, and often can name
the foreign minister of France, they tend to live in neighborhoods where everybody has a college degree (only about a

quarter of adult Americans do), and they often don't know much about the rest of the country. They might not know who Tim LaHaye and Jerry Jenkins are, even though these men are among the nation's best-selling authors, with over fifty million books sold. They often don't know what makes a Pentecostal a Pentecostal, even though Pentecostalism is the most successful social movement of the twentieth century, starting in Los Angeles with no members a hundred years ago and growing so fast there are now roughly four hundred million Pentecostals worldwide. They can't name five NASCAR drivers, though stock-car races are the best-attended sporting events in the country. They can't tell a military officer's rank by looking at his insignia. They may not know what soy beans look like growing in the field. Sometimes they can't even tell you what happens in Branson, Missouri, though, as sort of the country music Vegas, it is one of the top tourist destinations in the country. On the other hand, they are really good at building attractive and interesting places to live. This is, after all, the red-hot center of the achievement ethos, and while few people in these neighborhoods have fought in wars, many have endured extensive home renovations.

So if you are in an inner-ring suburb, you are likely to be amid people who have developed views on beveled granite, and no inner-ring dinner party has gone all the way to dessert without a serious conversational phase on the merits and demerits of Corian countertops. People here talk about their relationships with architects the way they used to talk about their priests, rabbis, and ministers. Bathroom tile is their cocaine; instead of blowing their life savings on narcotic white powder, they blow it on the handcrafted Italian wall covering they saw at Waterworks.

The sumptuary codes in these neighborhoods are always shifting. Highly educated folk don't want to look materialistic and vulgar, but on the other hand, it would be nice to have an in-house theater with a fourteen-foot high-definition projection screen to better appreciate the interviews on *Charlie Rose*. Eventually these advanced-degree moguls cave in and buy the toys they really want: the heated bathroom floors to protect their bare feet, the power showers with nozzles every six inches, the mudrooms the size of your first apartment, the sixteen-foot refrigerators with the through-the-door goat cheese and guacamole delivery systems, the cathedral ceilings in the master bedroom that seem to be compensation for not quite getting to church. Later, when they show off to you, they do so in an apologetic manner, as if some other family member forced them to make the purchase.

Inner-ring people work so arduously at perfecting their homes because they dream of building a haven where they can relax, lay aside all that striving, and just cocoon. They have deep simplicity longings, visions of having enough money and space so they can finally rest. Yet you know they are wired for hard work, because they feel compelled to put offices in every room in the house. Mom has an office in the kitchen, Dad has an office off the bedroom, the kids have computer centers near the family room, and it's only a matter of time before builders start installing high-speed Internet access in bathrooms. That dream of perfect serenity and domestic bliss will just have to be transferred to the vacation home.

Inner-ring people tend to have omnivorous musical tastes. They're interested in zydeco and that Louisiana dance music they heard on *Fresh Air*, even if they do tend to drift back to Melissa Etheridge and Lyle Lovett. They prefer independent bookstores, and they bend down and read the recommendations in the staff-picks section. That's how they stumbled across Anita Diamant, Paul Auster, and Wally Lamb before they got really popular.

If they are not perpetually renovating their properties, inner-ring people are off on allegedly educational vacations improving their minds. When Christopher Columbus returned from the New World, he didn't go to Queen Isabella and say, "Well, I didn't find a trade route to India, but I did find myself." That, however, is exactly what highly educated inner-ring people are looking for in a vacation. They go on personal-growth Greek cruises sponsored by alumni associations, during which university classics professors lecture on the Peloponnesian wars while the former econ majors try to commit adultery with the lifeguards.

As you sit with them intimately in their reading alcove (not the one in the master bedroom suite; rather, the one beside the office, near the nanny suite) they tell you about the weeklong painting seminar they took with Comtesse Anne de Liedekerke in Belgium, the cooking seminar in Siena, the tiger-watching adventure in India, or the vineyard touring week in Bordeaux. When they put all this hard-won knowledge to work by using the word "geometric" in reference to a cabernet, you want to applaud their commitment to lifelong learning, but you are distracted because your butt is shaking as a result of the eighteen-inch woofer their architect cleverly embedded in the built-in divan you are resting upon.

When people in their twenties are surveyed on where they want to live, more of them answer inner-ring suburbs than any other place. It's easy to see why. These places combine the sophistication of the city with the child-friendly greenery of the suburb. The people here are well educated, lively, and tolerant (unless you want to, say, build a school in their neighborhood, in which case they turn into NIMBY-fired savages ripping the flesh from your bones with their bare hands).

Immigrant Enclaves

As you drive out from the inner-ring suburbs, you find yourself on these eight-lane commercial pikes with strip malls up and down either side, a Taco Bell every four hundred yards, and so many turn signals and left-hand turn lanes that crossing the street is nearly impossible because you never know where the cars are coming from. These avenues are just about the ugliest spots on the face of the earth. You're stuck at one red light after another, with views of fast-food drive-through lanes, grungy convenience stores, storage-center warehouse facades, and more fluorescent-lit nail salons than the mind can comprehend. The strip malls have names like Pike Center or Town Plaza, because no one even bothered to think up a distinctive title. Every half mile or so, in between the car lots, cell-phone stores, and discount mattress outlets, there will be a lone five-story office building that has all the aesthetic charm of a sixty-foot water heater. Turn onto a side road, and you may find yourself in one of those suburban light-industry districts where, after a few years, everything comes to look like the inside of an auto garage. Most upscale suburbanites come to these neighborhoods only when they are selecting new floor surfaces for their renovated kitchen, since most of the companies in this zone distribute things most people never have to think about: truck hitches, flexible packing foam, and cut-rate sprinkler equipment.

But if you look closely, you begin to see something else: big restaurant signs with names like China Star Buffet, small Oriental groceries offering cellophane noodles, live tilapia fish, and premade bibim bap salad. Then you see Indian grocery stores with videocassettes from Delhi, boxes of crackers from Bombay, and imported spices in big brown barrels. You notice the taiga Japanese bookstore, newspaper boxes offering the *Korean Central Daily*, Pakistani cyber cafés, Bosnian banks, and a Shiseido cosmetics outlet offering "movie-star brown" hair coloring for Asians. Perhaps there is a Vietnamese diner featuring bunh mih xui mai, which is "sloppy joe" in Vietnamese.

These stores often have advertising posters taped to the front door—for DynaSky calling cards to Peru, or a Christian prayer meeting hosted by Shim-San Jung and his worship team. We have crossed over into the land of the invisible. In stark contrast to the nearby inner-ring suburbs, no mass-market lifestyle magazines are geared to the people who work in these suburban distribution zones. TV shows are never set here. The big daily newspapers don't do features on the trends that sweep through the strip malls and the industrial areas. These places just have their own customs and patterns that grew up largely unnoticed by the general culture. At a scraggly playing field on Saturday mornings, there will be a crowd of Africans playing soccer, then on Sunday it will be all Hispanics. Somehow it just got established that one day was for Africans and the other day was for Hispanics, and you never see them playing each other. Then you go over to the basketball courts, and maybe the Pakistanis have ripped down all the rims so they can play cricket without any interference from the basketball players.

These places are growing. One out of every nine people living in America was born in a foreign country—roughly 32.5 million people, according to the last census—which means there are now more foreign-born Americans than ever before in the country's history. Traditionally, immigrants settled first in cities. But that's no longer true. Today they are more likely to go straight to midsize towns and underutilized suburban gaps. The 2000 census revealed that minorities were responsible for the majority of suburban population gains made in the 1990s, so now you'll see little Taiwanese girls in the figure-skating clinics, Ukrainian boys learning to pitch, and when I opened the Loudoun County paper one day and came across the National Scholar Award winners, these were some of the names that were listed: Kawai Cheung, Anastasia Cisneros Fraust, Dantam Do, Hugo Dubovoy, and Maryanthe Malliaris.

Over the past decade, immigrants from Asia have flooded into the Hickory and Charlotte areas in North Carolina; Lincoln, Nebraska; and the Grand Rapids area in Michigan. There are huge numbers of Asian immigrants in New Jersey's Middlesex and Somerset counties. The San Gabriel Valley in California is the largest center of Chinese immigrants in the country.

Meanwhile, Hispanics have moved in large numbers to places like Fresno and Bakersfield in California, as well as Orlando and Las Vegas. It is still true that 50 percent of the counties in the nation are over 85 percent white (if you take a brush and sweep it from Maine down through western New York, Pennsylvania, and Ohio, across the Midwest through Wisconsin, Iowa, and into the Dakotas and Montana, you are—excepting the big cities—basically covering Caucasianville), but the southern and western parts of the country are quite diverse, and there are immigration pockets everywhere: Arabs in Michigan, Iranians in Orange County, and so on.

In the older northeastern and midwestern areas, the immigration residential patterns are distinct. There are certain immigrant zones and certain native zones. Old cities like Detroit and Hartford are clearly segregated. But in the new suburbs, and in the booming towns of the South and West, different groups merge. Neighborhoods in these parts of the country are less likely to have reputations or fixed points on the status system. Families are more likely to shop for homes strictly on the basis of price. So in places like Arlington or Garland, Texas; Stockton, California; Albany, New York; Saint George or Fort Lauderdale, Florida, whites, native minorities, and immigrants tend to live and work side by side.

These immigrant-heavy places defy generalization. Most of the new arrivals are just scraping by, scrounging for day labor at the contractor pickup points, lacking health insurance, crammed into split levels four to a room. Others are doing well, running a barbershop with twenty Vietnamese and Filipino coworkers and then driving home each day in a Lexus SUV. If you tour the open houses in a McMansion neighborhood of, say, Great Falls, Virginia, or Orange County, California, you will be stunned by how many of the luxury homes belong to immigrants who own businesses in these light-industrial zones. They have faded pictures of Mom and Dad in China on the grand piano, and Islamic prayer rugs from Lebanon in the basement. These peoples' attitudes about their millions are roughly the same as Pamela Anderson's attitude about her breasts: They worked damn hard to get them, and now that they've got them they are sure as hell going to show them off.

These immigrant zones are among the most baffling places in the country. Market-research firms have to scramble to help companies make sense of them. They've discovered that Hispanics spend a far greater percentage of their income on footwear and clothing for children under two, and a far lower percentage on stationery and tobacco products than the average American consumer. Whites spend much more on entertainment and much less on clothing for teenage boys. Blacks spend more on poultry and telephones and less on furniture and books. Whites are the most likely of all racial groups to visit a home-furnishing store but the least likely to visit an electronics store. These aggregates don't get you very far. You've got new groups of people in new sorts of places, so of course everyone is creating temporary ways of living.

But you can see that some powerful transforming energy is being let loose. And we can be fairly sure that the traditional immigrant entrepreneurialism will give birth to new companies and new fortunes. (Interestingly, five of the nine immigrant groups most likely to produce millionaires come from the Middle East, according to a study done by Thomas J. Stanley, the author of *The Millionaire Mind.*) We know that thanks to the current immigration wave, the U.S. population will surge over the next few decades; we can project, thanks to Bill Frey, that in 2050 the median age in the U.S. will be 35, while the median age in Europe will be 52; and we can be reasonably sure that the new immigrants will climb into middle-class life, using and changing established institutions as they go.

Suburban Core

We have now driven deep into the heart of suburbia. Here there are split-level communities, cul-de-sacs, soccerplexes, regional shopping malls with ever more grand titles (plaza, galleria, court), edge cities (which have city skylines but no actual city life), and all the other stereotypical appurtenances of Homo suburbianus. When you get out here in the postwar suburbs that are now around a half century old, you can see why they've discombobulated so many social critics. All the other places we've been on our drive would be familiar to our ancestors. The city neighborhoods and inner-ring areas are organized according to the patterns and models of past great cities and towns. The immigrant clusters hearken to homelands across the globe. But the split-level/rancher suburb is an entirely self-contained civilization. These places were designed to be utopias set apart from the crowding and congestion and customs of the old places, from the problems of the past and the flow of human history. They are immune to time, geography, life, and death.

Even today, suburban streets are never just streets—they are terraces, courts, drives, and circles. You drive by home after tidy home, each on its well-tended quarter or eighth or sixteenth acre, and you see the same icons of suburban life development after development: Big Wheels, swing sets, adjustable-height basketball hoops, garden-hose storage rolls, pink and purple girls' bikes with sparkly handlebar tassels, stay-at-home dogs barking behind the bay-shaped picture windows, allegedly squirrel-proof bird feeders, vinyl siding, rusting tool sheds, RE/MAX for-sale signs posted by the mailboxes, holiday-theme banners over the doorways, faux gaslight lanterns staked in the front yard.

Thanks to their owners' relentless commitment to home maintenance, even the older houses do not bear the mark of time. Generations have come and gone, individuals have lived and died, and yet these neighborhoods still carry the whiff of Eisenhower America. The Oldsmobiles may have been replaced by PT Cruisers. Chuck Berry is out and Eminem is in. The brick ramblers now have second-story additions, but the lawns look the same. The shrubs still get pruned, the gutters get cleaned, the cars get washed in the driveways, the weeds get killed, the driveways get patched and repaved, the decks get waterproofed and coated, and the garage doors go up and down and up and down.

The same rituals are observed, and all those things that once seemed hopelessly outré—cheerleaders, proms, country clubs, backyard barbecues, and stay-at-home moms—still thrive, in some ways more than ever. The trick-or-treaters are still greeted with oohs and ahs, the mischief-night eggings get reenacted, the storm windows come out and the screens go in season after season, year after year, and decade after decade.

No wonder artists are offended. Individuals don't seem to matter here. These places do not appear grand and glorious, like a canyon or mountain or a teeming metropolis, and yet they are humbling because they are so impervious to you and me. We might rail against this cul-de-sac culture, we may hate it and curse it. But it will remain this way through all the passage of time, committed to the same values: tidiness, tranquility, domesticity, safety, predictability. These hard-core suburbs will stay what they have always been: bourgeois values in real estate form. This ethos is awesomely powerful. The postwar suburbs allow families earning around $51,000 a year—about the median income in the U.S. today—to establish a sense of respectability, financial security, and comfort. This split-level civilization would not have remained so coherent for so long if it didn't solve certain human problems and appeal to the aspirations of many sorts of people who have moved to precisely these locales.

If you want to understand these places, you have to start with golf. You won't get suburbia right—in fact, you won't get America right—if you underestimate the powerful cultural influence of golf. Sometimes middle America seems shaped more by golf than by war or literature or philosophy.

I'm not talking about the game of golf, the actual act of walking through eighteen holes and striking a little white ball. For most people, the game is too expensive and time-consuming. I'm talking about the golf ideal, the golf vision of perfection, the golf concept of chivalry, valor, and success. At least in its American incarnation, golf leads to a definition of what life should be like in its highest and most pleasant state.

In the ideal world as defined by golf, everything is immaculate. The fairways are weedless stretches of soft perfection. The greens are rolling ponds of manicured order. The sand traps are raked smooth. The homes along the fairways look scrubbed and affluent. Even the people are neat; everybody is dressed casually but nicely.

But golf is more than just an environment. It suggests its own state of spiritual grace, a Zenlike definition of fully realized human happiness. In the realm of golf, that state of grace is called par. And par is the established suburb's version of nirvana.

When a golfer is playing at par, his swing is sweet and his manner is confident. He has slipped away from the tensions that usually bedevil him on the course, and he has achieved a state of harmony. He is still competitive, driven, and success-oriented, yet he feels an inner calm. He has defeated his primary foe—anxiety—and operates in a mystical groove. Everything seems simple, manageable. In this victorious state, it seems almost normal that he is wearing a pastel yellow sweater and comfortable-looking green slacks.

Like Tiger Woods, Arnold Palmer, Jack Nicklaus, and Lee Trevino, each in his own way, the chivalric golfer has mastered the fine art of false modesty. Golfers never puff themselves up, as boxers do. They fill the air with half-humorous declarations of their own shortcomings. The chivalric golfer, when playing at par, has a narrow emotional range. He does not lose his temper and throw his clubs in the pond; neither does he dance on the green. He may punch the air once or twice in an approved and highly Protestant manner. After the round, he may allow that he felt good out there. But every comment will be three notches more modulated than it needs to be.

The chivalric golfer is able to look calmly at the problem in front of him and focus his concentration on it. He is backed, as all American life is, by a great body of management theory, personal advice, and self-help takeaways. The golf life is filled with clinics, advice columns, and personal coaching. The golfer is also equipped with state-of-the-art technology. Everything he owns is made from titanium; the club he swings on the long tee has a head roughly the size of an oil drum and the technical pedigree of an Exocet missile.

Yet out there on the course, he alone is the master of his fate. He spends a good part of his time looking at things. First he looks at the fairway, then he looks at the ball. Then he looks at the green. He is manifestly good at looking at things. His face is calm yet focused. He makes subtle calculations in that engineering-like brain of his. He consults with his caddy in the ego-massaging manner of a far-seeing CEO at a board meeting. He has that slacks-and-pastels thing going. Then he decides and strides manfully up to the ball, exuding purpose. He strikes the ball, and the ballet begins all over again.

Much of traditional suburban America aspires to golf's paradisiacal vision. The modern suburb enshrines the pursuit of par. It is not a social order oriented around creativity, novelty, and excitement. The suburban knight strives to have his life together, to achieve mastery over the great dragons: tension, hurry, anxiety, and disorder. The suburban knight tries to create a world and a lifestyle in which he or she can achieve that magic state of productive harmony and peace.

When you've got your life together, you can glide through your days without unpleasant distractions or tawdry failures. Your DVD collection is organized, and so is your walk-in closet. Your car is clean and vacuumed, your frequently dialed numbers are programmed into your cordless phone, your telephone plan is suited to your needs, and your various gizmos interact without conflict. Your spouse is athletic, your kids are bright, your job is reward-

ing, your promotions are inevitable, everywhere you need
to be comes with its own accessible parking. You look
great in casual slacks.

You can thus spend your days in perfect equanimity.
You radiate confidence and calm. Compared to you, Dick
Cheney is bipolar. You may not be the most intellectual or
philosophical person on the planet, but you are honest and
straightforward, friendly and good-hearted. As you drive
home, you observe that the lawns in your neighborhood
are carefully tended, so as to best maintain the flow of par.
Your neighbors all know that one cannot allow too much
time to pass between mowings, and one cannot mow when
the grass is wet, lest it lead to clumpings and unevenness.
One cannot cut the grass too short, lest one stress the lawn.
One cannot leave one's garbage can out at the end of one's
driveway long after the garbage has been collected, lest one
disturb the par of the streetscape.

All of these things are done in the name of good order,
so essential to the creation of par. Perhaps in your area, the
members of the community association serve as defenders
of the par. They might be the ones who guard against
disharmonious housepaint hues and overly assertive flag-
poles. In other areas, sheer social pressure might direct
everybody in the common pursuit of par. Bitter sarcasm is
frowned upon, for it represents a crease in the emotional
surface of the neighborhood. Brightly colored annuals in
the window boxes are praised, for they enhance cheeriness.
Loafers are approved of, for they send off relaxation vibes.
Kids in the cul-de-sac are jointly monitored, for kids are at
once the suburbs' whole point, yet the focus of so many
anxious thoughts, that they are a potential chasm in the
flow of par.

This common pursuit of the together life leads to the conformity that the social critics have always complained about. On the other hand, the pursuit of tranquility is also a moral and spiritual pursuit. It is an effort to live on a plane where things are straightforward and good, where people can march erect and upward, where friends can be relaxed and familiar, where families can be happy and cooperative, where individuals can be self-confident and wholesome, where children can grow up active and healthy, where spouses are sincere and honest, where everyone is cooperative, hardworking, devout, and happy.

That's not entirely terrible, is it?

The Exurbs

Now we are out in the outer suburbs, the great sprawling expanse of subdevelopments, glass-cube office parks, big-box malls, and townhome communities. This new form of human habitation spreads out into the desert or the countryside, or it snakes between valleys, or it creeps up along highways and in between rail lines. This kind of development seems less like a product of human will than an organism. And you can't really tell where one town ends and the other begins, except when, as Tom Wolfe observed, you begin to see a new round of 7-Elevens, CVS's, Sheetzes, and Burger Kings.

We don't even have words to describe these places. Over the past few decades, dozens of scholars have studied places like Arapahoe County, Colorado; Gwinnett County, Georgia; Ocean County, New Jersey; Chester County, Pennsylvania; Anoka County, Minnesota; and Placer County,

California. They've coined terms to capture the polymorphous living arrangements found in these fast growing
regions: edgeless city, major diversified center, multicen-
tered net, ruraburbia, boomburg, spread city, technoburb,
suburban growth corridor, sprinkler cities. None of these
names has caught on, in part because scholars are bad at
coming up with catchy phrases, but in part because these
new places are hard to define.

You can't even sensibly draw a map because you don't
know where to center it. Demographer Robert Lang tried
to draw a map of a zone north of Fort Lauderdale, Florida.
He located all the roads and office parks and arbitrarily
drew the borders. If he'd slid his map north, south, east, or
west, some roads and buildings would have disappeared,
and others would have appeared. But there would have
been no noticeable change in density, no new and definable
feature, just another few miles of suburban continuum.

And yet people flock here. Seventy-three million Americans moved across state lines in the 1990s, and these
places—across Florida, north of Atlanta, shooting out
beyond Las Vegas, Phoenix, Denver, and so on—drew
them in. You fly over the desert in the Southwest or above
some urban fringe, and you notice that the developers build
the sewers, roads, and cul-de-sacs before they put up the
houses, so naked cul-de-sacs to nowhere spread out
beneath you. One day I stood and watched a crew carve a
golf course out of the desert near Henderson, Nevada, one
of the fastest-growing cities in America. A year later, and
fifty thousand people are living where there was nothing.

People move to these centerless places in search of the
things people have always sought in a home: extra counter
space in the kitchen, abundant storage space in the base-

ment, and plenty of closets. Those are the three most important amenities to home buyers, according to market research. More grandly if more ironically, people move because they want order. They want to be able to control their lives. They've just had a divorce with their old suburb because it no longer gave them what they craved. They've had it with the forty-five-minute one-way commute in northern California. They're tired of wrestling with the $400,000 mortgage in Connecticut. They don't like the houses crowded with immigrants that are appearing in their New Jersey neighborhoods. They want to get away from parents who smoke and slap their kids, away from families where people watch daytime talk shows about transvestite betrayals or "My Daughter Is a Slut," away from broken homes, away from gangs of Goths and druggies, and away from families who don't value education, achievement, and success.

The outer-ring suburbs have very few poor people, and relatively few rich people. While many of the successful people in inner-ring suburbs are professionals—doctors, lawyers, professors, and journalists—many of the people in outer-ring suburbs are managers in marketing, sales, execution, and planning. The professionals don't think of themselves primarily as capitalists; as competitive, revenue-maximizing machines oriented toward the bottom line. Managers are much more likely to measure their success this way. The subtle distinction leads to a whole shift in attitudes, opinions, and political preferences. Managers are more likely to be competitive, sports-oriented, and, as political analysts Ruy Teixeira and John Judis have noticed, Republican. Professionals are more likely to be verbally skilled, university-oriented, and Democratic.

Sometimes people move to the exurbs to get away from the upscale snobs moving into the inner-ring neighborhood where they grew up. I recently ran into a woman in Loudoun County, Virginia, where AOL is located, who said she had spent most of her life in Bethesda, Maryland, today an affluent inner-ring suburb next to Washington. "I hate it there now," she said with venom in her voice. As we spoke, it became clear that she hated the gentrification, the new movie theater that shows only foreign films, the explosion of French, Turkish, and new-wave restaurants, the streets full of German cars with Princeton and Martha's Vineyard stickers on the back windows, the doctors and lawyers and journalists with their educated-class one-upsmanship.

She sensed they looked down on her, and she was probably right. So she did what Americans always do when something bothers them. She moved on. The philosopher George Santayana once observed that Americans don't solve problems, they leave them behind. If there's an idea they don't like, they don't bother refuting it, they simply talk about something else, and the original idea dies from inattention. If a situation bothers them, they leave it in the past.

The exurban people aren't going to stay and fight the war against the inner-ring traffic, the rising mortgages, the influx of new sorts of rich and poor. They're not going to mount a political campaign or wage a culture war. It's not worth the trouble. They can bolt and start again in places where everything is new and fresh. The highways are so clean and freshly paved you can eat off them. The elementary schools have spick-and-span playgrounds, unscuffed walls, and all the latest features such as observatories, computer labs, and batting cages.

The roads in many of these places are huge. They have names like Innovation Boulevard and Entrepreneur Avenue. They've been built for the population levels that will exist in two decades, so today you can cruise down flawless six-lane thoroughfares in trafficless nirvana, and if you get a cell-phone call, you can pull over to the right lane and take the call because there is no one behind you.

People who move out here are infused with a sense of what you might call conservative utopianism. On the one hand, those who move to the exurbs have made a startling leap into the unknown. They have, in great numbers and with great speed, moved from their old homes in California, Illinois, Wisconsin, New York, and elsewhere to these places that didn't exist ten years ago. The places have no past, no precedent, no settled conventions. The residents have no families or connections here. There are no ethnic enclaves to settle into, and no friends. Sometimes people move here without even a job.

When they make the decision to move, they are picturing for themselves what their new lives will be like. They are imagining waterskiing buddies and Little League teams. They are imagining happy high school graduations, even though that high school may still be nothing but a steel frame. They are imagining outings with friends at home-style Italian restaurants that don't exist yet, outings to Science Olympiads with unformed teams, road trips to spring training with friends they haven't met, who are now sitting in their old suburb and haven't contemplated moving here. But they will.

And while they are making a radical change in their lives, they are really pursuing a conservative vision. It is no accident that people in the exurbs, while instinctively apolitical and often cynical about the political process, are, when they vote, overwhelmingly Republican. These places are sometimes seventy-thirty Republican, and if you look at every state where Republicans scored an upset senatorial victory in 2002—Georgia, Colorado, and Minnesota, to name a few—they did so with huge gains from the fast-growing exurbs.

The exurbs are built to embody a modern version of the suburban ideal. Demographic studies show that they look like 1950s suburban America—intact two-parent families, 2.3 kids, low crime, and relatively low divorce rates. You sometimes get the impression that these people have fled their crowded and stratified old suburbs because they really want to live in an updated Mayberry with BlackBerries.

There is nobody here who is socially far above or below you (at least until the country clubs get built and the tennis rankings come out). Unlike in the cities or the inner-ring 'burbs, there is relatively little social competition. You can go through your entire life—at home, at the office, in church—wearing comfortable, conservative nonthreatening casual wear that emphazises khaki, navy blue, and other unobtrusive colors. Postmen get hernias lugging all the Lands' End catalogs.

This is, after all, where those cheery people who broadcast on the morning drive-time radio shows live. The exurbs are the new epicenters of competitive cheerleading and other sports that you can do while smiling. Theology is too troubling a topic for general conversation, and politics is not that interesting, so the new neighbors converse happily about how much better the traffic is here than wherever they used to live. People talk a lot about sports, the kids' ice-hockey league, NBA salary levels, college football, or the local over-sixty softball league—the one in which everybody wears a knee brace and it takes about six minutes for a good hitter to beat out a double. Since nobody can understand what their neighbors actually do—she does something with cell phones, he's involved in some sort of marketing—residents are likely to be known by their leisure-time interests: He's the one who spends his life e-mailing practice schedules to the soccer parents, she organizes the drill team, she's scuba woman and perpetually off in the Caribbean underwater, he's Carnival Cruise man, longing to tell you how many restaurants there were on his last vacation boat.

When these exurban communities started exploding in the early 1990s, people wanted to live around golf courses, because that was part of the suburban ethos they grew up with. During that decade, the number of golf communities nearly doubled to 2,386, according to the National Golf Foundation, even though the number of golfers scarcely budged. But by the year 2000, there had been an interesting shift in values, according to surveys done for the building industry. Prospective home buyers were less likely to demand country clubs in their new neighborhoods. Instead, they wanted walking paths, coffee shops, Kinko's, clubhouses, parks, and natural undeveloped land. In other words, they wanted community.

They come here, remember, with visions of friendships and happy barbecues. They want everything new but also a sense of place. They also want community; and, confronted with a Bowling Alone world, they have shifted their priorities. So they have been ideal customers for the new but burgeoning theming industry. Themists are people who can take something bland and give it a personality and a sense of place. They are hired by builders and retailers to make sure people have a more intense experience when they visit a store, a restaurant, a mall, or a residential development.

The most influential exurb communities are Kentlands or King Farm in Maryland; Ladera Ranch in Orange County; Belle Creek in Colorado; Celebration, Florida; and the Parks of Austin Ranch in Texas. These are attractive new urbanist communities with front porches on almost every house, and people are so community-oriented and friendly that as you walk down the sidewalks, they're going to make damn sure they say "Howdy!" These are places that have village greens, wooded playgrounds, community centers with neighborhood spas, protected-view corridors, Transit Tot day-care centers next to light-rail commuter stations, faux antique tower clocks in recently constructed town squares. There are more pagodas and koi ponds in these places than in all of Asia.

The new-urbanist ethos started in socially conscious communities like Portland, Oregon, but it has spread nationwide. It's made life better and more community-oriented. A man can wake up on a Sunday morning and take his family to the seeker-sensitive nondenominational Willow Creek–style megachurch, which has a 3,800-seat multimedia worship auditorium that was completed the month before. If he's in the mood, the man can watch the service via video in the outdoor café by the parking lot, or if he's feeling traditional, he can watch the video in the faux-Gothic basement stone chapel. After services, which he can watch on the projection-TV screens hanging from either side of the stage, with hymn lyrics projected helpfully below, he can take his wife and kids out to the lifestyle cen-

ter ten minutes up the road. That's the Italian piazza
streetscape that a shopping-mall developer plopped down
in the middle of nowhere. You park on the fringe, near the
retro-design eighteen-screen movie theater, and walk down
Main Street, which has a Barnes & Noble, a Crate and Barrel, a Galyan's, an artisanal bread store, a few Cosis or a
Starbucks, a Restoration Hardware, and of course a brew
pub. The stores all have awnings, different brick-and-stucco
storefronts, and maybe a few loftlike mixed-residential
apartments up above, to give them the streetscape feel that
Jane Jacobs, an urban theorist, described. There's a cell-
phone transmission tower designed to look like a cam-
panile, and the street has been artfully curved so there are
no long view lines of the surrounding parking lots, thereby
allowing the pedestrians to feel comfortably enclosed.

The man and his family can eat outside at one of the
Europeanized panini grills, under wicker shade umbrellas,
and the servers will fill their iced-tea glasses every thirty
seconds or so. They can watch the trolley go by, wait for a
concert by the Dixielanders, the senior-citizen jazz band, or
be entertained by one of the street jugglers hired by the
development firm to give the place the vibrant street life
that is required if the builder has any hope of winning
national development awards.

Later, the man and his family can go over to the town
rink, which has ice skating in the winter and mini golf in the
summer; or browse through the pomegranates at the
farmer's market, featuring real live Mennonite agriculturists.

Then the family can split off to take care of the Sunday-
afternoon chores. Mom takes the girl off to her stick-
handling clinic at the ice rink before heading off to run her

errands, and Dad takes the boy to baseball practice before going off to buy that new barbecue grill they need.

The Grill-Buying Guy

I don't know if you've ever seen the expression of a man who is about to buy a first-class barbecue grill. He walks into Home Depot or Lowe's or one of the other mega-hardware complexes, and his eyes are glistening with a far-away visionary zeal, like one of those old prophets gazing into the promised land. His lips are parted and twitching slightly.

Inside the megastore, the man adopts the stride American men fall into when in the presence of large amounts of lumber. He heads over to the barbecue grills, just past the racks of affordable house-plan books, in the yard-machinery section. They are arrayed magnificently next to the vehicles that used to be known as riding mowers but are now known as lawn tractors, because to call them riding mowers doesn't fully convey the steroidized M1 tank power of the things. The man approaches the barbecue grills with a trancelike expression suggesting that he has cast aside all the pains and imperfections of this world and is approaching the gateway to a higher dimension. In front of him is a scattering of massive steel-coated reactors with names like Broilmaster P3, Thermidor, and the Weber Genesis, because in America it seems perfectly normal to name a backyard barbecue grill after a book of the Bible.

The items in this cooking arsenal flaunt enough metal to survive a direct nuclear assault. Patio Man goes from machine to machine comparing their various features—the cast-iron/porcelain-coated cooking surfaces, the 328,000-Btu heat-generating capacities, the 2,000-degree tolerance linings, multiple warming racks, lava-rock containment dishes, or built-in electrical meat thermometers. Certain profound questions flow through his mind. Is a 542-cubic-inch grilling surface enough, considering he might someday get the urge to roast a bison? Can he handle the TEC Sterling II grill, which can hit temperatures of 1,600 degrees, thereby causing his dinner to spontaneously combust? Though the matte-steel overcoat resists scratching, doesn't he want a polished steel surface so he can glance down and admire his reflection while performing the suburban manliness rituals such as brushing tangy teriyaki sauce on meat slabs with his right hand while clutching a beer can in an NFL foam insulator in his left?

Pretty soon a large salesperson in an orange vest—looking like an SUV in human form—comes up to him and says, "Howyadoin'," which is "May I help you?" in Home Depot talk. Patio Man, who has so much lust in his heart, it is all he can do to keep from climbing up on one of these machines and whooping rodeo-style with joy, still manages to respond appropriately. He grunts inarticulately and nods toward the machines. Careful not to make eye contact at any point, the two manly suburban men have a brief exchange of pseudo-scientific grill argot that neither of them understands, and pretty soon Patio Man comes to the reasoned conclusion that it would make sense to pay a little extra for a grill with V-shaped metal baffles, ceramic rods, and a side-mounted smoker box.

But none of this talk matters. The guy will end up buying the grill with the best cup holders. All major purchases of consumer durable goods these days ultimately come down to which model has the most impressive cup holders.

Having selected his joy machine, Patio Man heads for the cash register, Visa card trembling in his hand. All up and down the line are tough ex-football-playing guys who are used to working outdoors. They hang pagers and cell phones from their belts (in case a power line goes down somewhere) and wear NASCAR sunglasses, mullet haircuts, and faded T-shirts that they have ripped the sleeves off of to keep their arm muscles exposed and their armpit hair fully ventilated. Here and there are a few innately Office Depot guys who are trying to blend in with their more manly Home Depot brethren, and not ask Home Depot inappropriate questions, such as "Does this tool belt make my butt look fat?"

At the checkout, Patio Man is told that some minion will forklift the grill over to the loading dock around back. He is once again glad that he's driving that Yukon XL so he can approach the loading-dock guys as a co-equal in the manly fraternity of Those Who Haul Things.

As he signs the credit-card slip, with its massive total price, his confidence suddenly collapses, but it is revived as wonderful grill fantasies dance in his imagination:

There he is atop the uppermost tier of his multilevel backyard dining and recreational area. This is the kind of deck Louis XIV would have had if Sun Gods had had decks. In his mind's eye, Patio Man can see himself coolly flipping the garlic-and-pepper T-bones on the front acreage of his new grill while carefully testing the citrus-tarragon trout filets simmering fragrantly on the rear. On the lawn below, his kids Haley and Cody frolick on the weedless community lawn that is mowed twice weekly courtesy of the people who run Monument Crowne Preserve, his townhome community.

Haley, the fourteen-year-old daughter, is a Travel-Team Girl who spends her weekends playing midfield against similarly ponytailed, strongly calved soccer marvels such as herself. Cody, ten, is a Buzz-Cut Boy whose naturally blond hair has been cut to lawnlike stubble, and the little that's left is highlighted an almost phosphorescent white. Cody's wardrobe is entirely derivative of fashions he has seen watching the X Games. Patio Man can see the kids playing with child-safe lawn darts alongside a gaggle of their cul-de-sac friends, a happy gathering of Haleys and Codys and Corys and Britneys. It's a brightly colored scene—Abercrombie & Fitch pink spaghetti-strap tops on the girls and ankle-length canvas shorts and laceless Nikes on the boys. Patio Man notes somewhat uncomfortably that in America today the average square yardage of boyswear grows and grows, while the square inches in the girls' outfits shrinks and shrinks. The boys carry so much fabric they look like skateboarding Bedouins, and the girls look like preppy prostitutes.

Nonetheless, Patio Man envisions a Saturday-evening party—his adult softball-team buddies lounging on his immaculate deck furniture, watching him with a certain moist envy as he mans the grill. They are moderately fit, sockless men in Docksiders, chinos, and Tommy Bahama muted Hawaiian shirts. Their wives, trim Jennifer Aniston lookalikes, wear capris and sleeveless tops, which look great on them owing to their countless hours on the weight machines at Spa Lady. These men and women may not be Greatest Generation heroes, or earthshaking inventors such as Thomas Edison, but if Thomas Edison had had a

human-resources department, and that department organized annual enrichment and motivational conferences for
midlevel management, then these people would be the marketing executives for the back-office support consultants to
the meeting-planning firms that hook up the HR executives
with the conference facilities.

They are wonderful people. Patio Man can envision his
own wife, Cindy, the Realtor Mom, circulating among
them serving drinks, telling parent-teacher-conference stories and generally stirring up the hospitality; he, Patio Man,
masterfully wields his extra-wide fish spatula while absorb-
ing the aroma of imported hickory chips—again, to the
silent admiration of all. The sun is shining. The people are
friendly. The men are no more than twenty-five pounds
overweight, which is the socially acceptable male-paunch
level in upwardly mobile America, and the children are
well adjusted. This vision of domestic bliss is what Patio
Man has been shooting for all his life.

Patio Man has completed his purchase, another triumph in a lifetime of conquest shopping. As he steps into
the parking lot, he is momentarily blinded by sun bouncing
off the hardtop. He is no longer in that comfy lifestyle center where he and his family took their lunch. Now he is
confronted by the mighty landscape of a modern big-box
mall, one of the power centers where exurban people do
the bulk of their shopping.

Megastores surround him on all sides like trains of
mighty pachyderms. Off to his right there's a Wal-Mart, a
Sports Authority, and an Old Navy large enough to qualify
for membership in the United Nations. Way off on the horizon, barely visible because of the curvature of the earth, is a
Sneaker Warehouse. Just off the highway beyond, is a row

of heavily themed suburban chain restaurants, which, if they all merged, would be known as Chili's Olive Garden Hard Rock Outback Cantina—a melange of peppy servers, superfluous ceiling fans, free bread with olive oil, taco-salad entrées, and enough sun-dried-tomato concoctions to satisfy the population of Tuscany for generations.

This parking lot is so big you could set off a nuclear device in the center and nobody would notice in the stores on either end. In fact, in the modern American suburbs, there's often not just one big-box mall, there are archipelagos of them. You can stand on the edge of one and look down into a valley and see three more—huge area-code stretches of parking area surrounded by massive shopping warehouses that might be painted in racing stripes to break up the monotony of their windowless exteriors. If one superstore is at one mall, then its competitor is probably down the way. There's a PETsMART just down from a PETCO, a Borders near a Barnes & Noble, a Linens 'n Things within sight of a Bed Bath & Beyond, a Target staring at a Kmart staring at a Wal-Mart, a Best Buy cheek by jowl with a Circuit City.

Patio Man doesn't know it yet, but cutting diagonally across the empty acreage in the very lot he is standing in, bopping from megastore to megastore, is his very own beloved wife, Realtor Mom. She's cruising across the terrain in her minivan, but it's no ordinary minivan. If crack dealers drove minivans, this is the kind they'd drive. It's a black-on-black top-of-the-line Dodge Grand Caravan ES, with phat spoilers, muscle grillework, road-hugging fog-lights, and ten Infinity speakers that she controls with little buttons on the back of her steering wheel because reaching over to the knobs is too much effort.

Her eyes narrow as she heads for the Sam's Club mega-store. She sees an empty parking spot just next to ones set aside for pregnant women and the handicapped, not over twenty yards from the front door. As she zooms in, she notices competition coming from the northeast. There's a rule in the suburbs: The bigger the car, the thinner the woman. And sure enough, here comes a size-six Jazzercise wife in a Lincoln Navigator, trying to get her spot. But the Navigator woman has made two horrible mistakes. First, she's challenged a minivan driver who is in no mood to appear even more tame and domesticated. And second, she doesn't seem to realize that in America it is acceptable to cut off any driver in a vehicle that costs a third more than yours. That's called democracy. So Realtor Mom roars her massive kid-hauling Caravan and swerves into the spot just ahead of the Navigator. If the Navigator woman wants to park this close to the store, she'll have to put on her turn signal and wait behind that family piling into the Odyssey, the one that will take till sundown to strap everybody in and read a few chapters of *Ulysses* before they pull out.

Realtor Mom is halfway through her shopping expedition. She's already trekked through the Wal-Mart Supercenter to pick up a CD head cleaner and a can of Dust-Off. America clearly entered a new phase in its history when Wal-Marts started supersizing; it was as if somebody took a blue whale and decided that what it really needed was to be quite a bit bigger.

Though Realtor Mom likes Wal-Mart, it's the price club that really gets her heart racing, because price clubs are Wal-Mart on acid. Here you can get laundry detergent in 41-pound tubs, 30-pound bags of frozen Tater Tots, frozen waffles in 60-serving boxes, and packages of 1,500

Q-tips, which is 3,000 actual swabs since there's cotton on both ends. These stores have been constructed according to the modern American principle that no flaw in design and quality is so grave that it can't be compensated for by mind-boggling quantity. The aisles here are wider than most country lanes. The frozen-food section looks like a university-sized cryogenics lab, and the cutlery section could pass as a medieval armory. The shelves are packed from the linoleum floor clear up to the thirty-foot fluorescent-lighted ceilings with economy-sized consumer goods on massive wooden pallets. Sometimes you look up and consider what would happen if there were an earthquake right now, and you think, Great, I'm going to be crushed to death under a hillside of falling juice boxes.

The first time Realtor Mom went into one of the places and got a load of the size of the household goods, she naturally wanted to see what kind of person would come here shopping for condoms. But what's truly amazing is that wherever you go in a price club, everybody in every aisle is having the same conversation, which is about how much they are saving by buying in bulk. Sometimes you overhear "If you use a lot, it really does pay" or "They never go bad, so you can keep them forever" or "It's nice to have fifteen thousand Popsicles, since someday we plan on having kids anyway . . ." All the people in all the aisles feel such profound satisfaction over their good deals that they pile the stuff into their shopping carts—which are practically the size of eighteen-wheelers, with safety airbags for the driv-er—so that by the time they head toward the checkout, they look like the supply lines for the Allied invasion of Normandy.

But they feel they've accomplished something. In pur-

chasing Post-it notes by the million, they have put something over on the gods of the marketplace. They have one-
upped the poor nonclub members who have betrayed their
families by failing to get the best deal. They are the savvy
marketplace swashbucklers who have achieved such
impressive price-tag victories that they will return home in
glory to recount tales of their triumphs to tables of rapt
dinner guests. Bragging about what a good deal you got is
one of the many great art forms that my people, the Jews,
have introduced to American culture.

This trip, Realtor Mom is saving a bundle on frozen
sausage-and-pepperoni Pizza Pockets. She's making a
killing on tennis balls and vermouth-flavored martini
onions. She has triumphantly advanced in the realm of
casual merlot and inflatable water-wing acquisition. She
has stocked up on so many fat-free, salt-free, lactose-free,
and cholesterol-free items that the boxes she's carrying
might as well be empty.

She, too, heads back to her vehicle with a sense that she
has shopped victoriously. In this complicated and time-
stressed world, she has demonstrated, at least for an
instant, her mastery of everyday life. She has achieved par.

As it transpires, she finishes her rounds just as Patio
Man is pulling out of the mall with his backyard wonder-
grill tucked snugly into the back of his Yukon. She recog-
nizes his DADSTOY vanity license plate (she has the
MOMSCAB companion plate), and she honks brightly to get
his attention. Pretty soon they've both got their cell phones
with the walkie-talkie features out four inches in front of
their noses, and they chat affectionately about their
tremendous purchases.

They drive home together. They turn left on Executive

Avenue and head past the Chez Maison apartment complex and the Falcon Preserve gated-home community
toward their own townhome cluster.

The town fathers in their suburb have tried halfheart-
edly to control sprawl. As Patio Man and his wife cruise
over a hilltop and look down on the expanse of suburb
below, they can see, stretched across the landscape, little
puffs here and there of brown smoke. That's bulldozers
kicking up dirt while building new townhomes, office
parks, shopping malls, firehouses, schools, AmeriSuites
guest hotels, and golf courses. As a result of the ambiva-
lently antigrowth zoning regulations, the homes aren't
spread out with quarter-acre yards, as in the older, more
established suburbs; they're clustered into pseudo-urbanist
pods. As you scan the horizon, you'll see a densely packed
pod of townhouses, then a half-mile stretch of investor
grass (fields that will someday contain thirty-five-
thousand-square-foot Fresh Mex restaurants but are now
being kept fallow by investors until the prices come up),
then another pod of slightly more expensive but equally
dense-packed detached homes.

Realtor Mom and Patio Man's little convoy is impressive—8,000 pounds of metal carrying 290 pounds of
human being. They finally bear right into their community—their street has been given the imperious but baffling
name Trajan's Column Terrace—and they pull into their
double-wide driveway in front of the two-car garage and
next to the adjustable-height Plexiglas backboard.

Their home is a mini-McMansion gable-gable house.
That is to say, it's a 3,200-square-foot middle-class home
built to look like a 7,000-square-foot starter palace for the
nouveaux riche. On the front elevation is a big gable on

top, and right in front of it, for visual relief, a little gable juts forward so it looks like a baby gable leaning against a mommy gable.

These homes have all the same features of the authentic McMansions (as history flows on, McMansions have come to seem authentic), but everything is significantly smaller. There are the same vaulted atriums behind the front doors that never get used and the same open-kitchen/two-story great rooms with soaring Palladian windows. But in the middle-class knockoffs, the rooms are so small—especially upstairs—that the bedrooms and master-bath suites wouldn't fit inside one of the walk-in closets of a real McMansion.

As the happy couple emerges from the vehicles, it is clear that they are both visibly flushed and aroused. With the juices still flowing from their consumer conquests, it's all they can do to keep from humping away like a pair of randy stallions right there on the front lawn under the shade of the seasonal holiday banner hanging above the front door. But that would violate the community association's public copulation guidelines. So, with the kids away at their various practices, and not due to get carpooled home for another hour, the two erotically charged exurbanites mischievously bound up to the master suite and experience even higher stages of bliss on the Sealy Posturpedic mattress, on the stainproof Lycron carpeting, and finally and climactically, atop the Ethan Allen Utopia-line settee.

This today is one version of the American Dream: wild, three-location suburban sex in close proximity to one's own oversized motor vehicles and a brand-new top-of-the-line barbecue grill. In the course of our drive through middle- and upper-middle-class suburbia, we've seen other contemporary versions of the dream. But still, in all our segmented diversity, there are certain traits that Americans tend to share, traits that join the many flavors of suburban culture and distinguish us from people in other lands. We'll get a glimpse of some in the next chapter.

CHAPTER TWO

Thyroid Nation

WE'VE LEFT OUT LARGE swaths of America in the course of our drive. We've scarcely peered into urban America, and we haven't even ventured into rural America. If we had continued our drive outward from the exurbs, we would have crossed the meatloaf line, that invisible divide in the landscape across which restaurants are far less likely to have sun-dried tomato concoctions and far more likely to have gravy.

If we'd gone out there, we would have come across more American-made cars and different sorts of bumper stickers: "Friends Don't Let Friends Drive Fords" and "Warning: In Case of Rapture, This Vehicle Will Be Unmanned." We would have found an entirely different attitude toward money. A lot of people don't have much, even though they don't exactly look poor. Rural America has suffered some appalling economic blows over the past few decades—falling commodity prices, the decimation of small manufacturing plants, farm after farm going bankrupt. While many young people move away, those who remain decide that money is not their god. There is intense social pressure not to put on airs. In many rural precincts, if you had some money and tried to drive a Mercedes, you'd be asking for trouble. If you hired a cook for a dinner party, people would wonder who died and made you queen.

If we'd continued to rural America, we would have entered a giant deflation machine. Gas is somehow fifty cents cheaper a gallon, parking tickets are three dollars, and there are racks and racks of blouses at the Dollar General for $9.99. There are no Saks Fifth Avenues, Neiman Marcuses, or Tiffanys in these rural regions, just Kohl's and Value City, and it's nice to be in a place where you can afford nearly everything for sale (when you're in a city or an inner-ring suburb, you are constantly afflicted with high-end products ridiculously out of your price range).

In many small towns, you can set yourself a goal: Try to spend twenty dollars a person on dinner. You can order the most expensive thing on the menu—steak au jus, seafood delight, "slippery beef" pot pie, whatever—and you probably won't be able to do it. You can ask the locals to direct you to the nicest restaurant in town; they'll send you to a Red Lobster or an Applebees. You'll spy a restaurant that seems from the outside to have some pretensions—maybe a "Les Desserts" glass cooler for the key lime pie and tapioca pudding. But you'll check out the entrée prices and realize that you didn't crack that twenty-dollar barrier.

This truly is a segmented country. In rural America, they love QVC, Danny Gans, and the Pro Bowlers Tour; high schools close the first day of hunting season. In the inner-ring suburbs, they love Tavis Smiley, David Brancaccio, and socially conscious investing; and the farmers' markets empty out for gun-control marches. In rural America, churches are everywhere; in suburban America, Thai restaurants are everywhere. In rural America, it's unwise to schedule events on Wednesday night, because that is the night for prayer meetings. In inner-ring suburbs, you can schedule events any night, but you probably don't want to go up against *Sex in the City*.

Forty percent of Americans consider themselves evangelical Christians, according to the Barna Research Group. In cities and inner-ring suburbs, you don't hear much God talk (people are quiet about it), while in the exurbs, they are loud and proud. America is segmented politically, too. In 2000, Al Gore won among big-city voters by over three to one, while George Bush won among rural and exurban voters by nearly as big a margin. Ethnically, we remain split. SUNY demographer John Logan analyzed the 2000 census data and found that racial segregation by neighborhood is stubbornly persistent. Despite increasing numbers of middle-class African-Americans, people congregate in ethnic enclaves. We all loudly declare our commitment to diversity, but in real life, we make strenuous efforts to find and fit in with people who make us feel comfortable.

More menacingly, social and economic stratification seems to intensify every year. The sociologist Seymour Martin Lipset once observed that two great themes run through American history—the desire for achievement and the desire for equality. These days you might look around and get the impression that we have embraced the ideology of achievement and forsaken equality. The highly educated make more and more money, while the less educated struggle harder and harder. I recently heard a McKinsey consultant give a presentation to senior executives on how to retain star employees. You have to pay them far more than regular employees, he advised. Then he added, "Sometimes companies in the Midwest resist a little before they do this." You could hear an entire cultural code cracking under the weight of that aside.

Business consolidation widens the inequality. The banking system used to be decentralized. Small towns had their own banks, with their own executives and boards of directors. Hence, each small town had its own executive class. But now banks have consolidated, as have so many other businesses. The executives are congregated at the corporate headquarters in affluent areas, the loan decisions are made by formula, and small towns no longer have much of a local upper class.

The American education system has become a vast inequality machine as well. The National Assessment of Educational Progress shows that the gap between the best and worst fourth-grade readers is widening as the good schools extend their lead on the lagging ones. Go to an affluent inner-ring suburb—such as Lower Merion, Pennsylvania; Bethesda, Maryland; or Palo Alto, California—and you will find that graduating seniors at the local public high schools have average SAT scores over 1200 combined. The average student in these upper-middle-class public schools is in the top 10 percent nationwide. But in a rural high school or an inner-city school, the average SAT score might be around 800 or 900.

High-achieving parents are marrying each other and breeding kids who are high-achievement squared, who will in turn make a lot of money and breed their own kids who are high-achievement cubed. Studies show that as the meritocracy purifies, Americans are even more likely to socialize with and marry people at education levels similiar to their own. It begins to look like an inherited educational caste system, except that it's somewhat voluntary. A survey done for *American Demographics* magazine revealed that 34 percent of female high school grads said they would prefer to marry someone with only a high school degree, while only 4 percent would like to even date someone with a doctorate. They wouldn't feel comfortable spanning that vast cultural divide.

The Social Structure in the Age of Sprawl

Some people look across this segmented landscape and see signs of an incipient class war. The rich are getting richer, and the wages of the middle class are stagnating, or worse. Surely, people say, there will be some sort of explosion or reaction sooner or later. Others look across the landscape and see a slow-boiling culture war. In the conservative heartland, people are religiously observant, traditionalist, and moralistic. Along the liberal coasts, people are secular, liberation-minded, and relativist.

But people who predict class or culture wars misunderstand the social structure in an age of sprawl. Because of its vast space and money, America is not a hierarchical place. It doesn't have the sort of easily understood social structure that allows people to locate where they are on a bottom-to-top pecking order. America doesn't divide neatly into two or three massive social classes.

Perhaps there was once such a pecking order, with the Vanderbilts and the Rockefellers on top, along with a few blue-blood families, the old-line firms, and the rest of the Protestant elites. Perhaps there was once a single economic power structure, along with a dominant set of mainstream and hegemonic cultural understandings and standards of behavior. Perhaps there was once a definable and coherent political establishment that lived in Georgetown or Manhattan and silently ran things.

But in the era of great dispersal, everything spreads out. With all these vast, growing suburbs, there is even more geographic space. If you don't like the neighbors moving into town, you get out. With the panoply of channels, specialty magazines, and Internet sites, there is social space. With the explosion of alternative-lifestyle enclaves, there is cultural space. If the southern Baptists don't really sympathize with your decision to be a Wiccan, then you find your own Wiccan cluster. With the spread of fund-raising channels, there is political space. Power in Washington is no longer wielded by a few master powerbrokers in Georgetown. There are now thousands of interest groups and donors spread around the country, and it is up to each aspiring politician to cobble together a coalition.

In other words, living in an abundant society that's rich in financial and technological possibilities, you don't have to fight over scarce land and cultural space. You can move on and build your own milieu. Everything that was once hierarchical turns cellular.

As you look across the landscape of America—from hip bohemia to ethnic enclaves such as South Boston, through the diverse suburbs into exurbia and the farthest farm towns—you don't see a lot of conflict. You see a big high school cafeteria with all these different tables. The jocks sit here, the geeks sit there, the drama people sit over there, and the druggies sit somewhere else. All the different cliques know the others exist, and there are some tensions. But they go to different parties, have slightly different cultures, talk about different things, and see different realities. Although individuals may live in two or three overlapping cliques, the cliques don't know much about one another, and they all regard the others as vaguely pathetic.

In America, too, people find their own social circles, usually with invisible buffer zones. You may have moved to suburban Des Moines, but then you find a quilting club, and there are quilting meetings, national quilting conventions, and quilting celebrities such as Ike Winner, the Quilting Cowboy, and Marianne Fons and Liz Porter, hosts of the PBS show *For the Love of Quilting*. You've found your community, and as in every clique, it has its own status system, its own causes, its own validation systems, and its own exaggerated sense of its role in society.

There is no one single elite in America. Hence, there is no definable establishment to be oppressed by and to rebel against. Everybody can be an aristocrat within his own Olympus. You can be an X Games celebrity and appear on ESPN2, or an atonal jazz demigod and be celebrated in obscure music magazines. You can be a short-story master and travel the nation from writers' conference to writers' conference, celebrated for your creativity, haircut, and style. Perhaps you are an NRA enthusiast, an ardent Zionist, a Rush Limbaugh dittohead, a surfer, a neo-Confederate, or an antiglobalization activist. Your clique will communicate its code of honor, its own set of jokes and privileges. It will offer you a field of accomplishments and a system of recognition. You can look down from the heights of your own achievement at all those poor saps who are less accomplished in the field of, say, antique-car refurbishing, Civil War reenacting, or Islamic learning. And you can feel quietly satisfied about your own self-worth.

"Know thyself," the Greek philosopher advised. But of course this is nonsense. In the world of self-reinforcing clique communities, the people who are truly happy live by the maxim "Overrate thyself." They live in a community that reinforces their values every day. The anthropology professor can stride through life knowing she was unanimously elected chairwoman of her crunchy suburb's sustainable-growth study seminar. She wears the locally approved status symbols: the Tibet-motif dangly earrings, the Andrea Dworkin–inspired hairstyle, the peasant blouse, and the public-broadcasting tote bag. She is, furthermore, the best outdoorswoman in the Georgia O'Keeffe Hiking Club, and her paper on twentieth-century Hopi protest graffiti was much admired at last year's Multidisciplinary OutGroup Research Conference. No wonder she feels so righteous in her beliefs.

Meanwhile, sitting in the next seat of the coach section on some Southwest Airlines flight, there might be a midlevel executive from a postwar suburb who's similarly rich in self-esteem. But he lives in a different clique, so he is validated and reinforced according to entirely different criteria and by entirely different institutions.

Unlike the anthropologist, he has never once wanted to free Mumia. He doesn't even know who Mumia is. But he has been named Payroll Person of the Year by the West Coast Regional Payroll Professionals Association. He is interested in college football and tassels. His loafers have tassels. His golf bags have tassels. If he could put tassels around the Oklahoma football vanity license plate on his Cadillac Escalade, his life would be complete.

These people sit on the plane, hip to hip, and they would be feeling mutually superior if they gave each other a moment's thought. One of the great observations about this country is that here, everybody can kick everybody else's ass. The crunchies who hike look down on the hunters who squat in the forest downing beers, and the hunters look down on the hikers who perch on logs smoking dope. The fundamentalists look down on the Jewish Buddhist Taoist liberals who think redwoods are a religious shrine, and the Jewish Buddhist Taoist liberals look down on the fundamentalists who think natural-history museums are filled with evolutionist propaganda.

As you may have noticed, 90 percent of Americans have way too much self-esteem (while the remainder has none at all). Nobody in this decentralized, fluid social structure knows who is mainstream and who is alternative, who is elite and who is populist. Professors at Harvard think the corporate elites run society, while the corporate elites think the cultural elites at Harvard run society. Liberals think their views are courageously unfashionable, and conservatives believe they are bravely dissenting from the mainstream media.

Most people see themselves living on an island of intelligence in a sea of idiocy. They feel their own lives are going pretty well, even if society as a whole is going down the toilet. They believe their children's schools are good, even if the nation's schools in general are terrible. Their own congressperson is okay, even if most of the others should be thrown out of office. Their own values are fine, even if civilization itself is on the verge of collapse. We all live in Lake Wobegon because we are all above average. We are all okay; it's the vast ocean of morons who are mucking things up.

Ours is not a social structure conducive to revolution, domestic warfare, and conflict. The United States is not on the verge of an incipient civil war or a social explosion. If you wanted to march against the ruling elite, where exactly would you do it? The problems we're more likely to observe during our drive through suburbia are withdrawal, segmentation, and disunion. Seduced by the splendor of our glorious great rooms and the insular comfort of our validation groups, we're more likely to take advantage of all the space and ignore everybody else, become detached from public life, and even more ignorant of the other cliques and communities all around. Then what happens to this common enterprise we call America? And will our tendency to disperse ruin this wonderful union we call America?

Full Throttle

When you step back and think about it, this tendency is not breaking up America; it *is* America. It was in 1782 that an astute visitor to these shores, the Marquis de Chastellux, observed, "In a nation which is in a perpetual state of growth, everything favors this general tendency; everything divides and multiplies." That's been true ever since.

We may not all be chasing the same thing, but we are all chasing something. What defines us as a people is our pursuit, our movement, and our tendency to head out. Today's movement to ever more distant suburbs is merely the current iteration of the core American trait.

In 1910 a man named Henry Van Dyke wrote a book called *The Spirit of America,* which begins with the sentence "The Spirit of America is best known in Europe by one of its qualities—energy." That is what you see across this country. Wherever we are heading, we are getting there at great speed and with great energy. It's not the steering wheel that distinguishes us, it's the throttle. The mystery of America is the mystery of motivation. Where does all the energy come from?

It was the energy to move that brought many people here in the first place. During the twentieth century, the population of France increased by 52 percent, the population of Germany increased by 46 percent, and the population of the United Kingdom by 42 percent, but the population of the United States increased by 270 percent. About 120 million Americans, 46 percent of the country, moved between 1995 and 2000. The number of local moves has actually decreased with increased home-ownership rates. But the number of long-distance moves has remained constant.

When we are not striving to move outward, we are striving to move up. Americans are the hardest-working people on the face of the earth. We work more hours per year than even the Japanese. The average American works

350 hours a year—nearly ten weeks—longer than the average European.

Furthermore, this work is not compulsory. For the first time in history, people at the top of the income ladder work longer hours than people at the bottom. Over the past twenty years, the proportion of American managers and professionals who work over fifty hours a week has increased by a third. If you present people with this statement: "I make a point of doing the best work I can even if it interferes with the rest of my life," 60 percent of Americans say it applies to them, compared to only 38 percent of Germans, who are not pikers when it comes to hard work.

We switch jobs frequently. The average job tenure in the U.S. is 6.9 years, compared to 10.4 years in France, 10.8 years in Germany, and 11.3 years in Japan.

If we are not rushing to work, we are rushing to church or softball or tutoring. The American tendency to switch religions—sometimes several times over the course of a lifetime—is probably unprecedented in world history. Nearly a fifth of adult Americans have converted at some point in their lives, according to the 2001 Religious Identification Survey. Although the exact numbers are under heavy dispute, Americans attend religious services at rates well above those of all comparable nations. Fifty-eight percent of Americans say their belief in God is very important to their lives, compared to only 12 percent of the French and 19 percent of the British, according to a UNESCO survey. About 86 percent of Americans believe in heaven, twice the German percentage. Our tendency to donate time to community service and voluntary associations such as Big Brother programs is also unmatched. Global surveys reveal that about 80 percent of Americans belong to some sort of voluntary association, compared with only 36 percent of, say, Italians and Japanese. About one-third of Americans do unpaid work for religious organizations, compared to 5 percent of the French and 6 percent of the British.

Nearly three-quarters of Americans make charitable contributions, with those toward the lower end of the income scale donating a higher percentage of their income than any other group. We have tailored our tax system to reinforce this national trait. Americans donate more money per capita than any other people, about $1,100 per year on average, with evangelical Christians giving about $3,600 a year per adult. No other nation has such a private non-profit sector.

The fabric of our everyday lives is frenetic. We are the nation of the take-out coffee cup. In most other countries, people drink their coffee out of porcelain cups. According to a GfK Ad Hoc Research Worldwide study, 57 percent of Americans eat out in a given week, compared to 12 percent of the French and 10 percent of the Germans. We eat out because we don't have time to cook, and the restaurant of choice is often someplace cheap, casual, and fast. When Europeans, for example, eat out, it tends to be at someplace slow, expensive, and fine. Only 8 percent of Americans say they typically spend thirty dollars or more when they eat out. Half of all Dutch people do.

We have constructed our society so that we have a relatively open field in all directions, so our energies can take us to both good and bad extremes. We have high marriage rates and very high divorce rates. High incomes but also high spending, and hence low savings. We are productive but also wasteful. We are quick to embrace innovations such as credit cards and e-commerce, but also quick to jump at get-rich-quick manias and dot-com bubbles. We have high job-creation rates but also high layoff rates. We have income mobility but also high violent-crime rates and high incarceration rates. We spend more money per school pupil than any other nation, have the highest high school and college graduation rates, and offer some of the best universities in the world but also some of the worst elementary and secondary schools. We devote a higher percentage of GDP to health care than any other people, and have the best hospitals, but more than 40 million of us are uninsured. We are incredibly rich, but our distribution of income is strikingly unequal, and the American welfare state is much smaller than that of comparable nations. Because Americans are relatively allergic to restrictions, regulations, and restraint on their mobility, our government is smaller. The American government collects about a third of the national GDP in taxes, compared to 52 percent in Sweden and 40 percent in Belgium and France, and these gaps are increasing. Only 38 percent of Americans say that government should work to reduce income inequality, compared to 80 percent of Italians and 70 percent of Austrians.

As Seymour Martin Lipset observes in his book *American Exceptionalism,* "America continues to be qualitatively different. To reiterate, exceptionalism does not mean better. This country is an outlier." I suspect that every nation, like every person, is unique and exceptional. Our exceptionalism takes the form of energy and mobility and dreams of ascent. As Lipset documents, we are the most individualistic, the most rights-oriented, the most optimistic, and the most committed to personal liberty. Of course, many people in America are risk-averse, and go to their secure bureaucratic jobs until they can retire and live out the rest of their days safely and happily. But on balance, and compared to people in other cultures, we don't want barriers in the way of our ambitions and desires, and we seem more willing to tolerate the risks, insecurity, and inequality that come as freedom's downside.

Whether in the city or the inner-ring suburb or the outer-ring exurb or beyond, we are witnessing different effusions of the same impulse to move out and up.

Rhino of the Earth

The energy and mobility of average Americans translates into many things. It translates first into money. All those thrusting, aspiring people in the downtown lofts, the suburban town centers, the immigrant zones, the exurban office parks, and the rural factories have made this country outlandishly affluent. With under 5 percent of the world's population, the U.S. accounts for about 31 percent of the world's economic activity. American gross domestic product per worker is about 30 percent greater than that of Germany or Japan.

The affluence of the upper class isn't the amazing thing. It's the affluence of the middle class. Americans spend $40 billion on lawn care each year, more than the total tax revenues of the federal government in India. The average American family spends $2,000 a year on food in restaurants. According to Cotton Incorporated's magazine, *Lifestyle Monitor,* American women between the ages of sixteen and seventy have, on average, seven pairs of jeans in their wardrobes. Nearly three-quarters of the new cars on the road have cruise control and power door locks.

American homes are by far the largest in the world. According to data compiled by the UN and the U.S. Department of Energy, the typical American occupies a house with 718 square feet per person. Australia comes in second, with 544 square feet per person. In Canada, the average person has 442 square feet; in crowded nations such as Holland, the average person has 256 feet, and in Japan, the average person has only 170 square feet.

Ours is a country with six hundred certified pet chiropractors. The average household headed by someone with a college degree has an income of about $72,000 a year. If you live in that household, you are richer than 95 percent of the people on the planet. You are probably richer than 99.99 percent of the people who have ever lived. In comparative terms, you are stinking rich.

This affluence translates into power. Americans in their townhome communities and subdivisions didn't seek to dominate the world. Many of them have rarely been abroad and are comfortably oblivious to much of what goes on at other latitudes and longitudes. But through their incredible hard work, their entrepreneurial zeal and creative energy, they have propelled the United States upward to occupy an unprecedented position in world affairs.

Thanks to the unexplained and unquenchable energy of all those different lifestyle seekers, the United States dominates the globe. Three-quarters of recent years' Nobel laureates in economics and the sciences live and work in the United States. The U.S. is responsible for 40 percent of the world's spending on technological research and development. American movies account for about 83 percent of world box-office revenues. American drug companies bring more new drugs to market than all the other drug companies in all the other nations combined. American venture-capital firms dwarf the venture-capital firms in all other nations of the globe. The U.S. military spends more on defense than the next fifteen nations combined. As the Yale historian Paul Kennedy recently noted, never before in human history has one nation been so dominant in the world; never before has one nation's economic and military might so eclipsed that of its closest rivals and allies.

If there were a rhino in the middle of your room, you wouldn't be reading this book, you'd be staring at the rhino. The United States is the rhino of the world. And when you get down to it, all that might is based on the work, the creativity, and the mysterious inner drive of the Patio Men and Realtor Moms, the inner-ring litigators and the bohemian software geeks. We are living in the age of the American Empire, and America is a suburban nation, so we are living in the age of the First Suburban Empire. And what the heck is that?

The paradox of suburbia is that people move there to pursue their private dreams. They want to live in a nice house with a nice yard and have a nice career and nice kids who go to nice schools. Yet because of their energy and productivity, they have propelled the United States into its rhino position.

Suddenly, people from other parts of the world are reacting to us and confronting us and demanding our attention. Whether it is Osama bin Laden or Saddam Hussein or the antiglobalization protesters or politicians in places as diverse as France, Israel, North Korea, and China, everybody is trying to do something to the United States, trying to flatter it, attack it, humiliate, it, mold it, or improve it. All sorts of world problems end up landing in the American lap, whether it is crises in the Middle East, AIDS in Africa, or weapons of mass destruction anywhere. The middle-class suburbanites chased private happiness, but their country has an inescapably public role. The people who live in the most powerful nation on earth don't really control their own agendas. They find themselves under attack for reasons they haven't thought much about. They have to act on the world stage, which is a place that doesn't interest most of them.

Our Nation, Our Selves

In normal circumstances we don't really think about it: how being American shapes our personalities and who we are and the path our lives take. But in extraordinary circumstances, we become acutely aware of what it means to be a member of a nation and a people. Thousands of Americans were killed on September 11, 2001, simply because they were American or worked in America. In the months and years since, we have become more aware of our nationality, of other peoples' perceptions of America, and the distinct and problematic role that America plays in the world.

The British writer George Orwell began to think about the significance of nationality during the early years of World War II. He was living in London, and at night German planes would try to destroy his city. He wrote an essay called "The Lion and the Unicorn," which began, "As I write, highly civilized human beings are flying overhead trying to kill me." He knew that those highly civilized German human beings were trying to kill him not because of who he was personally, but because he was English, and he began to wonder what that meant. "Till recently it was thought proper to pretend that all human beings are very much alike," Orwell wrote, "but in fact anyone able to use his eyes knows that the average of human behavior differs enormously from country to country. Things that could happen in one country could not happen in another."

What is this identity, Englishness? Orwell wondered. What can the England of the mid-nineteenth century have in common with the England of the mid-twentieth? But, he continued, "What have you in common with the child of five whose photograph your mother keeps on the mantelpiece? Nothing, except that you happen to be the same person."

Your nation, Orwell went on, "is your civilization. It is you." It changes. "But like anything else it can change only in certain directions, which up to a point can be foreseen. That is not to say that the future is fixed, merely that certain alternatives are possible and others are not. A seed may or may not grow, but at any rate a turnip seed never grows into a parsnip." It is important, he concluded, to know what England is before guessing what part England can play in the world.

In some ways, each of us is like nobody else. In some ways, each of us is like everybody else on earth. And in some other ways, each of us is like our countrymen. We have inherited and been molded by some shared mentality. Our personalities, in ways we appreciate or not, approve of or not, have been shaped by America. We are not detachable creatures who have been formed in absentia from the culture in which we were raised. Across the polymorphous perversity of our landscape, and even across the transformations of our history, there are some assumptions and attitudes that bind us together.

Despite all the changes, what Alexis de Tocqueville wrote about this country in the 1830s remains eerily applicable today. And it's not only Tocqueville's descriptions that still seem to fit, it's those of Crèvecoeur, who lived here in the eighteenth century; of James Bryce, who came here in the late nineteenth, and of many others. When we drive through suburbia and out to the exurbs, we are seeing much that is unprecedented, but the new aspects are the most recent embodiments of centuries-old ideas, impulses, and aspirations.

As we observe people in their townhomes, home theaters, and luxury pickup trucks, with their donut holes, their Dippin' Dots ("The ice cream of the future"), their baggy jeans and laceless sneakers, we do begin to wonder: What drives Americans to cram their hours and minutes with activity, to spend and move and disperse? What impels Americans to spread so quickly, to buzz so feverishly, and to spread vibrations out across the globe? What is the source of all this energy?

Observers, foreign and domestic, have tried to answer these questions. Some have interpreted our tendency to move and work and disperse as part of a noble and utopian effort to realize certain ideals—freedom, happiness, and spiritual fulfillment. Others have argued that our energy is merely part of some manic drive to avoid the deep and profound issues of life, to skate along the surface of existence and wallow in material luxury and incessant gain. In Chapter 4, we'll take a look at those who believe we are driven by a spiritual wind. But first let us probe into the depths of superficiality and consider the case made by those who consider Americans the spoiled blond bimbos of the earth.

CHAPTER THREE

Americans: Bimbos of the World

IF GOD IS OMNIPOTENT, omniscient, and good, why does He allow morons to succeed? One notices this phenomenon constantly; the most empty-headed, asinine individuals float helium-like ever higher into the firmament of success, from plum post to plum post, without ever demonstrating extraordinary talent, original intelligence, or even a noteworthy grasp of the matters at hand. Often they have pleasant faces and a certain animal magnetism, and their ascent seems to be accelerated by the fact that they are not burdened by the weight of an interesting personality. They've somehow acquired the reputation as One Who Is Chosen, so when leadership jobs open up and selection committees meet, they are called.

Their unbearable lightness is pleasing to the selectors, who either want somebody safe and manipulable or are themselves members in the community of the eminently vapid. So the zero-gravity hero ascends one more level in his merit-free rise to greatness, where he will be in a position to promote other empty eminentoes, who will promote still more hollow leaders, so that gradually, day by day, they will all find themselves in a golden circle of high-cheekboned innocuousness—girded on left and right by a band of pleasing, unoriginal, stress-free, talentless paragons radiating benign self-satisfaction upon one another without end. Amen.

This phenomenon represents a gaping flaw in the structure of the universe. It is a cosmic screw-up in the Divine Plan. How in this universe can it be that those who have a critical sensibility roughly equivalent to a golden retriever's, and who are so manifestly spiritually inferior to oneself, nonetheless manage to rise and rise? What's galling is not the undeserving success of this person, nor that he drives around in a Porsche Boxster, nor that he lives with his coldly gracious wife and her buttery-chunks hair and their blandly perfect and effortlessly slender children on an immaculately manicured horse farm with a helipad. No, the material trappings of success are not what gall. Maybe you wouldn't want such niceties even if you could afford them.

The infuriating thing is that he is not even aware of his shortcomings. Vapidity is the one character flaw that comes with its own missile defense system. The vapid person by definition does not possess the mental wherewithal to be aware of his own vapidity. This person has a blessed imperviousness, a milk-and-honey obliviousness to the meagerness of his actual merit. It hasn't occurred to him that he is not the richest, the fullest, the deepest emblem of human accomplishment and worthiness. His conscience, like everything else about him, is clean.

Nine times out of ten, the universe is structured in such a way that he is never forced to come face-to-face with his true self. He is born to grace, grows up in the land of charm, is nurtured in the fraternity of self-confidence, floats up through the career of plush paneling, fund-raising networks, and golf resorts, rests in the paradise of garrulous companionship, and retires at long last to Aspen, where he finally dies of happiness. The reckoning never comes! The moment of truth is avoided. Moreover, he is untouchable by the likes of you. You could scream tirades at him, write long essays denouncing his hollowness, construct mathematical formulae proving his mediocrity. He would whiz by in his golf cart to play out the back nine, and you'd be left spluttering into the void. Look at his résumé! Look at his impressive shoulders, graying temples, slender nose, and perfectly trimmed nails. And then look at you in your scuffed shoes, spluttering.

You stand there praying: If he would stop his cart just once, and turn to acknowledge, "Yes, I am shallow! I am undeserving!" then you would gladly grant him his Boxster and his buttery-chunks wife and his effortlessly slender children and the weedless horse farm, and you would be at peace with the world. But it will never happen. This paragon of success is the Lord of Self-esteem—the unapproachable, the all-powerful, the one who will not be brought low.

The inescapable fact is that the universe is divided between Blondes and Brunettes. This is not a matter of the color of one's hair. This is a cosmic trait. The Cosmic Blonde floats through life on a beam of sunshine, from success to success. The Cosmic Brunette obsesses and reflects,

frets and fumes, turns inward, and clings to the view that
the examined life is the only life worth living, despite all the
evidence to the contrary. The Cosmic Brunette writes and
reads books, worries, condemns and evaluates, judges, dis-
cerns and doubts. The Cosmic Blonde water-skis.

Go into any town, and you can see the Blondes and
Brunettes engaged in their rival spheres. This is, I empha-
size, not a matter of physical traits; many people who are
born with fair hair are actually Brunettes of the soul, and
vice versa. Nor is it a matter of intelligence. Some people
with the highest IQs also possess a sunny imperviousness,
an innate sense that life is to be enjoyed and that anything
complicating fun and ascent can be safely ignored on the
highway to Telluride. And some of the world's dumbest
people have Brunette personalities—hence the appeal of
sensitively suffering pop singers. You see them in any town,
rich or poor, suburb or city. The Cosmic Blondes slip from
health club to country club with their power-of-positive-
thinking expressions, their BlackBerries clipped efficiently
on their fat-free hips, their laser-surgeried eyes carefully
tinted to match the leather interior of their Lincoln Navi-
gators, which are so big they look like the Louisiana Super-
dome on wheels, guzzle so much gas that Saudi princes line
the driveway gaping and applauding, and are so overbearing that they are scarcely out of the dealership before
they've got little Hondas and Toyotas embedded in their
grillework. The Brunettes, on the other hand, putter
around in their low-slung Japanese sedans with a clutter of
books and magazines on the backseat and bird-watching
equipment in the trunk, deriving their usual passive-
aggressive pleasure from their talent for looking down on
people who are their economic and political superiors.

Bimbo to the World

This phenomenon is relevant today, because for many people around the world, the United States is the Cosmic Blonde of nations. People around the world concede that American culture has a certain appeal. They don't deny that the United States is an awesomely powerful nation, or that Americans are economically successful. How could they?

What people around the world do deny is that the U.S. is the most profound of nations, or that we are the most intelligent and reflective of peoples, or that we have mastered the art of truly savoring the important things in life. America's image is to the world what southern California's image is to the rest of America. When many foreign observers look at America, they see the culture of Coca-Cola, McDonald's, Disney, boob jobs, Bart Simpson, and boy bands. They see a country that invented Prozac and Viagra, paper party hats, pinball machines, commercial jingles, expensive orthodontia, and competitive cheerleading. They see a slightly trashy consumer culture that has perfected parade floats, corporate-sponsorship deals, low-slung jeans, and Cinnamon Frosted Cocoa Puffs; a culture that finds its highest means of self-expression through bumper stickers ("Rehab Is for Quitters") or the kind of message T-shirts motorcyclists wear ("If You Can Read This, the Bitch Fell Off"). In short, people see the Universal Blonde of nations.

The anti-Americanism that flared up around the time of the 2003 war with Iraq didn't emerge out of nothing, and the rage was not fueled merely by a disagreement about policy. Anti-Americanism, as political theorist James W. Caeser has noted, is based on the belief that there is something deeply arrogant at the core of American life that threatens the rest of the world.

It's amazing how early America was stereotyped as a money-grubbing, empty-headed, shallow-souled, energetic, but incredibly vulgar land. François la Rochefoucauld-Liancourt, who traveled to the United States in the 1790s, declared, "The desire for riches is their ruling passion." In 1805, a British visitor, Richard Parkinson, observed, "All men there make [money] their pursuit." "Gain! Gain! Gain! Gain! Gain!" is how the English philosopher Morris Birkbeck summarized the American spirit a few years later. Around 1850 the disillusioned Russian writer Michail Pogodin lamented, "America, on which our contemporaries have pinned their hopes for a time, has meanwhile clearly revealed the vices of her illegitimate birth. She is not a state, but rather a trading company."

The judgment was reinforced by succeeding waves of foreign observers. Charles Dickens described a country of uncouth vulgarians chasing, as he put it, "the almighty dollar." Oswald Spengler worried that Germany would devolve into "soulless America," with its worship of "technical skill, money and an eye for facts." Matthew Arnold likewise fretted that global forces would Americanize England: "They will rule [Britain] by their energy but they will deteriorate it by their low ideas and want of culture."

By the start of the twentieth century, people around the world had concerns that America's brand of crass materialism would spread. In 1901 the British journalist William Stead published a book called *The Americanization of the World*. In 1904 the German Paul Dehns wrote an influential essay with the same title. "What is Americanization?" he asked. "Americanization in its widest sense, including the societal and political, means the uninterrupted, exclusive, and relentless striving after gain, riches and influence."

Many of these observers came to regard America as the money-mad Moloch of the earth, the corrupter of morals and vulgarizer of culture. Benjamin Franklin was viewed as the quintessential prosperous, smug American, the ultimate man on the make, Homo americanus. Gifted at piling up a fortune, and armed with a shrewd if perpetually self-interested intelligence, he was also seen as self-satisfied, unreflective, and complacent. "The *summum bonum* of his ethic," Max Weber famously declared, was "the earning of more and more money." D. H. Lawrence was even more vituperative. Sure, Franklin could produce, experiment, man the cash register of life, and maybe shave a few pennies from the ledger. "But man has a soul," Lawrence protested. "The wholeness of man is his soul, not merely that nice little comfortable bit which Benjamin marks out. . . . And now I, at least, know why I can't stand Benjamin. He tries to take away my wholeness and my dark forest, my freedom. For how can any man be free without an illimitable background? And Benjamin tries to shove me into a barbed wire paddock and make me grow potatoes."

These days, opposition to our alleged Cosmic Blondeness comes in two forms—the virulent and the merely nervous. Virulent anti-Americans see us as the blonde slut of the universe, seducing the young and subverting traditional values. These people sometimes teach at madrassas or join terror organizations. Some seek to expose our essential hollowness and weakness with a devastating act; they seek to contrast their heroic and self-sacrificing deeds with the materialistic mediocrity of American commercialism. "The Americans love Pepsi-Cola, we love death," an Al Qaeda leader observed after the attacks on the World Trade Center and the Pentagon. Others proselytize from radical group platforms or in universities and opinion journals. They feel spiritually superior to Americans but are economically, politically, and socially outranked. They conclude that the world is diseased, that it rewards the wrong values. They have no real strategy to bring the U.S. low, just their rage, their burning sense of unjust inferiority, their envy mixed with snobbery. As Avishai Margalit and Ian Buruma remarked in *The New York Review of Books,* "With some on the left, hatred of the U.S. is all that remains of their leftism; anti-Americanism is part of their identity." Jean-François Revel put it more broadly (no doubt too broadly): "If you remove anti-Americanism, nothing remains of French political thought today, either on the Left or on the Right."

The people in the merely nervous school distrust America because they see it as representing a particularly immature, aggressive, and imbalanced strain of democratic capitalism. Suspicious of our fevered energy, disliking our hormonal popular culture, discomfited by our gun ethos, our advertising harlotry, and our military might, they regard Americans as muscle-brained blond cowboys roughriding over the globe. They look on in horror as Americans charge off on John Wayne–style crusades: We dim boobies have no idea what sort of instability we are about to cause. We will go marching off as we always do, naively confident of ourselves, yet unaware of the situation's complexities.

In Graham Greene's novel *The Quiet American,* the

protagonist, Alden Pyle, is a well-intentioned, earnest man-child who dreams of inspiring democracy but stirs up chaos and destruction. "I never knew a man who had better motives for all the trouble he caused," one of the characters remarks about him.

With Friends Like These

That's the case for the prosecution. What about our friends? America does have its defenders. Most people in most countries in most times have been favorably disposed toward the United States. And these friends do rise up in our defense. They get on their feet, clear their throats, and speak, and we wait eagerly for their rebuttals. We wait for the soul-stirring encomiums to our greatness, gratitude for our gifts to the world, admiration for our democracy, freedom, generosity, and success.

What comes tumbling from their lips? Concessions. Yes, they allow, Americans are gum-chewing, synthetic, and childish. But look at how vibrant they are. Sure, they're naive and oblivious to history, but look how optimistic they are. Sure, their children are spoiled, their women too masculine, their sexual attitudes prudish, their friendliness phony, their foods fatty and fast, but look how amusing, crazy, and fun they can be. Yes, Americans have business contacts instead of deep friendships. Yes, they practice savage capitalism, have meager and callous welfare systems, and execute their minorities. Yes, they are incapable of contemplation and true enjoyment and live in the grip of puritanical religious fanaticism. Yes, they lack depth of character, and most of them lack any appreciation of the fine arts. Yes, they are terrified of real intellectual debate, and yes, they crudely try to impose their will on the world. But look at their delightful energy, their liberating freedom, their colorful personalities, their technological virtuosity, their military might, and they did bail us out during two world wars.

This is the defense. These are our character witnesses!

It's been this way all through history. The visitors who are most in love with America will feel compelled to slip in—amid all the adoring praise for our glorious future and our wonderful liberty—a little shiv of equivocation about our shallow souls. Alexis de Tocqueville, the most brilliant and unavoidable writer on this subject, noticed the hectic pace of life in the United States. A Frenchman, he wrote, felt connection to his land, his village, and his ancestors, and thus respected the long "woof of time," while an American had no such set of connections across the centuries. "Democratic man," he wrote, meaning Americans, "does not know how to orient his life. Material goods are the sole fixed point, the sole incontestable value amidst the uncertainty of all things." Therefore, Tocqueville continued, the longing and striving for wealth and possession come to dominate life in America, and to flatten character:

> Each of them, living apart, is as a stranger to the fate of the rest; his children and his private friends constitute to him the whole of mankind. As for the rest of his fellow citizens, he is close to them but he does not see them; he touches them, but he does not feel them. . . .

> If your object is not to create heroic virtues but rather tranquil habits, if you would rather contemplate vices than crimes and prefer few transgressions at the cost of few splendid deeds, if in place of a brilliant society you are content to live in one that is prosperous, and finally, if in your view the main object of government is not to achieve the greatest strength or glory for the nation as a whole but to provide for every individual therein the utmost well-being, then it is good to make conditions equal and establish a democratic government.

To some, this sounds remarkably like the comfortable but unheroic world of the American suburb.

Many of the foreign visitors who have admired and defended America have also feared its insidious pleasantness. During the Cold War, the Italian writer Luigi Barzini wrote a string of books with titles like *Oh, America!* and *Americans Are Alone in the World,* rhapsodizing about America and all things American, from our politics to our magazines. But at low moments, even he wondered about these "poor people who don't know what to do with themselves, who have everything money can buy and industry, science and advertising can provide—new machines, new diets, new medicines, new religions, wonderful movies, the best climate in the world—and [you] wonder whether they would be more or less miserable dead."

The contemporary British military historian John Keegan, as true a friend of America as can be imagined, can't fathom why Americans are so totally incapable of relaxing, pausing for reflection, or even dawdling leisurely over a meal. In his book *Fields of Battle,* he describes the scene at the Princeton University faculty club, where he'd go during his visiting professorship in hopes of relaxing with some colleagues over a lunchtime gin and tonic. Instead, "descending to the restaurant floor, I would spend an hour mesmerized by the sight of distinguished academics trans-fixed by their lonely reading, raising their heads only to take savage canine bites at enormous indigestible sand-wiches clutched in a free hand. Strange zoo-like feelings possessed me, as if I were present at the feeding time of a species of superintelligent primates hitherto unknown to science."

This isn't exactly what you want to hear from your advocates. It isn't the patriotic banner you want to march under when you go to defend your nation: "God Bless America! Energetic Vulgarity Is Our Cause! Affluent Medi-ocrity Is Our Way!"

It's always the same: We are vital but spiritually stunted. The American historian Henry Steele Commager studied the vast foreign literature on America and found that most people who came here liked what they saw. He summarized the bundle of traits that show up again and again in descriptions—first and foremost, observers see America as the land of equality, as the land of the future. It's the land of opportunity, the land of industry and hard work, the land of plenty. But there is the inevitable parade of flip sides. In *America in Perspective,* Commager noted that just as foreign visitors tend to identify the same posi-tive traits in America, they also repeat the same criticisms decade after decade, generation after generation:

> The passion for equality, it was charged, made for mediocrity, for a general leveling down of distinc-

tion and of talent. The concern for material well-being produced a materialistic civilization, one in which the arts flourished only by indulgence, as it were. The passion for work, or for mere activity, left little time for the amenities of life, and Americans were rude. An easygoing tolerance played into the hands of the vulgar and corrupt, permitted the invasion of privacy, the exaltation of the mediocre, the violation of law and order. An excessive nervous vitality made for instability and rootlessness, gave an air of impermanence to almost everything that Americans undertook.

In other words, our foreign friends don't exactly deny our Cosmic Blondeness; they just savor the silver lining, our eager openness to everything, our capacity for mindless fun. They come from time-scarred, serious civilizations where sophisticated people spend their time keeping up with the Kafkas. And they're enchanted by us, the convertible nation, ripping off our tube tops, yipping like banshees as we cruise down the freeway from cineplex to surf shop. How charming! How wild! How seductive the Americans are, with all their careless money and ingenuous vitality!

"There is no pessimism in America regarding human nature and social organization," the French existentialist Jean-Paul Sartre sniffed. The United States, Georges Clemenceau wittily observed, is the only nation in history that "has gone directly from barbarism to degradation without the usual interval of civilization."

Indeed, it is French intellectuals who have mastered the art of the pro-American insult. A great French writer, say, arrives in the United States and is greeted by a throng of our leading thinkers. Dinners are arranged at sophisticated townhouses, local academics are assembled, subtle sauces prepared. But the French writer will have none of it. "Please," he insists, "take me to your Elvis impersonators." The French writer, you see, is on safari for puerile paradoxes. He wants to explore the meaning of vapidity, the exquisite sadness of glitter, and the penetrating tranquility of violence. He wants to head straight for the hyperreality, for Vegas, for Orlando.

The quintessential French love letter to the U.S. is Jean Baudrillard's 1986 book, *America*. It is of course a brilliant book. That is to say, the subject of the book is Baudrillard's brilliance. There are scenes of Baudrillard being brilliant in Utah, being brilliant in Los Angeles, being brilliant in New York. America has only a minor supporting role. "Americans believe in facts, but not in facticity," he writes. Aah! Brilliant! A Puerile Paradox! One pictures him posing like a great Gallic hunter next to this bon mot he has bagged on the American desert. It is a marvelous stuffed insight, a trophy mot he can hang on his wall at home.

One imagines him thumbing a ride through Nevada. A trucker picks Baudrillard up, and he begins unfurling some of the observations he will put into his book. "Here in the most conformist society the dimensions are immoral. It is this immorality that makes distance light and the journey infinite, that cleanses the muscles of their tiredness," Baudrillard intones as the trucker barrels the big rig down the asphalt. Baudrillard is pleased with the string of words, but the truck driver is looking sideways at him, trying to figure out what this French guy is talking about. Baudrillard continues his soliloquy. His self-regard radiates out in waves, putting a strain on the air-conditioning system. He is inhabiting a higher realm, the realm of the seer of supple things. He pictures himself repeating these ironic profundities on French TV, holding the microphone up to his mouth like a seductive cigarette, with one of those "God Is Dead but My Hair Is Perfect" looks that French intellectuals have mastered in the presence of febrile undergraduates.

Baudrillard drones on to the trucker: "The pigmentation of the dark races is like a natural make-up that is set off by the artificial kind to produce a beauty which is not sexual, but sublime and animal." The truck driver glances about for a baseball bat. But Baudrillard, lost in the glory of his oracular brilliance, goes on: ". . . extreme heat, the orgasmic form of bodily deterritorialization. The acceleration of molecules in the heat contributes to a barely perceptible evaporation of meaning. . . ." In another second, the trucker has gunned it to 85 mph, and with a flick of the opposite door handle and a shove, the soliloquizing semiotician has been pushed onto the highway, where he has been transformed into a rolling, bouncing postmodernist ball, thrilled in his last brilliant thought to have been the object of such a daring countertextual act, a purity of will, a jejune comment on the transgression of meaning.

The Inner Sociologist, the Self-Lacerator of the Soul

But Americans never actually react that way. How one reacts to the international critique depends on where you sit on the Blonde/Brunette divide. The Cosmic Blondes are amazed. Amazed! That anyone could not see the true nature of our own splendid American selves! Amazed that anyone could misinterpret our warmth, generosity, idealism, and nobility! Their reactions come in phases. America is at some level the Sally Field of nations—"You like me! You really really like me!"—and so the Cosmic Blondes wonder what the hell the problem is with our marketing department. We do a lousy job of communication, they say. If we could only polish our brand, tell our story, craft our message. If the truth were ever allowed out, if it were presented just right, then all the world would see us and love us, and history would end in a chorus of exultation.

Then, when that reaction gets stale, there is the other classic Cosmic Blonde reaction—that these hostile judgments about us are unpleasant, and since they are unpleasant, they must be unimportant. The Blondes grunt at the peculiarity of the sour losers who dislike us so. They figure vaguely that these people must have some problem or something, and retreat behind their milk-and-honey obliviousness to go on with the great sunshine beam of their lives.

The Cosmic Brunettes in America do not act this way. These, recall, are the people who write, read, and reflect (you are quite probably one yourself, as am I). The Brunettes look at the foreign critique of American society and think, Why do they hate us? Once you ask that question, you can always find something wrong with America with which to answer it. The Brunettes wheel out the inner sociologist, the deep dark self-lacerator of the soul, and they come to the measured judgment that the foreigners have a point. They are not completely right, for the Cosmic Brunette never finds anybody else's opinion 100 percent perfect. But with caveats, with equivocations, with amendments and cavils, it must be conceded that the basic posture of our observers has some merit.

Indeed, America's Cosmic Brunettes have been saying many of the same things themselves. American culture is essentially the history of Cosmic Brunette reactions to the crude driving energy of mainstream Blonde success. The transcendentalists, the Bohemians, the Marxists, the beatniks, the hippies, the academics, the indie-film screenwriters, the literati, the MacArthur genius-grant culturati, the religious activists, and the conservative think-tankers have all taken their turn on the national stage, rebelling against the Blondeness of America's bitch goddess success. The Cosmic Brunettes sit in coffeehouses, make movies, consume novels, hold conferences, and nibble European sorbets while contemplating the soul-crushing self-satisfaction that is middle-American life.

Sometimes it appears as if the Brunette mind of America went off in one direction and the Blonde body went off in another. The body is all about getting and gaining, climbing and making, blind optimism, catchpenny opportunism. The mind stands aside, vaguely repelled by what it sees as narrow selfishness, smug complacency, and synthetic culture. It's as if there's an unbridgeable chasm, and you have to choose which side you're on. On the one side there is money, acquisitiveness, success, and SUVs. On the other side there is spirit, imagination, creativity, and tenure.

Just as Europeans were quick to see America as a vulgar, money-mad land, many American writers and artists have been quick to decide that the way middle Americans live is an insult to the noble ideals that our country is supposed to represent. "The cursed hunger of riches," Cotton Mather thundered in 1706, "will make man break through all the laws of God." His kinsman, Eleazer Mather, looked at Boston life and called for "less trading, buying, selling but more praying, more watching over hearts, more close walking, less plenty and less inequity." He concluded, "Outward prosperity is a worm at the root of godliness, so that religion dies when the world thrives." The Shakers also rejected abundance and ever increasing prosperity. Their vision of the simple, honest life remains attractive to millions of Americans who buy the simple yet tasteful armoires, television stands, and dining room sets inspired by their creed.

Thomas Jefferson argued that America must renounce manufacturing and remain a land of independent yeoman farmers in order to retain its virtue. He feared America would become a nation of "gamblers" and "jugglers" doing "tricks with pieces of paper." Around the time of the American revolution, the founders—students of classical history—had imbibed a depressing view of the life cycle of great nations. Simplicity leads to strength and power. Strength and power lead to wealth and luxury. Wealth and luxury lead to corruption and decline. "Human nature, in no form of it, could ever bear prosperity," John Adams wrote in a letter to Jefferson.

Americans feared their own material success and the corruptions it might breed. The country was identified from the first as blessed with plenty and hungry for more. Yet its moral leaders have always regarded wealth and success as a potential poison that shrivels the soul and eventually devours itself. And so has arisen the tension that propels American culture: America hungers for success, and manifestly is a success, and at the same time suspects that worldly success will be its undoing.

By the early nineteenth century, the southern cavaliers

saw themselves as a moral antidote to the acquisitive commercialists of Yankee industrialism. Western pioneers were also depicted, mainly by easterners, as straight-talking adventurers who would serve as remedy for the crowded and moneyed corruptions of the coastal cities.

Henry David Thoreau emerged as the most important dissident against the American longing for success. In *Walden,* he posited that the way Americans live is a mistake. "The mass of men lead lives of quiet desperation," he argued, in one of the most famous lines in American literature. "They are employed, as it says in an old book, laying up treasures which moth and rust will corrupt and thieves break through and steal. It is a fool's life." The goods and luxuries that Americans toil so hard to acquire don't make them happier. "Most of the luxuries, and many of the so-called comforts of life, are not only not indispensable, but positive hindrances to the elevation of mankind. With respect to luxuries and comforts the wisest have ever lived a more simple and meager life than the poor."

In 1863, in the midst of the Civil War, Thoreau published an essay in *The Atlantic Monthly* called "Life Without Principle," in which he protested the workaholism of American life. "This world is a place of business. What infinite bustle! I am awaked almost every night by the panting of the locomotive. It interrupts my dreams. There is no Sabbath. It would be glorious to see mankind at leisure for once. It is nothing but work, work, work." If you spend a day alone in the woods, you are called a loafer, Thoreau lamented. And yet "The ways by which you may get money almost without exception lead downward." The people who hustle in the mainstream of American life, he continued, are shallow, mosquitolike creatures. Their conversation is inconsequential, their concerns are trivial, their politics are inhuman.

Americans have always read and admired Thoreau, and the millions who have never read him are influenced by his ideas and nod when they hear echoes in sermons, in movies, and at dinner-party conversations, or when they read them in the pages of simplicity magazines. But reformation never comes. America still continues to hustle and prosper. The money piles in, and the homes and the cars and the media centers grow finer and more luxurious. The American producer and consumer is an anxious but unstoppable whirlwind.

The result is that idealists, the Cosmic Brunettes, tend to withdraw and feel themselves alienated from mainstream American life. Thoreau's companions purified themselves of the materialism and ambition of the world. They either retreated literally, as he did (very briefly) into the forest; opted for a life shorn of luxuries and frantic getting and spending; or they ascended intellectually, as Ralph Waldo Emerson did at one point in his life, onto the Olympus of high ideals and moral abstractions. "It is a sign of the times," Emerson observed, that "many intellectual and religious persons withdrew" from "the market and the caucus"—capitalism and politics—to find something "worthy to do." They looked at life as it was actually lived, with corrupt politicians, growing and greedy businesses, and vulgar mass culture, and they were prone to fits of despair. "Ah my country!" Emerson wailed in one dark mood. "In thee is the reasonable hope of mankind not fulfilled. . . . When I see how false our life is . . . all heroism seems our dream and our insight a delusion."

If optimism was compulsory in Blonde America, then

short-term pessimism became nearly compulsory in Brunette America. The founding fathers' "really great and noble dream had become a good deal like a stampede of hogs to the trough," Henry Adams lamented.

Henry James had a character say in his short story "The Madonna of the Future": "An American, to excel, has just ten times as much to learn as a European. We lack the deeper sense; we have neither taste, nor tact, nor force. How should we have them? Our crude and garish climate, our silent past, our deafening present, the constant pressure about us of unlovely circumstances are as void of all that nourishes and prompts and inspires the artist as my sad heart is void of bitterness in saying so!"

No wonder the foreign critique hit home. If you go back over the past half century of novel writing and social criticism—during the time when American success was most obvious—you find that the anxieties of success have produced a long Chorus of Bemoaning. America goes through a wave of declinism about every seven to ten years. As I look over my bookshelves at the books, essays, and novels of the last fifty years, I could build, if I had sufficient balancing ability, a pile of books that would loom high over my head, a mountain of cultural pessimism attesting to the hollowness of contemporary life.

To keep the pile manageable, I wouldn't include any books written before, say, 1950, leaving off such classics as *Babbitt* and *The Man in the Gray Flannel Suit.* I'd choose David Riesman's *The Lonely Crowd,* with its portrait of the other-directed man who subordinates his own inner nature so he can conform to the habits of his neighbors. Then there'd be Richard Hofstadter's *Anti-Intellectualism in American Life,* and William Whyte's *The Organization*

Man, which describes the modern American as a bureau-
cratized cog in the corporate machine. Just for variety's
sake, I might throw in *The Catcher in the Rye,* on the sen-
sitive person's inability to make connections in contemporary society; a video of *Rebel Without a Cause,* on the
stifling banality of middle-class parents; a copy of *Death of
a Salesman,* on the emptiness of the American version of
success.

From the 1960s, there'd be the Port Huron Statement,
the founding document of the New Left and a manifesto
against the stifling technocratic banality of the modern
order; and Theodore Roszak's *The Making of a Counter
Culture.* Of course, I'd have to include Eldridge Cleaver's
Soul on Ice, which puts an Afrocentric spin on the frigidity
of mainstream American life. At one point Cleaver paints a
vivid picture of white people dancing: "They gyrated and
whirled and flailed their little dead asses like petrified zom-
bies trying to regain life's warmth, and to spark a bit of life
into their dead limbs, cold asses, stony hearts and those
stiff mechanical, inert joints."

Now the pile is up to my waist, and here we begin to
see an interesting change. Up to this point, the general
theme has been that Americans' shallow materialism turns
them into bland conformists. But from here on up, the general theme will be that Americans' shallow materialism
turns them into self-absorbed individualists. The first book
in this new mode is Daniel Bell's *The Cultural Contradictions of Capitalism,* which decried "the tedium of the unre-
strained self." Then comes Christopher Lasch's *The
Culture of Narcissism:* "Self-absorption defines the moral
climate of contemporary society." I'm just up to the mid-
1970s, and already the pile is around my neck, and I'm

afraid it might burst through the ceiling, so I leave out all the 1970s New Age efforts to escape arid, rationalized American life into higher realms of est, Zen, Eastern mysticism, crystals, and spiritual grace.

In 1985, Robert Bellah et al. published *Habits of the Heart,* which portrayed the disintegration of communities as people retreated from the meaninglessness of their jobs and public lives into the lonely comfort of their homes. By the 1980s, conservatives as well as liberals were likely to decry the banality of American culture. In *The Closing of the American Mind,* published in 1987, Allan Bloom argued that students live in a world of "easygoing nihilism." Floating in a warm bath of relativism, fearing conflict, picking up one value one day and an opposite value the next, they are comfortably untroubled by their lack of firm beliefs and guiding principles. "I fear that spiritual entropy or an evaporation of the soul's boiling blood is taking place."

By the time we get to the 1990s, the pile is over my head. I'm peering up at books such as Francis Fukuyama's *The End of History and the Last Man,* which warns of the arrival of the Last Man, the lukewarm child of comfort, afraid of conflict, obsessed by health and safety, untroubled by any disturbing passions, content in his world of money, mildness, and easy pleasures. I see Robert Putnam's *Bowling Alone,* which documents the decline of community and healthy human bonds throughout American society. Nonetheless, I grab a stepladder and stack on top Al Gore's *Earth in the Balance,* to represent the environmentalists' concern that in our cold, arrogant effort to pile up more belongings, we are losing touch with nature and our truest selves. I'd include Robert Bork's gloomy bestseller *Slouching Towards Gomorrah,* on the decline of just about everything, and Michael J. Sandel's *Democracy's Discontent,* which explores the concern that "the moral fabric of community is unraveling around us"; also nearly everything ever written by Gore Vidal, Susan Sontag, Kevin Phillips, Noam Chomsky, Juliet Schor, Michael Lind, Jonathan Kozol, Lewis Lapham, Michael Moore, Pat Robertson, Jerry Falwell, E. L. Doctorow, Thomas Pynchon, and the Unabomber.

I also throw a video of *American Beauty* onto the pile, to represent all the thousands of movies and millions of TV episodes detailing either the mediocrity of American suburban life or the sickness festering beneath its bland and hypocritical surface. Naturally, I include the vast literature on suburban sprawl, which protests the ugly, monotonous, soul-destroying landscape of modern suburban life.

By this time the pile is so high, I've been through so many gloomy and depressing books, that I'll probably want to go in the kitchen and suck the gas pipe.

Many of these books are brilliant, some of the best that have been published in our lifetime. And they do not all say the same thing; you could discern several categories. There is the left-wing gloom from writers who think that American-style capitalism has ravaged our souls. There is the conservative version, which says bourgeois mediocrity has undermined classical virtues and distracted us from religious truths, thus turning us into comfort-loving Last Men or godless, decadent hedonists. Then there is the conservative pessimism that purports to be a defense of American culture while showing little faith in it. Writers of this school—dissident conservative academics, mostly—argue that the noble American traits have been corrupted by intellectual currents coming out of France, Germany, and the universities, as if the American soul were such a delicate flower that it could be dissolved by the acid influence of Herbert Marcuse.

Finally, there are the freelance pessimists who believe that whatever condition made America great—the family farm, the Greatest Generation, the Depression mentality—has vanished or been forsaken in the land of shopping malls and theme parks.

If you scan these documents all at once, or even if, like a normal person, you absorb them over the course of a lifetime, you find that their depictions congeal into the same sorry scene. America, especially suburban America, is depicted as a comfortable but somewhat vacuous realm of unreality: consumerist, wasteful, complacent, materialistic, and self-absorbed. Sprawling, shopping, Disneyfied Americans have cut themselves off from the sources of enchantment, the things that really matter. They have become too concerned with small and vulgar pleasures, pointless one-upsmanship, and easy values. They have become at once too permissive and too narrow, too self-indulgent and too timid. Their lives are distracted by a buzz of trivial images, by relentless hurry instead of genuine contemplation, information rather than wisdom, and a profusion of superficial choices. Modern Americans rarely sink to the level of depravity—they are too tepid for that—but they don't achieve the highest virtues or the most demanding excellences; nor do they experience the grandest passions or the sublimest expressions of nature's grandeur. As W. E. B. Du Bois put it long ago, "Our machines make things and compel us to sell them. We are rich in food and clothes and starved in culture. . . . All delicate feeling sinks beneath floods of mediocrity."

CHAPTER FOUR

The Spiritual Wind

BUT WHAT IF THAT'S all wrong? What if Thoreau was wrong to think that the ordinary life most Americans choose is a mistake? What if Spengler was wrong to think that Americans are soulless creatures driven by their desire for the almighty dollar? What if even Tocqueville's fear that Americans are disoriented by their materialism, and driven to lonely lives of self-regard and muffled ambitions, was unfounded? What if Lasch was wrong about narcissism, Whyte was wrong about conformity, Bloom was wrong about nihilism, Bork was wrong about hedonism, and the radical Islamicists were wrong about decadence? What if all these writers, and the hundreds more who write along these lines, have failed to observe some crucial trait beneath the crass surface of American life that redeems and corrects for the obvious flaws?

After all, most of these criticisms come enshrouded in predictions of American decline. The pessimists have long predicted that a cultural catastrophe would crash upon this nation and fracture it; or that some other nation—the Soviet Union, United Europe, Japan—was on the verge of overtaking the sagging U.S. as the globe's top dog. But America has an amazing ability to not decline. American standards of living surpassed those in Europe around 1740. For about 260 years, in other words, America has been rich and allegedly money-mad and materialistic. Yet Edward Gibbon would have nothing to write about here, because economic, military, or even social decline hasn't come. On the contrary, despite the supposed sickness of the American soul and the vulgarization of American culture, there have been clear signs of regeneration over the past decades: Crime has dropped, illegitimacy has dropped, and teenage pregnancy has declined, as have teenage suicide rates, divorce rates, and poverty rates.

Americans have shown a remarkable tendency to remain undecadent. Look, for example, at how we spend our money. The Consumer Expenditure Survey reveals that during the 1990s—the wondrous fizzy decade of splendiferous stock-market returns and walloping prosperity—Americans spent less on just about every item in the Hugh Hefner/Larry Flynt/*Maxim* magazine/*Robb Report* repertoire. Americans in 2000 spent less than they did ten years before on steaks, martinis, cigars, jewelry, watches, furniture, toys, and sound equipment. They increased their spending on education, housing, transportation, and computers. Americans spent 10 percent less on food in general but 15 percent more on fresh vegetables. They spent 14 percent less on clothing, the largest decline in any category, though they did spend 12 percent more on shoes. They spent less on entertainment, as baby boomers went less frequently to rock concerts, and chose to go, less expensively, to the movies.

Overall, this is not the picture of a nation of superficiality and self-indulgence. American beaches still aren't Rio-style thong expos; nor are they Southern European nudist zones, where seventy-year-old women who grew up with corsets and propriety suddenly get the urge in advanced retirement to throw off the vestments of civilization and let their vein patterns hang out in the breeze. Despite leadership from the top, we haven't learned to relax about adultery, and serious sex surveys do not depict a culture of serious kinkiness and sensuality. Picture a typical American man going on the Internet looking for some pornography. In a few minutes, he can't help himself, he's clicked over to LendingTree.com, and he's checking out the latest mortgage rates.

Obviously, huge problems remain, but if you go back and read the leading social scientists of the past few decades, you are struck by the fact that they were invariably too pessimistic, too stuffed with gloomy predictions and forebodings of catastrophe, the vast majority of which never came true. America is a country that goes every year to the doctor and every year is told that it has contracted some fatal disease—whether it is conformity, narcissism, godlessness, or civic disengagement—and a year later, the patient comes back with cheeks still red and muscles still powerful. The diagnosis is just as grim, and the patient is just as healthy.

It brings to mind a question: If middle America is so stupid, vulgar, self-absorbed, and materialistic, which it often is, then how can America itself be so great?

The Counter Tradition

Quietly, alongside the torrent of writing about the crassness of American life, there is another, less crowded intellectual tradition. This line is advanced by writers who believe that the materialist baubles—the sport utes and the clip-on nails—are surface products of a deeper spiritual striving. They argue that America is an exceptional nation infused with unique purpose and spirit.

In one of his later and generally neglected essays, "The Fortune of the Republic," Emerson put it most succinctly: "They [who] complain of the flatness of American life have no perception of its destiny. They are not Americans." They don't see that America is "a garden of plenty . . . a magazine of power. . . . Here is man in the garden of Eden; here, the Genesis and the Exodus." And here, Emerson continued, would come the final Revelation.

Walt Whitman, who was not blind to his nation's many faults, also perceived that America's "extreme business energy," its "almost maniacal appetite for wealth," was just part of its "vast revolutionary" drive. "My theory includes riches, the getting of riches, and the amplest products," Whitman wrote in his essay "Democratic Vistas." "Upon them, as upon substrata, I raise the edifice [of revolution] . . . the new and orbic traits waiting to be launched for in the firmament that is, and is to be, America."

For writers in this tradition, material striving blends with spiritual aspiration. The race for riches is just a manifestation of a deeper metaphysical striving that's in the midst of realizing its glorious destiny. American life, by this account, is amphibious. It is crass but also visionary, practical but also fantastic. America is the most moralistic nation on earth and also the most materialistic. As the historian Sacvan Bercovitch put it in his book *The American Jeremiad*, "A crucial distinction was *not* made in this country"—the distinction between the sacred and the profane.

Other writers have hinted at the same phenomenon. An American, according to George Santayana, is "an idealist working on matter." Santayana spent much of his life in the U.S. but never felt at home here and returned to Europe in his later years. But his book *Character and Opinion in the United States* remains one of the most intelligent inspections of the American spirit. Santayana believed it was a complete mistake to think that Americans are driven by a love of money. If Americans truly cared about material things, they would hoard and protect them. But they are loose and careless with their stuff, eager to move on to the next new thing: "The American talks about money, because that is the symbol and measure he has at hand for success, intelligence and power; but as to money itself he makes, loses, spends, and gives it away with a very light heart." Instead, there is some deeper impulsion: "To be an American is of itself almost a moral condition, an education and a career."

Later, Luigi Barzini, in his essay "The Baffling Americans," made this argument at slightly greater length:

> What few imitators have understood is that the secret of the United States' tremendous success was in reality not merely technology, know-how, the work ethic, the urge to succeed or plain greed. It

was a spiritual wind that drove the Americans irresistibly ahead from the beginning. What was behind their compulsion to improve man's lot was an all-pervading sense of duty, the submission to a God-given imperative, to a God-given code of personal behavior, the willing acceptance of all the necessary sacrifices, including death in battle. Few foreigners understand this, even today. The United States appears to them merely as the triumph of soulless materialism.

These writers are on to something, but they are always maddeningly vague. They almost never explain in an overarching or specific way what they mean when they say Americans are driven by a "spiritual wind," or that being American is a "moral condition." Their observations come in fragments, aphorisms, and stray notes. They sense a spiritual force motivating Americans. They feel that somehow the materialism is infused with moralism, but they seem unwilling to investigate or nail down its features and effects.

That's probably because most of us are trained to think and write about society as a collection of social conditions, economic forces, or—at the most abstract—political and philosophical ideas. We are not quite comfortable crossing over to the religious and the transcendental. After all, sophisticated people in the past few centuries have tended to assume that the world is becoming more secular as it becomes richer and better educated. The most influential thinkers have sought to explain behavior largely by "hard" and "scientific" secular terms. Writers from Adam Smith and Karl Marx to Sigmund Freud have worked up sophisticated and brilliant social-science models to describe why people behave the way they do, and these tools have tremendous explanatory power.

Yet there is something else out there, some religious or mythical or metaphysical yearning that refuses to die, and that shapes everyday life in ways that cannot be predicted easily by journalists, social scientists, or even philosophers. Writers in this second tradition of writing about America— and I am thinking about Barzini, Santayana, and above all, Whitman—sense the religious impulses that infuse American society, but they don't quite lay it out for us.

The Idealistic Nation

In the old days, preachers did it better. America, historians remind us, was born in a seedbed of religion. There is a vast and ever growing literature on Puritan belief, on the sermons of Edwards and Mather and so on. I suspect so many writers are drawn to this subject because in the seventeenth, eighteenth, and even the nineteenth centuries, Americans were articulate about their guiding religious and transcendental beliefs. We are still shaped by such beliefs, we just don't know how to talk about them as well.

When you read early American sermons, you find much that is alien now, but it is also possible to infer—and historians such as Sacvan Bercovitch seem to have spent their careers doing precisely this—which metaphysical passions still influence us. For example, seventeenth- and eighteenth-century ministers were explicit in their belief that America was the redeemer nation. As the historian Perry Miller put it, the Puritans felt that God had assigned them to run an errand into the wilderness and thus create a new society and a new church that would fulfill His plan for the human race.

America, in the minds of these preachers, was a new Jerusalem, the setting for the final salvation, and the settlers themselves were a new chosen people who, in rejecting the corruptions of the Old World, would help create a second paradise in the New World. America, in other words, had a sacred mission, in their eyes, to fulfill the biblical prophecies. "There are many arguments to persuade us that our Glorious Lord will have an Holy City in America; a City, the street whereof shall be pure gold," Cotton Mather preached in his 1709 sermon "God's City: America." By the time of the revolution, the theme had been secularized. John Adams declared: "I always consider the settlement of America with reverence and wonder, as the opening of a grand scene and design in providence, for the illumination of the ignorant and the emancipation of the slavish part of mankind all over the earth."

In the eyes of these early Americans, the United States was not merely a nation, it was an eschatology. It was a vision of human fulfillment. This sense that America had a divinely ordained mission did not diminish with the years. "Our whole history appears like a last effort of the Divine Providence in behalf of the human race," Emerson wrote. In 1865, Edward Beecher observed, "Men in all walks of life believed that the sovereign Holy Spirit has endowed the nation with resources sufficient to convert and civilize the globe, to purge human society of all its evils, and to usher in Christ's reign on earth."

Or, as Herman Melville famously summarized the creed in his novel *White-Jacket*:

The future is endowed with such a life, that it lives to us even in anticipation . . . the Future is the Bible of the Free. . . . We Americans are the peculiar chosen people—the Israel of our time. . . . God has predestined, mankind expects, great things from our race; and great things we feel in our souls. . . . We are the pioneers of the world; the advance-guard, sent on through the wilderness of untried things, to break a new path in the New World that is ours. . . . Long enough have we been skeptics with regard to ourselves, and doubted whether, indeed, the political Messiah had come. But he has come in us.

Today few believe that Americans are God's new chosen people. But Americans are different enough from other peoples to consider themselves an exceptional nation, with an exceptional mission in the world. Whether they know it or not, they have inherited a certain style of idealism, a faith, and a fulfilling and chiliastic creed.

It is often declared that America is not only a plot of land but also an idea and a cause. As the political theorist Martin Diamond has observed, words like "Americanization," "Americanism," and "un-American" have no counterparts in any other language. Nobody says that a country or culture is being Italianized or Japanized or Chinese-ized, yet the Americanization of the world has been a topic of debate for a century. This doesn't mean just that there are McDonald's and Tom Cruise movies sweeping the landscape; it means some distinctive creed, mentality, and way of life is felt to be overrunning earlier patterns and cultures.

As Leon Samson, a radical socialist, put it in his 1933 book *Toward a United Front*:

When we examine the meaning of Americanism, we discover that Americanism is to the American not a tradition or a territory, not what France is to a Frenchman or England to an Englishman, but a doctrine—what socialism is to a socialist. Like socialism, Americanism is looked upon . . . as a highly attenuated, conceptualized, platonic, impersonal attraction toward a system of ideas, a solemn assent to a handful of final notions—democracy, liberty, opportunity, to all of which the American adheres rationalistically much as a socialist adheres to his socialism—because it does him good, because it gives him work, because, so he thinks, it guarantees him happiness. Americanism has thus served as a substitute for socialism. Every concept in socialism has its substitutive counter-concept in Americanism, and that is why the socialist argument falls so fruitlessly on the American ear. . . . The American does not want to listen to socialism, since he thinks he already has it."

Or, as Sacvan Bercovitch argues in *Rites of Assent*:

Only "America," of all national designations, took on the combined force of eschatology and chauvinism. Many forms of nationalism have laid claim to a world-redeeming promise; many Christian sects have sought, in open or secret heresy, to find the sacred in the profane; many European Protestants have linked the soul's journey and the way to wealth. But only the "American Way," of all modern symbologies, has managed to circumvent the contradictions inherent in these approaches. Of all symbols of identity, only "American" has succeeded in uniting nationality and universality, civic and spiritual selfhood, sacred and secular history, the country's past and paradise to be, in a single transcendent ideal.

The Exceptionalists

Few writers explore this line of argument today. It's deeply unfashionable to talk about a distinct national character. But even if Americans are not united by a creed, they are united by the fact that they are creedal. While they have many different ways of defining a proposition that the nation should stand for, they share a mentality that assumes the nation should stand for something—something working toward perfection. What Americans share, in other words, is an inherited sense that history has a story line; and that each of us, individually and as a citizen of the nation, plays a role in bringing the story to its happy ending.

This mentality leads to a few behavioral traits. For example, historians point out that a tremendous strain of anxiety runs through U.S. history, the nagging and sometimes panicked sense that we are failing to live up to our ideals and mission, that if we Americans fail, then that will be the most terrible failure in human history.

This anxiety propels Americans to strive and reform perpetually. It helps account for the periodic awakenings and moralistic crusades that recur throughout American history—the Great Awakenings, the abolitionist movement, the temperance movement, the civil rights, antiabortion, even anti-smoking movements. America is not only the nation where you can get a super-size tub of french fries to go with your thirty-two-ounce double cheeseburger, it is also just about the only nation where people blow up abortion clinics. Whether it is fatty food or moral crusades, nothing here ever stops at its logical conclusion; some crusading fervor propels things a few steps beyond.

Historians have often noted a strain of perfectionism running through American life. As Richard Hofstadter once wryly remarked, "The United States was the only country in the world that began with perfection and aspired to progress." This trait has its roots as a religious and, more specifically, Protestant perfectionism, the striving to be finished Christians. "Nothing short of the general renewal of society ought to satisfy any soldiers of Christ," declared the nineteenth-century Methodist author William Arthur. But it soon pervades society in a generalized sense that one must perpetually strive to eliminate the tensions inherent in a world caught between promise and fulfillment.

So Americans developed an elaborate faith in education and a zeal for political causes that promise to purify the nation and the world. They are gripped sometimes by a zeal for purgative wars that will cleanse the world of some evil. Most of all, they have a zeal for permanent self-improvement, an impulse to move constantly toward the realization of one's perfect self.

When he arrived on these shores, Luigi Barzini was immediately struck, as others have been, by this strange compulsion "to tirelessly tinker, improve everything and everybody, never leave anything alone." He was amazed by the incredible profusion of self-help manuals in every bookstore, in every pharmacy, on every magazine rack:

One could learn for a few dollars how to speak masterfully in public, be irresistible, dominate a meeting, mesmerize superiors or opponents, make friends, sell everything to everybody, and in the end, with the first million in the bank, spot prodigious investment opportunities, investments that multiplied themselves like amoebas. . . . People hopefully bought these books by the millions, as true believers buy sacred relics or bottles of miraculous holy water.

In *Character and Opinion in the United States,* George Santayana argued that Americans go through life with two worlds in their heads. In one part of their brain, they see the real world; but in the neighboring part, they see the perfect imagined world, assumed to be close by and realizable. These two worlds sometimes get confused and intermingle. Americans' "moral world always contains undiscovered or thinly peopled continents open to those who are more attached to what might or should be than to what already is. Americans are eminently prophets; they apply morals to public affairs; they are impatient and enthusiastic."

An American is thus imbued with a distinctive orientation: future-mindedness. "His enthusiasm for the future is profound; he can conceive of no more decisive way of recommending an opinion or a practice than to say that it is what everybody is coming to adopt. This expectation of what he approves, or approval of what he expects, makes up his optimism." He continues:

At the same time, the American is imaginative; for where life is intense, imagination is intense also.

Were he not imaginative he would not live so much in the future. But his imagination is practical and the future it forecasts is immediate; it works with the clearest and least ambiguous terms known to his experience, in terms of number, measure, contrivance, economy and speed. He is an idealist working on matter. . . . All his life he jumps into the train after it has started and jumps out before it has stopped.

The Mystery of Motivation

Over the past two chapters, I've sketched two broad ways of describing life in the United States. One sees middle-American life as essentially mediocre, materialistic, driven by worldly longing. The second sees a life that is primarily metaphysical and imaginative, in which everyday Americans are driven to realize grand and utopian ideals *through* material things. These two views are different answers to the mystery of motivation. Everybody agrees that Americans are driven by some impulsion to be energetic, hardworking, and radioactive. They disagree about the nature of that impulsion. Those who suspect America see it, with the German philosopher Martin Heidegger, as "the most dangerous form of boundlessness, because it appears in a middle-class way of life mixed with Christianity, and all this in an atmosphere that lacks completely any sense of history." Others see the impulsion as a noble and salvific force pushing history toward a glorious material and spiritual fulfillment.

I would like to think that the second way of looking at

America is the true way. I would like to think that an idealist flame does burn in every American split level, that everyday American life is shaped by grand metaphysical visions, a holy sense of mission, and a commitment to redeem the failures of the present by committing oneself to a glorious future. I would like to believe that we are all driven by some spiritual impulsion of which we are perhaps not even aware. This condition of mind is simply the water in which we swim. This worldview is so ingrained in our culture that it isn't even necessary to pass it down consciously from parent to child.

But it's hard to be sure that normal American life truly is that heroic. W. H. Auden once wrote that "The Commuter can't forget / The Pioneer." Possibly every commuter, or at least some commuters, really are pioneers pushing into the wilderness of the future, driven by a radical hopefulness, a green light shimmering across the water that redeems, Gatsby-style, all the shallow fleshiness of life. Maybe America is in fact enflamed and ennobled not by a creation myth but by a fruition myth, a noble vision worth striving for.

But maybe a commuter is just a commuter. Maybe he or she is just the person you see through the rearview mirror in the car behind you at the red light—spilling coffee, applying her lipstick, picking his nose. Maybe all that stuff about utopian visions and missionary causes was just made up by some of our more poetically minded writers and romanticists. Or maybe what was a grand mentality has been gradually buried under layers of trivial concerns. Maybe the forces of affluence or selfishness or modernity or triviality have smothered what were once admirable ideals. Maybe middle-class American life *is* shallow and uninspiring.

Let's look into the matter. Let's move away from the writing about America and get back to looking at life as it is actually lived in America. Let's take a few dips into the stream of normal American behavior, looking for signs of materialistic crassness but also imaginative hope. Maybe even among the barbecue grills and the big-box malls, we'll find some reflections of that redeeming fire or signs of that spiritual wind.

It's not necessary to be too solemn during our little excursions into American life. Sometimes a little satire is in order. In any case, here we go.

CHAPTER FIVE

Growing

I'M TRYING TO PERSUADE my kids to go into the soon-to-be-lucrative field of playdate law. I'm convinced that in a few years, parents are going to be suing each other because their child received insufficiently nutritious afternoon snacks while visiting playmates' homes.

The way I see it, the role of the playdate lawyer will begin long before the actual playdate. First the attorney will offer advice on which of, say, a second-grader's classmates would be a good fit for a developmentally appropriate and cognitively enhancing play session—which classmate has sufficient conflict-resolution skills and toy-sharing capacities and the sort of at-home recreation resources necessary to provide an experientially diverse afternoon. Then the attorney will work with the other party to make the playdate overture and explore whether the two children have any free afternoons in common, or whether their soccer league/ballet/SAT prep/recorder lesson/hockey practice/therapist schedules make *any* playdate impossible.

Assuming the two children have a free afternoon within the next four-year period, the playdate lawyer will begin negotiating the predate agreements, which are parent-to-parent contracts setting down clear guidelines on all of the normal playdate issues: GameBoy preferences, mean-older-sibling control measures, food-allergy concerns, pet anxieties, and early-pickup contingency plans in case one of the parties decides in the middle that this playdate simply isn't enriching enough.

Within the larger field of playdate law, I suspect a subspecialty will emerge around the VSIs (video-screen issues). Attorneys in this niche will negotiate separate predate protocols on whether there should be a Nintendo ban or Nickelodeon consumption limits during the playdate, and whether computer games should be prohibited, and if so, whether that includes the ones that teach phonics and typing skills. Some parents will prefer to sign a Document of Joint Understanding forbidding the viewing of all Disney videos, while others will deem it acceptable for the children to spend time watching videos from the *Little Mermaid/Lion King* era but none after *Pocahontas*.

Finally, the playdate lawyer will accompany the parent on the predate inspection, ensuring the host family adheres to the conventional safety norms. In other words, making sure that they have childproof devices over every outlet, cabinet handle, and stove control; that they have motion sensors within fifteen feet of any stairway; that the corners of any hard surface have been rounded to prevent gouging;

that all construction paper in the house is made from specially treated flame-retardant fibers; that the lawn has been aerated to make it soft in case of falls; and that all LEGOs are water-soluble to guard against choking.

Once the county inspector has verified that the home is a peanut-free zone, and that the air contains none of the ambient food-additive particulates that have been found to induce hyperactivity and ADHD in laboratory rats, the attorney will do a final walk-through and certify that the playdate is officially arranged. The parents then exchange pager numbers and medical records, and the kids are all set to have a fantastic time—unless either party offers to pick up the other family's child from school, in which case a whole other range of transportation security measures must be dealt with.

The way I see it, the issues inherent in playdate law are sufficiently complex, and the parents' stake in their child's development is sufficiently overwrought, that before long the Ubermoms will be litigating against each other in droves. I suspect parents of all sorts will be tempted to go to court to resolve playdate conflicts, but the Ubermoms will be especially likely because of their superior parenting skills.

Ubermoms

Ubermoms are women who graduated Phi Beta Kappa in economics and engineering, earned MBAs with honors, and rose to the level of senior vice president for corporate strategy at Fortune 500 companies before giving up the job to raise a family, thus channeling their enormous drive, massive intelligence, and $950,000 worth of education on the nurturing of their junior achievers.

You see the Ubermoms at the board and parent-association meetings of most high-achieving elementary schools. You can spot them easily, because they generally weigh less than their children. They may have given birth to their youngest one, say, twelve hours before, but they still have washboard abs and buttocks firmer than footballs. That's because even at the moment of conception, which occurs during highly aerobic multiorgasmic intercourse, the prospective alpha mother is doing special breast exercises to prevent sagging. While her love partner is contentedly dozing by her side in postconnubial bliss, as his sperm is breaching the membrane of her incredibly fit and fertile egg, she is staring at the ceiling calculating which year her child will be ready to enter nursery school and when she can run for chairperson of the school auction.

During pregnancy, Ubermom—assuming she decides not to enter that year's Tour de France—is generally found in tranquil yoga positions, performing special pregnant-woman weight-lifting exercises, and devoting the energies she formerly spent on career advancement to walkathons that raise awareness of life-threatening and other diseases. During the second trimester, she'll be marching, biking, jogging, and running for lupus, leukemia, MS, heart disease, breast cancer, and the flu. When a friend gets the flu, Ubermom puts on her lycra and goes around the block raising money. Her lapels are ablaze with so many pink, green, black, yellow, and red awareness ribbons she looks like the UN headquarters when she stands still.

She also spends her prebirth months altering society's conceptions of female beauty, studying medical textbooks on amniotic fluids, reading thoughtful articles by trained psychologists in magazines such as *Child* and *Parenting* ("Could Your Praise Be Hurting Your Child?" "How Safe Is Your Drinking Water?"), calculating how many children to have (three is the new two, one parent informed me recently), coming up with prebirth colic-prevention strategies and selecting pretentiously nonpretentious names she thinks will look good on preschool cubbies. (If she has a girl, she's thinking of naming her Campbell, Griffin, McKenzie, or one of the other clan names from *Braveheart*. If it's a boy, she's vacillating among Max, Sam, Caleb, and a few other names that she associates with stylishly retro 1930s ethnic deli owners.) In 1951, 25 percent of American babies had one of the ten most popular names—John, Mary, Mike, and so on. But by 1999, when significant numbers of Ubermoms and Uberdads had identified baby naming as one more realm of individuation and self-expression, only 12 percent of American babies were given one of the ten most popular names.

Ubermom babies generally weigh more than Saint Bernards. The mothers have been ingesting so many vitamin-enriched soy-based dietary supplements during pregnancy, and their baby's resulting growth has been so phenomenal, that the little creatures enter the world looking like toothless defensive linemen.

In the delivery room, the Ubermoms generally cut the umbilical cord themselves (assuming they're not busy adjusting the video lighting) and then, focusing their attention on the delivery doctor, utter the words that mark the highest stage of Ubermomism: "So, is her Apgar score above average?"

As you know, Americans live to be tested. From the

first gulp of breath, the little American boy or girl has his or her aptitude prodded, poked, measured, evaluated, and compared. This basic system of comparing, grading, and evaluating does not cease so long as the heart continues its pitter-patter. The baby who begins life with the Apgar score continues through years of grades, elementary school accountability tests, SAT exams, workplace-aptitude measures, and retirement-plan evaluations unto death. The American is conceived amid a flurry of quality-control evaluations ("Was it good for you, honey?"), lives in an atmosphere of progress reports, and dies amid a carefully calibrated burst of obituaries, funeral evaluations, and testimonials. If God were an American, the Last Judgment would be a multiple-choice questionnaire with one of those bubble answer forms you fill out with a number-two pencil, and American babies would be scoring 680 or 720 minimum because of their superior test-taking skills.

Ubermom is not yet done with her delivery-room gasping and heaving, and already she's got one of those *What To Expect . . .* books in her hands. She's reading the chapter "What to Expect After Three and a Half Minutes," which tells her that at this point in its development, her child should be able to mewl, may be able to wheeze, and might possibly be able to puke, and when she sees her little one vomiting up a storm, she looks around at the assembled medical professionals, expecting them to announce that this baby is the best they've ever seen and that she is to be moved immediately over to the special gifted-and-talented ward for Ivy-bound infants and their mothers. I've long contemplated writing a book called "What to DEMAND When You're Expecting: Pregnancy for Fascists," but that probably won't sell, because new parents are in a temporary soft, fuzzy stage.

The first day of her baby's life is an exciting one for Ubermom, because it is also her first session with the lactation consultant. Since 1995 the number of consultants in the U.S. accredited by the International Board of Lactation Consultant Examiners has more than doubled, so there are now at least eight thousand lactation experts advising American mothers on how to breast-feed. As the activists at La Leche League, a pro-breast-feeding advocacy group, put it, "Breast milk is liquid gold, and it's yours to give." So the Ubermoms take the time for thorough nipple and areola preparation. They know what positions will produce superior latching between their baby's gums and their breast. They know what it feels like when their baby has achieved an effective seal, the leak-free suction environment that will make for steady milk flow. And they know all this not only because they take the time to master the proper skill set, but because their culture has produced hundreds of thousands of experts, advisers, child psychologists, social scientists, and medical researchers to analyze every aspect of child rearing and embalm the whole nurturing process with advice, findings, warnings, books, and gear.

The furnishing of a newborn's room these days is roughly comparable to the construction of an orbiting scientific laboratory. Space must be found for all the requisite air-filtering mechanisms, odor-free diaper-disposal systems, stereos for the *Mozart for Babies* CDs that will be playing constantly to enhance the little one's early-life brain functions. Hanging over the baby's crib will be a black-and-white graphic mobile to enhance spatial-recognition skills. The patterns on this mobile should complement the patterns on the flash cards that modern parents flash before babies at mealtime and during car trips in the hope of generating a few extra IQ points.

American women are having their first children later and later. The rate of first births for women in their thirties and forties has quadrupled over the past thirty years, while rates for women who have their first child in their twenties have dropped by a third. People in their early twenties are still too stupid and horny to get overwrought about raising their kids. But the Ubermoms in their late thirties and early forties are smart enough to know how to shape their children into being perfect, without being overbearing about it, like some of those other parents one could name.

So in the first few weeks of life, Ubermom will measure her child's walking reflexes, begin the baby-massage regimen her personal coach recommended, and get the little tot his or her first aerobics instructor. I once saw what looked like an Ubermom roundup on one of the lawns in New York's Central Park. There was an outer ring of Hispanic nannies standing next to empty strollers. In the inner ring was a circle of white mothers sitting on blankets with their babies; and in the center was a fitness counselor showing mothers how to move their babies' arms around for maximum firmness and flexibility.

By the time her child is in the pre-preschool years, Ubermom is boosting her junior achiever's prephonics-acquisition skills. She's patiently counting Cheerios at the breakfast table to accelerate number recognition, she's working with her baby on the extra-large pudgy-fingers computer keyboard lest the infant fall behind in alphabet mastery, and she's reading multicultural animal tales so her child grows up prejudice-free.

All of this will allow Ubermom to hold her head up in the most ruthless jungle of all, the nursery school parents' social. In this Hobbesian state of nature, competing Ubermoms drop broad hints about their child's budding musical abilities; the stay-at-home moms give parenting pointers to the working moms, who are quietly contemplating homicide; and the overweight moms huddle in the corner feeling like they are the walrus display at the zoo. One uber-Ubermom, who, after months of careful positioning, has gotten herself named class parent, is busy voicing her concerns over the school's fire-drill policy, while two other Ubermoms face off at the punch bowl. Ubermom A secretly reflects that while her three-year-old can sing the entire alphabet song, identify six of the ten first numerals, and was clearly the most promising student in the parent-toddler poetry workshop, Ubermom B's little boy spends all day on the ground staring at toy-truck wheels. Meanwhile, Ubermom B is thinking that while her little guy is so mature he leads the class in tearless drop-offs, every time Ubermom A tries to kiss her daughter good-bye, the girl sobs hysterically and clings to her mother's legs as if she's being abandoned to the Khmer Rouge.

Great Expectations

Dorothy Parker once said that American children aren't raised, they are incited. They are given food, shelter, and applause. It is true that since time immemorial, observers of the United States have commented on how indulgent and deferential Americans are toward their children.

That's because, as we tirelessly tell one another, our

children are our future. "Every child begins the world again," Henry David Thoreau declared. A newborn's life seems (and much of the time is) radically open, with potentialities limitless and vast. With our loose social structures and geographic dispersion, the future of an American child is unknowable. It's impossible to know if the child will keep his or her parents' religion (possibly not), live in the same state (probably not), follow in his parents' career footsteps (almost certainly not). The greatest successes or the saddest failures seem possible.

As the anthropologist Margaret Mead observed, American children are expected to lead lives *unlike* their parents'. In many families, it is expected—and in some immigrant families, it is demanded—that children shall exceed their parents. Each generation understands that it shall surpass the last, and each generation has a duty to see that the next one can do the same. And so from age three, American kids grow up with a question ringing in their ears: What do you want to be when you grow up? Not what do you want to do, but what do you want to *be*. What divine future existence dances in your brain, what field of glory? While the answers may change over a kid's childhood—from astronaut to shortstop to rap star to veterinarian—subtle frowns of disapproval greet anything that is not lofty. Somewhere around nursery school age, kids are infused by their parents, teachers, and caregivers—by the whole adult establishment—with the ideology of potentiality. So many roads beckon. Life is plastic; one makes out of it what one wills. There is nothing you cannot do if you set your mind to it. Indeed, life is a quest, a climb to realize your fullest potential, and develop your capacities through perpetual improvement.

The Sloan Study of Youth and Social Development recently found that 80 percent of high school seniors expect to work in a professional job, 71 percent expect to become millionaires, and 40 percent expect to be millionaires by the time they are fifty. These are expectations of an insanely high level, and they are radically higher than the expectations similar students had four decades ago.

American children, raised in an atmosphere of hope, are also raised with the inevitable flip side of hope, anxiety. If you return to the U.S. after a long time abroad, you are immediately struck by how fraught American culture is on the whole subject of childhood. Stories of kidnapping fill the local news. Child-abuse scandals are prosecuted and misprosecuted with almost Salem-witch-trial fervor. Drugs, cigarettes, and Internet porn are seen as evil specters at the door and outside the windows, seeping through any crack into the sanctity of the home. Brain chemistry is destiny, so you'd better stimulate those synapses by the time the neurons either form or perish at age three. Newsmagazines are filled with ominous stories on Dangerous Day Care and Driveway Dangers. Child-rearing magazines are filled with perfectionist instruction on the most minute matters; *Parenting* magazine recently ran an article called "Nose Blowing 101," on how to hold a tissue under your child's mucus.

The names of activist groups such as the Children's Defense Fund and Focus on the Family suggest wartime preparedness. Libraries are filled with book upon book, report upon report, with such titles as *Stolen Childhood* and *The Threatened Child*. The most influential education report of our lifetimes was called "A Nation at Risk." It's not just that the schools are mediocre; the whole nation is at risk.

The most devastating evidence of American parenthood's overwrought nature is that most of the child-care books—which are written by experts who spend their entire lives thinking about child rearing—don't tell parents to concentrate more on child rearing. The experts—and there are more than ten thousand parenting books on Amazon.com—feel compelled to tell parents to relax. The entire literature of parental instruction can practically be summed up in the phrase "Don't worry. This happens to everyone."

Somehow this advice only sends parents deeper into the carpe-diem dilemma. On the one hand, childhood is supposed to be a happy, innocent time. It is the one time in life, the precious, never-to-return moment, when a person should be free to have fun, to not feel the insistent pressures of work, obligation, and responsibility. Yet there is an equal and opposite voice: Irresponsibility now will lead to failure and doom later on. If little Sarah doesn't develop the right work habits, what sort of life will she have? The future is lurking just ahead, making its demands. Parents are perpetually bouncing on the horns of the dilemma, making little guilty jokes about the amount of therapy their kids will someday need to correct for vague errors made in the character-molding years.

In 1844, Ralph Waldo Emerson wrote in his journal, "I wish to have rural strength and religion for my children, and I wish city facility and polish. I find with chagrin that I cannot have both." Today many parents wish spontaneity, eccentricity, and imagination for their kids, and also industriousness, self-discipline, and success. They long to inculcate their children with both sets of values, but they look up one day and notice that the values of achievement always take precedence. Preparation for success trumps spontaneity and eccentricity.

It's no wonder so many parents drive around in vehicles that look like tanks. It's no wonder that the inside of the average minivan looks like a battlefield that's hosted marauding armies wielding cracker crumbs, juice boxes, and candy wrappers. The whole country is on a war footing when it comes to raising kids.

The Most Supervised Generation

Roughly two-thirds of women with kids under three are in the workforce, compared to roughly one-third twenty years ago. At the same time, children—at least those in two-parent families—spend more time with their parents than they did before.

The University of Michigan's Institute for Social Research runs the most exhaustive and reliable studies on how parents and children spend their day. Today, the institute reports, the average child spends 31 hours a week with his or her mother, up from about 25 hours a week in 1980. The average child spends 23 hours a week with his or her father, up from 19 hours a week. This does not mean that families are able to dawdle together over the dinner table. But it does mean that parents have gone to extraordinary lengths not to let jobs get in the way of child rearing. They have added work time, but on average, they have not stolen those hours from child-rearing time. The time has come out of housework, relaxation, and adult friendships.

Middle-class families often become factories for producing happy and successful children. Parents become co-CEOs in the manufacture of junior achievers. They measure themselves by what sort of life preparation they are providing for their kids. They orient their vacations for maximum childhood pleasure. They sacrifice golf, socializing, reading, even their sex lives. And when a friend has a newborn, they give the following advice: "From now on, you won't have time to do the things you used to enjoy doing, but don't worry, you'll find a whole new set of things you'll enjoy more."

The University of Michigan time diaries reveal that over the past twenty years, there has been a quiet revolution in the way kids are raised in America. The amount of time spent in unsupervised play has declined dramatically, while the amount of time spent in adult-supervised skill-enhancing activities has gone up. Between 1981 and 1997, the amount of time children between the ages of three and twelve spent playing by themselves indoors declined by almost a fifth. The amount of time spent watching TV declined by 23 percent. The amount of time studying increased by a fifth. The amount of time doing organized sports increased by 27 percent.

Drive around your neighborhood. Remember all those parks that used to have open fields and undeveloped forests? They've been carved up into neatly trimmed soccer and baseball fields, crowded with parents in folding chairs who are watching their kids perform. In 1981 U.S. Youth Soccer had 811,000 registered players. By 1998 it had nearly 3 million.

This is the probably the most supervised generation in human history. Never before has such a high proportion of our young people been enrolled in school. Now 91 percent of five-to-fifteen-year-olds are in school, compared to 83 percent in 1950. Now there are fewer than thirteen students per teacher in school, compared to more than twenty-six students per teacher then, if you take the average of all the many different types of school districts.

School is tougher. During the 1960s and 1970s, schools assigned less and less homework, so that by 1981 the average six-to-eight-year-old was doing fifty-two minutes of homework a week. By 1997 the amount of homework assigned to the average child of the same age had doubled to over two hours a week. Meanwhile, the school day, which had shortened during the 1960s and 1970s, has steadily lengthened, as has the school year. Requirements have stiffened. Before 1983 the average school district required one year of math and one year of science for high school graduation. Now the average high school calls for two years of each.

The culture of schools has tightened, too. In the 1970s, rebelling against the rigid desks-in-a-row pedagogy of the 1950s, schools experimented with open campuses and schools without walls. The language of education has changed, and the emphasis is on testing, accountability, and order. Especially order. Zero tolerance is a mantra. Increasingly, and in surprising numbers, kids whose behavior subverts efficient learning are medicated so that they and their classmates can keep pace. The United States produces and uses about 90 percent of the world's Ritalin and its generic equivalents, and the number of students on the drug shoots upward every year—especially in the middle- and upper-middle-class suburbs. As Neil Howe and William Strauss observe in their book, *Millennials Rising*: "Ironically, where young boomers once turned to drugs to prompt impulses and think outside the box, today they turn to drugs to suppress their kids' impulses and keep their behavior inside the box."

In short, the childhood of unsupervised loitering, wandering, and exploring has been replaced by the childhood of adult-supervised improvement. Bike riding around town has given way to oboe lessons and SAT prep. Time spent hanging out on the corner is now spent in the backseat of the van, going from after-school tutoring to community service. More people are competing harder for those precious college-admissions slots and highly skilled job openings, and as a result, Americans are engaged in a massive cross-generational conspiracy to produce success. The urge to launch our children into marvelous futures of ascent and happiness makes Ubermoms of us all.

The System

There exists in this country a massive organic apparatus for the production of children, a mighty Achievatron. Nobody planned it. There is no central control deck. But all the anxious parents, child psychologists, teachers, tutors, coaches, counselors, therapists, family-centered activist groups, and social critics organically cohere into an omnipresent network of encouragement, improvement, advice, talent maximization, and capacity fulfillment. This system is frightening, when you step back and grasp its awesome power, its ability to mold little ones for frictionless ascent and smooth their eccentricities to maximize social aerodynamics. Worse than being run through the assembly line is not being run through it. The main tragedy of the country—and it is a genuine tragedy—is that millions of kids never make it onto the con-veyor belt. They are left behind.

But in many middle-class homes, kids perform so many self-enhancement tasks that they suffer from what toy manufacturers call "age compression." The toys, such as Barbies or Hot Wheels, that used to appeal to eight-year-olds now appeal to four-year-olds. The eight-year-olds have moved on to laptops. Parental conversation consists largely of quoting their children's brilliant aperçus to each other. The refrigerator door becomes a shrine to children's prowess. I look into my garage these days, and I see a vast landscape of protective gear. My daughter, who is nine, is already a four-helmet kid. She has a bike-riding helmet, a horseback-riding helmet, a batting helmet, and an ice-hockey helmet. These helmets serve as testimony to a cer-tain sort of active, scheduled, yet massively protected childhood.

Never underestimate the Achievatron's power to trans-form daily life. Go to a hockey rink at six A.M., and there will be kids lugging body-bag-sized equipment valises from the SUVs into the rink. By six-twenty they'll be doing belly flops across the blue line while a young woman in an Amherst Women's Hockey sweatshirt glides by at twice the speed of sound, offering pointers. Then the games start, and you've got these miniature humans, in hockey leagues with names like Squirt and Mite, zooming around at 30 mph, executing passes like the Toronto Maple Leafs.

Go up to any semirural Sheraton on a summer week-end, and parked outside will be pickup trucks with little trailers hitched on the back and travel-baseball-team logos painted on the outside: the Bethesda–Chevy Chase Heat, the Florida Lightning, the San Diego Stars. (Communities tend to name their teams after weather systems or astronomical features, since it's no longer politically acceptable to use ethnic groups.) The hotel pool area will be teeming with kids who have baseball tans—brown on their necks and faces and pale on their foreheads, where their caps protect them from the sun. On one side of the pool will be groups of middle-aged women with "Baseball Mom" T-shirts; on the other side, the dads will be gathered in serious consultation over the scouting notes on their eleven-year-olds' next opponents.

The entire weekend economy of small-town America seems to depend on prepubescent sports tournaments with boxing-bout names—Beast of the East, Clash of the Champions, Fling in the Spring—to which teams travel hundreds or even thousands of miles to play. The teams arrive in great convoys, with exclamation-laden cheers and admonitions ("Go Jordan! #6! Goin' to the 'ships!") painted on the rear windows of the SUVs. Parents exist mainly to drive their kids places and carry their kids' gear, haul out hitting tees, practice nets, professional-quality baseballs by the bucket, and banners with résumé-like championship results to hang over the dugout. The kids have sports bags that would make major leaguers blush, different gloves for different positions, and two-hundred-dollar big-barrel bats with names like the Power Elite—because even radical writers like C. Wright Mills get their book titles co-opted by the competitive sports industry.

These kids practice three nights a week. They play 80 to 140 games a year. In the winter, they work out in gyms and get special tips from former minor leaguers turned eighty-dollar-an-hour youth baseball instructors offering specialized wisdom on the right elbow angle to adopt as you begin your trigger motion, or on the proper slide step to come to the plate with when there are runners on base.

When did it become normal that by age ten, kid athletes should be specializing in one sport year-round? But few parents pull their kids out of competitive sports, because they see—it is impossible not to see—that their kids love it. Studies from the Institute for Social Research (yes, there have been studies on this, too) show that most kids enroll in these activities because one of their friends was doing it, so they asked their parents if they could do it also. The kids initiate the activity, not the adults. Moreover, the kids love the team, the camaraderie, the fun of playing and practicing and achieving and learning. They are happy creatures in the land of achievement.

The Achievatron is easy to ridicule but not easy to reject. Hardly a dinner party goes by without somebody noting how kids' sports are out of control. But what's really happening is that the spirit of improvement has taken over sports, just as it has taken over every sphere of life. How can one reject getting the most out of your abilities on the sports field when one accepts that regimen in everything else? While everyone can point to examples, there are few parents who are maniacally overpressuring their kids. The kids are still kids. They love goofing around with one another and forget the losses five minutes after they have occurred (with the parents, it takes about an hour). The coaches, far from being martinets or drill sergeants, are mostly remarkably generous human beings.

In fact, sports coaches have become the leading moral instructors in America today. They are the only ones who dare to tell kids to tuck in their shirts, say please and thank you, and be respectable. They are the ones who get kids who have trouble cleaning their rooms to polish their shoes and clean their equipment. They are the ones who confront kids at a moment of humiliating failure—a goal between the legs, an interception—and give them specific advice on how to handle adversity. They're the ones who talk unabashedly about character, sportsmanship, old-fashioned politeness. The best coaches insist on a code of chivalry that has somehow survived untarnished in an age of scoffing and irony. They still demand deference to authority, loyalty, and individual subordination to the team in ways that nobody else does outside of the military. Most coaches preach a code of effort, hard work, and discipline so straightforward that it seems archaic when it comes out of the mouth of anybody else in American society.

As for the parents, most are decent and only want their kids to learn and have a good time, and they freely make asses of themselves as their way of contributing to the upbeat spirit that is obligatory at all youth sporting events.

Say a normal Little Leaguer comes up to bat and finds himself facing one of these man-childs so common these days—a six-foot-tall eleven-year-old with shoulders roughly the width of Manhattan who throws the ball at 70 mph and looks like he began shaving at age four. As the batter approaches the batter's box, all the team parents will begin incanting his name, "Hey, Danny, Danny, Danny!" and the coach, utilizing the baseball savvy that elevated him to this position of authority, will offer advice such as "Okay, Danny, be a hitter up there," as if the kid were going up there to be a snow shoveler if he hadn't been offered that proper wisdom. Then the man-child will throw a four-seam fastball on the inside corner that Danny can barely see, let alone swing at. At this point, kids, who are realists, will say to themselves, "I can't hit this. I guess I'll be striking out this time." But the parents, who have given themselves the responsibility of offering encouraging inanities no matter what the situation, will scream out things like "Okay. Now you've seen it. Now you've got the timing down" or "No problem. You can do this!" So the man-child throws an even faster pitch on the outside corner at the knees, and the batter, too stunned to swing, is trying to remember where he left his bag of sunflower seeds on the bench. The parents have switched to a new line of insanely upbeat propaganda: "That wasn't your pitch anyway" or "Little line drive here. Don't try to kill it. Just meet the ball." Danny's parents are deep in prayer, silently offering to trade God five years of their lives if only Danny could jack one into left-center field, and the coaches and the other savvy baseball parents are barraging the kid with advice: "Square your feet up . . . keep your head down . . . hands straight to the ball . . . move back in the box."

The kid hears none of this, because while he is at bat, he is deep in his own zone of concentration, and the parents and coaches vaguely know this, but they have to keep shouting, because how else are they going to disguise their own irrelevance? So the man-child throws a ball two feet over Danny's head, and Danny, who has decided to begin his swing fifteen seconds before the ball is released on the freak hope that he might catch up with it, swings lamely and misses, and it's strike three and all the parents, who all display a capacity to ignore reality and lie like dogs such as would impress even a political consultant, greet him as he walks back to the dugout with a chorus of spin: "Good at-bat, Danny . . . you were right on it . . . you'll get him next time . . ." The coach gives him an encouraging tap on the top of the helmet, and pretty soon Danny is cheerfully ensconced on the bench with his sunflower seeds while the next batter goes up for his whiffing, and the parents, like a Greek chorus overdosing on Prozac, repeat their reality-free cries of support.

The Theology of Achievement

The achievement ethos is built on an idealistic premise: There is, at the core of each human being, a wonderful destiny waiting to be realized. It is not just the talented few who have great potentialities lurking within. Each person has a noble destiny that can be realized, given the right output of effort, direction, and support. Each person was born with promise, and each has a God-given right to a chance to achieve the fullest of his or her capacities.

Not all societies give such prominence to this belief. In some civilizations, people are more inclined to seek the harmony that comes with total submission to God's will. Others are built on the love for the nurturing presence of loved ones and community. It is better to stay home with one's kin than to venture forth in search of achievement and success. But American civilization encourages us to strive to realize our best self. Our identity, we often assume, is formed not by where we are born or who our ancestors are. Our identity is defined by what we do and accomplish. Each of us has a gift to offer the world. Just as Marx wrote that "Milton produced *Paradise Lost* as the silkworm produces silk, as the activation of his own nature," so each of us has some contribution, if only we can find it, to offer our fellows.

Each personality is perpetually in the process of unfolding, of fulfilling itself through energy and exploration. Life becomes a journey. We don't know what our individual destinations look like, much less the destinations of our sons and daughters. But it is through our efforts to forge ahead that we discover who we are, what direction we are trying to travel, what gift we might have to share. As the theologian Jürgen Moltmann put it when describing the Christian eschatology in *Theology of Hope,* "Man has no subsistence in himself, but is always on the way towards something and realizes himself in the light of some expected future whole."

There is an exalted noble dream of democratic greatness buried at the core of our achievement ethos. There is an optimistic faith in the basic goodness of every individual, and it will show itself when the obstacles to achievement are removed, when people are given a chance to bloom. As so many foreign visitors have noticed, we are a people with an unbounded faith in the true inner self, in our own essential goodness.

As anybody who looks at meritocratic life knows, this creed is not easy on its disciples. There is no rest. Expectations don't sleep. There's a little voice saying, "Not there yet." Parents expect colossal things from their children, and from an early age kids feel the burden of those goals. They measure their progress by their prowess. Whatever you are doing, you should never be merely as good tomorrow as you are today. If you are a bird-watcher, you achieve a life list. If you are a punk musician, you become a better punk musician. If you are a swing dancer, your moves perpetually improve. Capacities are there to be cultivated, heading toward some never achieved perfection.

We tell ourselves and our children that the purpose of life is not merely to achieve worldly success—money, fame, prestige. Then we assign them a curriculum of self-improvement that makes mere worldly success look as easy as kindergarten. For example, Anna Quindlen, the novelist and *Newsweek* columnist, recently gave a commencement address at Villanova University that offered the students the sort of advice we are always giving the young and each other: "Get a life," she said. "A real life, not a manic pursuit of the next promotion, the bigger paycheck, the larger house."

She assigned a few tasks:

> Get a life in which you notice the smell of salt water. . . . Get a life in which you are not alone. Find people you love and who love you. And remember that life is not leisure, it is work. . . . Get a life in which you are generous. Look around at the azaleas. . . . Work in a soup kitchen. Be a big brother or sister. . . . Consider the lilies of the field. Look at the fuzz on a baby's ear. . . . Just keep your eyes and ears open. Here you could learn in the classroom. There the classroom is everywhere.

That's good advice. But consider how arduous it is. "It is so easy to exist instead of live," Quindlen said. You can rest assured that her listeners won't renounce their career goals. Nor did she say they should. She was invited to address the crowd precisely because she herself has had such a phenomenally successful career. The destitute are rarely asked to give commencement addresses. Yet she is asking us to pile goodness on top of plenty, patience on top of hustle, tranquility on top of aspiration. When does Anna Quindlen expect us to sleep?

This is the culture of upwardly mobile childhood. And when you look at the frantic strivings of today's young meritocrats, what you are seeing is the latest and maybe most fevered version of a long line of American strivings. It was the early settlers who established the code that life is a pilgrimage toward perfection. Jonathan Edwards told his flock never to be content with their virtues, never to feel satisfied. "The endeavor to make progress" in developing one's character, he declared, "ought not to be attended to as a thing by the bye, but all Christians should make a business of it. They should look upon it as their daily business."

Benjamin Franklin more or less invented the mode of childhood we see around us today. He was the original enterprising boy. "It was about this time," he wrote somewhat ironically of his childhood ambitions, "that I conceived the bold and arduous project of arriving at moral perfection." Franklin made a little scorecard of the thirteen virtues such as industry ("Lose no time. Be always employed at something useful") and temperance ("Eat not to dullness. Drink not to elevation"). Then he gave himself daily performance reviews, marking his scorecard when he found himself guilty of imperfection.

One of the first outstanding American sociologists, Lester Ward, described "this all-pervading spirit of improvement" that marks American life. The constellation of American stock characters is dotted with young people on the make: the Horatio Algers, the Sammy Glicks, the ambitious immigrant kids, the gangsters trying to rise from obscurity to success, the politicians ascending from log cabin to White House. There is no real resting spot. "It is provided in the essence of things," Walt Whitman acknowledged, "that from any fruition of success, no matter what, shall come forth something to make a greater struggle necessary."

Take one of these young meritocratic kids raised on *Mozart for Babies,* tutored at age six, coached at age eight, honed and molded and improved and enlightened every day of his life, and imagine telling him at some point in middle adulthood that the ascent is over. All his dreams have been realized. There is no more need to exert himself. Do you think he'd be happy? Of course not. Inertia would reduce him to the gravest misery. He is bred to want more and better and deeper, to ceaselessly reform and improve himself. He has become, for better and worse, an American.

CHAPTER SIX

Learning

As you know, the college-admissions process is the confirmation or bar mitzvah of American life, the central initiation rite when a boy becomes a man, or when a girl becomes a woman.

It is no easy ritual. Many students begin contemplating their college application around age twelve (roughly twelve years and nine months after their parents have begun worrying about it). By age fourteen, they are thoroughly immersed in the cult of the fat envelope. They are laboriously prepping for standardized tests, honing application essays—inspiring stories of personal growth and transformation downloaded from the Internet—all while girding themselves for the moment of ultimate judgment.

High school years, which once upon a time were devoted to cruising, malt shops, and necking, are increas-

ingly spent being corresponding secretary of this and trea-
surer of that. All around the country, one's peers and
college-admissions competitors are taking AP courses, winning trophies at Social Studies Olympiads, leading debate
teams, managing their a cappella group's international
tour, getting accepted into honor societies, and performing
hours upon hours of résumé-enhancing, legally mandated,
yet seemingly altruistic community service. "I don't know
where these kids find lepers," George Washington University president Stephen Trachtenberg has observed, "but
they find them and they read to them."

To get into top schools, students need to get straight
A's, or close. That means they must embrace the rigors of
the GPA mentality. They must learn not to develop a consuming passion for one subject, lest it distract them from
getting perfect marks across the board. They must carefully
and prudentially budget their mental energies. They must
learn the tricks of good studenting (without necessarily
developing a deep interest in the classes' actual content) so
that they can, to paraphrase Joseph Epstein, take whatever
their teachers throw out at them and return it back in their
warm little mouths.

In his memoir *My Early Life,* Winston Churchill wrote
that "where my reason, imagination or interest were not
engaged, I would not or could not learn." But that's not the
case with today's successful students, for they can learn—
or at least get good grades—in all circumstances. They
must become masters of the subtle suck-up, exhibiting
sycophantic skills just this side of nauseating, without ever
quite going over the line. They must apply themselves to
their homework, their career-building summer jobs, and
their after-school activities without ever letting their raging

hormones suck them into the fits of distracting passion and madness that Mother Nature intended for these adolescent years.

By the time they apply to college, the best of them have, to judge by their applications, founded a few companies, cured at least three formerly fatal diseases, mastered a half-dozen languages, and monitored human-rights abuses in Tibet while tutoring the locals on conflict-resolution skills and environmental awareness. Their résumés are so impressive, and the competitive standard they set is so high, that no American adult could get into the college he or she attended as a youth.

Then, having put their pubescent résumé in good order, they face the ultimate choice: What institution's window sticker will their parents be able to affix to the back of their car? It is with electron-microscope subtlety that they mea-sure and compare the quality and prestige levels of differ-ent universities. Which school has higher status, Brown or Columbia? Which school will be more fulfilling, Claremont or Occidental? During the course of your life, when people ask you where you went to school, which institution will come tripping more impressively off the tongue, Tulane or Vanderbilt? Which schools, in the vast academic pecking order, will you select as your "reach" schools, and which will be "safeties"? The society dames in Edith Wharton novels comprehend amazingly subtle social gradations, but nothing like the ones that separate America's institutions of higher learning. The ranking of these schools is at once so important, yet so fundamentally bogus, that it takes teams of university-trained status professionals at *U.S. News & World Report* to quantify the differences between Penn State and the University of Michigan.

Say a student survives this ordeal. Say he, or more likely she (since women earn a quarter more bachelor's degrees and a third more master's degrees than men), crosses the endless mountain chains of the application process, endures the long, isolating winters of study, activity, and SAT prep, and arrives at the promised land of college admissions—and is accepted! The fat envelope arrives! And the next fall she loads up the U-Haul for one of America's prestigious campuses, a university with an endowment that tops the GDP of 140 of the world's 200-odd nations. The trek is over. The land of milk and honey has been attained. The student is finally on her own, free from pressuring parents and overbearing guidance counselors. She can now let Dionysus out for a romp, kick back, and enjoy the mad magic of youth—never mind what the future may hold.

Does she? No, she kicks it up a notch. From the achievement-oriented movers and doers they were as teenagers, today's high-achieving Americans turn, once on campus, into the Junior Workaholics of America. The Achievatron, remember, rewards energy as much as intelligence. The ones who thrive are the ones who can keep going from one activity to another, from music to science to sports to community service to the library and so on without rest. Once that pattern of exertion has been established, it is not even possible, in the full bloom of youth, to slow down. The habits are ingrained. The internal reactor is humming along, pumping out gigawatts. The Holy Bee, the patron saint of busyness, must be served.

If you go to college campuses, especially competitive college campuses, you may run into the student who is heading off at six A.M. to crew practice, then a quick bite at the coffee shop, then class, the library, resident-adviser duty, science lab, class, tutoring, Bible study, work, choral practice, career-recruiting seminar, year-abroad information meeting, discussion group, and so on until midnight, when it is time to hit the e-mail. She will brag to her friends about how little sleep she gets, or about how much work she has ahead of her, or about how she never has a moment to get back to her room during the day, because there is simply too much going on.

I went to lunch a little while ago with a young man in a student dining room that by one-ten had nearly emptied out as students hustled back to the library and their classes. I mentioned that when I went to college in the late 1970s and early 1980s, we often spent two or three hours around the table, shooting the breeze and arguing about things. He admitted that there was little discussion about intellectual matters outside of class. "Most students don't like that that's the case," he said, "but it is the case." So he and a bunch of his friends formed a discussion group that meets regularly with a faculty guest to discuss serious subjects. If they can get it scheduled into their Palm Pilots, they can get it done.

One finds students applying time-quadrant techniques to maximize their mental efficiency. They read *The 7 Habits of Highly Effective Teens*. In 1985, 16 percent of freshmen told researchers at UCLA that they frequently felt stressed at school. By 1999, 30 percent of the respondents reported feeling "frequently overwhelmed by all I have to do." And many of them like it that way. They aren't living this frenetically because they're compelled to. It's not the sticks that drive them on, it's the carrots. Opportunity lures them, the glorious future. There's so much neat stuff to do.

American universities are diverse and enriching places, packed with learning, experiences, and opportunities. American young people are nearly twice as likely to attend college as young people in Western Europe, and American universities spend, on average, about twice as much money per student as their French, German, or British counterparts. Like gluttons in the candy store, students want to take advantage of it all, enjoy it all, experience it all, launch themselves into adulthood. Four-fifths of college students, according to a Jobtrack.com study, believe it will take them ten years or less to achieve their career goals.

With so many options and so little time, students must develop a strategizing, professional mind-set in order to allocate their energies efficiently. Interests must be judged and ranked. Which courses will help professionally? Which will be fun but won't require much work? What readings will really be on the test? Which activities can be jettisoned under stress, because while they might be interesting, they don't contribute to the process of personal-growth maximization? In the land of time pressure, one has to strive for personal fuel efficiency.

Students may be fuzzy about what destination awaits them, but they know they are heading for something. College is one step on the continual stairway to paradise, and they're aware that they must get to the next step (corporate job, law school, medical school, whatever). This professional mind-set gets more pronounced at community colleges and the less prestigious four-year schools, where getting a good job is more likely to be the main point of the exercise. In 1969, according to UCLA's annual survey of freshmen, developing a meaningful philosophy of life was listed by 76 percent of students as a key collegiate goal. By

1993 only 47 percent of students felt it necessary to say that. Meanwhile, 76 percent of students said that becoming "very well-off financially" ranks as a very important reason to go to college. At many community colleges, there are no frills, no Gothic architecture, no lineage, no arboretums, no ancient faculty rituals. There are just low brick buildings, linoleum floors, and aspiring students struggling with work, bills, and kids. They are hungry for skills, success, and advancement.

Today's college students, by and large, are not trying to buck the system; they're trying to climb it. Hence, they are not a disputatious group. One often hears on campus a distinct verbal tic: If someone is about to dissent with someone in a group, he or she will apologize beforehand, couching the disagreement in the most civil, nonconfrontational terms available. On the whole, professors love and admire their students, but they are a little disturbed by how noncontentious they are, how willing they are to jump through whatever hoop is placed in front of them for the sake of pleasing teachers, mentors, or the achievement system itself. These students are, in general, exceedingly deferential to authority. Very few will challenge or contradict a professor, any more than an employee would be likely to challenge or contradict the boss.

At Princeton I saw a recruiting poster from Goldman Sachs in the student center. Under a photograph of a group of wholesome-looking young people relaxing after a game of lunchtime basketball, the text read "Wanted: Strategists, Quick Thinkers, Team Players, Achievers." Nearby was a recruiting poster from the consulting firm KPMG, showing a pair of incredibly hip-looking middle-aged people staring warmly into the camera. The text read, "Now that you've made your parents proud, join KPMG and give them something to smile about." A few decades ago, recruiting posters wouldn't have appealed to a student's desire to make her parents happy.

The Unalienated

When you read about America's universities in the media, you might get the impression that the top colleges are left-wing hothouses filled with multicultural radicalism and fevered anti-American passions. That's not quite right. It's true that most professors are liberals, and in its wisdom, American society has decided to warehouse its radicals on university campuses—in departments that serve as nunneries for the perpetually alienated. But most students do not live in an overly politicized world.

There is, one must always remember, a large cultural gap between the students and the faculty. Remarkably few students—alarmingly few, actually—seriously contemplate a career in academia. They think of becoming high school teachers or reporters or even soldiers, but if you ask them what life is like in academia, they talk about the pedantic specialization of academic research, the jargon and impenetrable prose, the professor's cloistered remove from the real world and the low salaries.

The faculty at most schools is significantly to the left of the students. The students know this and accept it as part of the inevitable structure of the universe. They know who the radical professors are and regard their radicalism as an endearing blemish, the way a professor's absent-mindedness would have been regarded in an earlier generation. The weird thing is that while most students don't share the radical ideologies, they do find them convenient.

Truth is indeterminate, the (once) cutting-edge literary critics argued. Texts can be deconstructed in an infinitude of ways, and words are signifiers open to a diversity of meanings. Every point of view deserves respect. The enlightened person should be open to everything—opinions, lifestyles, and ideologies—and closed to nothing. One should never judge The Other harshly, but should respect minority or multicultural alternatives. These notions may have been promulgated by people who thought of themselves as radicals—they were French deconstructionists, tenured revolutionaries, or transgressive countercultural provocateurs.

But they are ideas perfectly suited to the ethos of the achievement-oriented capitalist. After all, why should the achiever want to make enemies or waste time in angry conflict? Why should the time maximizer struggle to find that thing called Absolute Truth when it is more efficient to settle for perception? Why should one get involved in the problematic rigor of judging? Easygoing tolerance is energy-efficient. The world of floating signifiers and upended cultural hierarchies, in which nothing has any fixed attachment to a universal truth, and in which it is as valid to write a paper interpreting denim as Dante, is a world of maximum fluidity and flexibility: just the sort of world the opportunity-seeking meritocrat wants to live in. In other words, the radical ideas that were first espoused in fits of protest and anger—ideas that were meant to tear down reactionary hierarchies and question the foundations of truth—now seem like convenient intellectual habits for people of mild disposition and strategizing minds.

The current generation of college students doesn't see itself as a lost generation or a radical generation or a beatnik generation or even a Reaganite generation. They have relatively little generational consciousness. That's because this generation is, for the most part, not fighting to emancipate itself from the past. The most sophisticated people in the preceding generations were formed by their struggle to break free from something. The most sophisticated people in this one aren't. Many of them are ambivalent about the extreme meritocratic system they grew up in, but they do not see an alternative. For those growing into adulthood during most of the twentieth century, the backdrop of life was a loss of faith in coherent systems of thought and morality. Educated people knew they were supposed to rebel against authority, reject old certainties, liberate themselves from hidebound customs and prejudices. Artists rebelled against the stodgy mores of the bourgeoisie. Radicals rebelled against the commercial and capitalist order. Feminists rebelled against the patriarchal family. And in the latter half of the twentieth century, a youth culture emerged that distilled these themes. Every rock anthem, every fashion statement, every protest gesture, every novel about rebellious youth—starting with *The Catcher in the Rye* and *On the Road*—carried the same cultural message: It's better to be a nonconformist than a conformist, a creative individualist than a member of a group, a rebel than a traditionalist, a daring adventurer than a careerist striver.

Though they might retain the youth-culture patina, today's college students don't live in that age of rebellion and alienation. Nothing in their environment suggests that the world is fundamentally ill-constructed or that life is made meaningful only by revolt. They have not witnessed senseless bloodbaths or seen any World War I– or Vietnam-type evidence that the ruling establishment is fundamentally incompetent, murderous, or corrupt.

During most of the twentieth century, the basic ways of living were called into question, but those fundamental debates are over, at least for most of today's college students. Democracy and dictatorship are no longer engaged in an epic struggle. Islamic extremists may challenge Western modes, but the mullahs have few allies in your average college dorm. Pluralistic democracy is the beneficent and seemingly natural order. The globalization protesters notwithstanding, no fundamental argument pits capitalism against socialism; capitalism is so triumphant, we barely contemplate an alternative. Radicals no longer assault the American family and the American home. Even theological conflicts have settled down. It's somewhat fashionable to be religious so long as one is not militantly so.

When I have taught on campus, I have amazed students with readings from eras when the frame of debate was not nearly so narrow as it is today, when people talked about radically restructuring the way average folks live. The students are interested in such visions, but they are surprisingly unromantic about the manifestos that used to come from communists, agrarians, or socialist utopians and other outsiders. "We saw what happens to those big ideas," these twenty-first-century students say. "They fail and they lead to disaster." It's better to be modest, realistic, and small-scale, they continue. That makes them wise, perhaps, but not confrontational. So authority does not seem threatening to them. They are less likely than previous generations to feel they must rebel against their parents. Responding to a 1997 Gallup survey, 96 percent of teenagers said they got along with their parents, and 82 percent described their home life as "wonderful" or "good." I'm not sure families are quite that healthy, but the results show what young people want things to be. Roughly three out of four teens said they shared their parents' general values. When asked by Roper Starch Worldwide in 1998 to rank the major problems facing America today, students aged twelve to nineteen named as their top five concerns: selfishness, people who don't respect law and the authorities, wrongdoing by politicians, lack of parental discipline, and courts that care too much about criminals' rights. It is impossible to imagine teenagers of a few decades ago calling for stricter parental discipline and more respect for authority. In 1974, for example, a majority of teenagers told pollsters that they could not "comfortably approach their parents with personal matters of concern." Forty percent believed they would be "better off not living with their parents."

The current college students live in a world that is more open to different lifestyles and callings, more fluid and flexible. According to a survey commissioned by the Independent Women's Forum, 87 percent of college students believe it is wrong to "judge anyone's sexual conduct but my own." They grew up in a world in which the racial and gender barriers were lower, and the mental categories of past generations have been washed away. For them, it's natural that an Ivy League administrator has a poster of the Beatles album *Revolver* framed on her office wall. It's natural that hippies work at ad agencies and found organic ice-cream companies, and that management consultants quote Bob Dylan atop their final reports.

They don't have the same awareness of mental barriers

between establishment and rebels, between respectable striving society and antistriving subversives. For them, all the categories are mushed together, so they can go work at Bank of America and support Greenpeace, trade overseas and sympathize with the antiglobalization protesters. All is fluid and free. They've learned that this open-ended world is one good for development. What those twentieth-century radicals were really trying to tear down, it now appears, were the structures that would inhibit the flowering of one's best self. Now it matters somewhat less if you are a man or a woman; you can achieve. Now it matters somewhat less if you are straight or gay; you can achieve. You can achieve, you can achieve, you can achieve.

If opportunities to succeed are more open, the competition has grown more fierce as a result.

Fuckbuddies

This competitive environment changes college life in all sorts of unexpected ways. Even the biological necessities get squeezed out. There is a fair bit of partying on campus, and a lot of drinking, but many students have found they have no time for dating and/or serious relationships. They are more likely to go out in groups—the group has replaced the couple as the primary social unit—and then they hook up for occasional sex. I've been amazed by the number of young women who come up to me after an event on campus to say, "I don't have time for a relationship, so of course I hook up." They say this in the tone one might use to describe commuting routes, the same tone they use when toting up lists of their hookup partners in late-night e-mails. At some schools you hear about buddy sex or fuckbuddies, the friends you go to for the occasional roll in the hay. At Princeton I ran across students who said they have friendships, and then they have friendships with privileges—meaning sex.

A study conducted by Peggy Giordano and Monica Longmore of Bowling Green found that 55 percent of eleventh-graders had had sex with a casual acquaintance. College students talk about prudential sex—the kind you have for leisure without any of that romantic Sturm und Drang, as a normal part of life (though many of them are lying).

Some bizarre rituals grow out of this new social scene. First, there no longer is a big-man-on-campus social structure. In the age of dispersal, remember, everything hierarchical turns cellular. So at most schools, there is no clear pecking order, with one clique of beautiful or rich or popular students on top and everybody else scattered in less prestigious social circles down below. I've been amazed by how few college students even know what the acronym "BMOC" stands for.

Instead, there is a profusion of groups defined by interest, dorm, or activity. Most students are casual members of several groups, to which they display different parts of themselves. A young man may reveal his inner doubts among the Fellowship of Christian Athletes and show his outer bravura on the track. Different groups don't even listen to the same type of music. A 1950s study by the University of Chicago sociologist James Coleman revealed that teenage musical tastes were similar, with half saying that rock and roll was their favorite kind of music. Now those musical tastes have been segmented into rock, classic rock, rap, alternative, hip-hop, folk, dance, rave, house, and a hundred other genres, and each clique has its own constellation of preferences.

Second, there is the weird return of chauvinist-piggism, as if in the age of prudential climbing, it suddenly became acceptable to play—in a suitably self-conscious manner— at being an *Animal House* frat boy. Highly educated college men read *Maxim, FHM,* or one of the other laddie magazines. Unlike *Playboy* or *Penthouse,* which had intellectual pretensions, these magazines are pure in their pursuit of horniness. Women in their pages are reduced to cleavage. Men exist solely at that crossroads where celebrity babes in lingerie meet power tools, plasma TVs, and serial-killer computer games. The articles, which tend to be within the "How to Score at Funerals" genre, are short but didactic shallowness primers. (In the world of *Maxim,* size matters in every aspect of human existence except attention span.)

This behavior is socially acceptable on campus, despite a generation of feminist consciousness raising, because it is all conducted in a mood of knowing irony (or at least faux irony), and because the new mores call on all of us to be liberated sexual beings together. We men can leer at your breasts, and you women can leer at our buns. We can be Bob Gucciones equally, and we'll call it gender equity.

Finally, ambiguity hangs over nearly every social bond. After the hookup, the sex partners enter what one of my students called the "Now that we've seen each other naked, we have to at least talk to each other" phase. There are infinite types of hookups—with friends, near-strangers, potential love interests—and infinite gradations of sexual activity. Afterward, the man and the woman will go back to their other buddies and wonder, What kind of hookup was it? What did it mean? Was it for fun? Was it serious? Or was it just another in the long string of wants and activities that fill a college student's day? In the midst of a political-science paper, another of my students, a woman, nicely captured how personal relationships blend into the smorgasbord of life-enhancing campus interests and activities, at least at one elite university:

> Most Yale women, for example, except for the premeds, aren't clamoring for equal rights or the chance to be called on in class anymore. They want a long wool coat for the winter, a Macintosh laptop computer with an MP3 player, a course load that doesn't include books by dead white men exclusively, a gay man for advice and a straight man for every other weekend or so, one good pair of Manolo Blahniks sometime in the future, to maintain a woman's right to choose, something to finally be done (for Christ's sake) for the women being circumcised in Africa and suffocated under burqas in the Middle East, a cigarette or a shot or a joint when the company is right, a husband at some point though no point soon, a good education, a GPA above 3.5, and a network of connections for when she graduates.

This is the point at which we fogies are supposed to lament the decline in courtship, the total absence of the romantic ideal, which says that there must exist one person in the world with whom each of us can unite at all levels, and that one should save oneself for that person and not sully intimacies in such a casual way. Indeed, I was out drinking late one night with a group of students at a small Midwestern liberal arts college, and the woman to my left, from Michigan, mentioned that she would never have a serious relationship with someone she wouldn't consider marrying. "That sounds traditional," I said to her.

"I didn't say I wouldn't fuck anyone I wouldn't consider marrying," she responded.

One young man at our table from an Indiana farm town heard the exchange, and for the next few minutes I could see him brooding. Finally, he exploded with a short tirade on how the women on his campus had destroyed romance by making it so transactional. He didn't quite call the three women on my left sluts, but he was heading in that direction.

As he spoke, I could feel them shaking with rage, making little growls of protest but politely not interrupting him. I knew they were only waiting to let rip. Eventually, they let him have it. They didn't deny his version of reality, that sex is sometimes transactional. Their main point was that guys have been acting this way all along, so why shouldn't they?

As we left the bar, the young man walked me part of the way to my hotel and commented that the Michigan girl who'd made the comment was really cute. He thought he might give her a call.

Now, the first thing to be said about this state of affairs is that every survey of youth sexual activity over the past several years reveals that young people are having less sex than their predecessors were ten and twenty years ago. Young women may talk more baldly about sex, but it is simply not true that they are more promiscuous or casual about it. Their conversational style is a reflection of the amazing self-confidence of the women on these campuses. The single most striking, if hard to define, difference between college campuses today and college campuses twenty years ago is in the nature and character of the female students. They are not self-confident just socially. They are self-confident academically, athletically, organizationally, and in every other way.

In general, the women carry themselves with an appearance of ease that must have been matched by only that of the old WASP bluebloods when schools were oriented around their desires. Twenty years ago, if memory serves, it was mostly we men who performed the role of seminar baboons—speaking up and showing off with knowledge, just as today it is mostly men who fill the op-ed pages with ideas and pontifications.

In my discussions with student groups, there were always several women who projected authority with a grace that was unusual two decades ago. These women— who were born around 1983—appeared uninhibited by any notion that either they shouldn't assert themselves for fear of appearing unfeminine, or that they should overexert themselves to prove their feminist bona fides. Those considerations appeared irrelevant. Of course, people in every group suffer from the normal insecurities, but in general, and at least on the surface, young women today carry themselves with a wonderfully straightforward assurance.

The changing character of women was bound to change the courtship rituals. One night over dinner at a northern college, a student from the South mentioned that at her local state university, where some of her friends go, they still have date nights on Friday. The men ask the women out, and they go as couples. The other students at the dinner table were amazed. The only time many young people have ever gone out on a formal date was their high school senior prom. You might as well have told them that in some parts of the country, there are knights on horseback jousting with lances.

One of the young men at the dinner table piped up and said that his generation happened to come along during a time of transition. A generation ago, there was one set of courtship rituals. Twenty years from now, he continued, there will be another. But now there are no set rules. There is ambiguity.

A literature professor told me that he had come to notice a strange pattern among his students. Many of the nineteenth-century novels he teaches, he said, end with the heroine leaving her family and friends and going off to marry her one true love. Recently, he continued, he had found his students rebelling against that choice. To them, it didn't make sense to sacrifice your relationship with your friends to build a marriage. To them, the friendship relationship was higher, more intimate, and more satisfying than the sexual or even the romantic relationship. Friendships are forever, whereas just look at romance . . . that breaks apart. As one male student put it, in a phrase I heard a few times, "Bros before hos." (The female counter to that phrase is "Chicks before dicks.")

It should be said that these students are idealizing friendships. Every longitudinal study of young people shows that Americans between sixteen and twenty-two build and abandon intimate friendships with astounding speed. The friends of freshman year are probably not the same friends of junior year. And yet it is that ideal—the happy, flexible clique with an undertone of sexual tension (just like on *Friends*) that beckons as the preferred social bond. This is an amazing inversion of decades-old, if not centuries-old, social norms.

The literature professor went on to say that his students think they're making life more efficient for themselves by having these loose, informal bonds. After all, the girl doesn't have to sit by the phone waiting to be asked out. There is no nervousness about when to start going steady. There are fewer traumatic breakup scenes. But on the other hand, the professor noted, nobody really knows where they stand. Relationships are abandoned without any formal end, sometimes without a fight or even a word. I heard about a few in which the guy thought he was going out with the girl, but the girl had an entirely different understanding. The ambiguity allowed each to interpret their friendship (or love affair) in contradictory ways, with trouble looming down the road. The professor concluded that on balance, the fluidity and ambiguity of the students' social lives led to greater misery.

I've bounced his observations off many students, and some think he is overstating the situation. Many students are involved in long-term relationships. But fewer, I believe, than two decades ago. And it's undeniable that students bring a prudential frame of mind to their romantic activities. College is a busy time. It's better, many of them reason, to put off serious relationships until such time as one's career is established and there's time to invest in love. Several mentioned that the best time to think seriously about it is at the ten-year reunion, after you're established on your career track and have the financial resources to start a family.

In fact, these students are merely following the advice of their parents, the same people who would be quick to condemn them for taking the magic out of love. How many parents do you know—liberal or conservative, atheist or evangelical—who would enjoy seeing their child devoting the bulk of his or her collegiate energies to a boyfriend or girlfriend, rather than to the vast array of activities and learning opportunities available at these phenomenally expensive schools? Very few. Parents who are ambitious for their kids imbue them with a calculating, strategizing mind-set. It's not surprising that they have carried this over, to some extent, into the arena of romance and sex.

Character

The students in America's colleges are bright, lively, funny, and generous. Their behavior is in many ways exemplary, especially compared to past generations. They are not the pains in the ass to their parents that many of their parents were to theirs.

Their commitment to community service is one of the marvels of the age. Their volunteer work may have started out as a way to impress admissions officers, but their interest in it has transcended shallow careerism. You go to schools and find that 20, even 30 percent of the students spend some meaningful time each week helping the less fortunate.

Today's college students are remarkably eager to try new things, to thrust themselves into unlikely situations, to travel the world in search of new activities. At the more elite universities, every other student you meet has just come back from some service adventure in remotest China or Brazil. During my conversations with them, I would sometimes realize with a start that they were two decades younger than I. With their worldliness, their sophisticated senses of humor, and their ability to at least fake knowledge of a wide variety of fields, they socialize just like any group of forty-somethings. Most of all, they have a passion for personal growth that is amazing. They want to make money and become successful, but they also want to become good people, inside and out, if only they had some clear idea of how that is achieved; if only they had a vocabulary that would enable them to talk about their moral desires.

And that is the part that gnaws. It is not that they have bad character or no character. I haven't yet seen a machine that allows us to peer into a generation's souls and measure whether they are deep or not. We are right to be skeptical about generalizations on the moral health of America's youth. But we can observe their public lives and the way they conduct themselves in social situations. It is not too hard to see that at the very least, talk about character has been crowded out amid all the rush, bustle, and achievement.

On the whole, college students are articulate on every subject save morality. When you talk to them about character, you notice that they are hesitant to say anything definitive, as if any firm statement about which lifestyle choice is conducive to firm character development might break the code of civility. When you ask if their school builds character, they inevitably start talking about legislation. They mention their school's honor codes, the sexual-harassment rules, or the antidrinking policies. This may be character in the negative sense—efforts to prevent students from doing bad things. But it doesn't get at what an earlier generation meant when they used the phrase "noble character."

Although today's colleges impose all sorts of rules to reduce safety risks and encourage achievement, they see passing along knowledge, not building character, as their primary task. If you ask professors whether they seek to instill character, they often look at you blankly. They are on campus to instill calculus, or nineteenth-century history, or whatever their academic specialty happens to be. "We've taken the decision that these are adults and this is not our job," Princeton professor Jeffrey Herbst once told me in an interview. "We're very conservative about how we steer. They steer themselves," said that school's dean of undergraduate students, Kathleen Deignan. "I don't know if we build character or remind them that they should be developing it," ruefully added the then dean of admissions, Fred Hargadon.

To put it at its baldest, the Achievatron micromanages the tiniest issues in young people's lives. Their SAT prep, their recycling habits, their brain chemistry, their drinking-and-driving tendencies. But when it comes to instilling character, the most difficult task of them all, suddenly it's "You're on your own, kiddo." The laissez-faire ethic reigns.

We assume that each person has to solve these questions alone (though few other societies in history have made this assumption). We assume that if adults try to offer moral instruction, it will backfire, because young people will reject our sermonizing (though truth be told, they more often seem to hunger for precisely this kind of big-question guidance). We assume that such questions have no correct answer that can be taught.

Or maybe the simple truth is that adult institutions no

longer try to talk about character and virtue because they simply wouldn't know what to say. It is interesting, by way of comparison, to go back a century or so ago, before the code of the meritocrat had fully established its hegemony over education and life. The most striking contrast between the college atmosphere of those days and these is that collegians then were relatively unconcerned with grades and academic achievements, but they lived in a web of moral instruction.

Americans are famously devoted to education. New England had its first college when the Massachusetts Bay colony was all of six years old. By 1910, the United States had nearly 1,000 colleges enrolling over 300,000 students (at a time when France had 16 colleges enrolling 40,000 students). The elite universities of that day aimed to take privileged men (or, at some institutions, women) and toughen them up, teach them a sense of discipline, right thinking, and social obligation. In short, universities aimed to instill in the students a sense of honor and chivalry.

Universities were intentionally short on the creature comforts. Rooms and living arrangements were Spartan— which must have been a rude shock for the boys who grew up in aristocratic mansions (unless they'd had a taste of such conditions at Spartan prep schools). Students passed through harrowing extracurricular challenges and ordeals. At Princeton, the freshman and sophomore class would stage annual snowball fights. In actuality, they threw rocks at each other, and in the university archives are pho-tographs of students after the contests. Their eyes are swollen shut, their lips are broken open, they have contu-sions across their cheeks, and there are signs of broken noses and broken jaws on many faces.

These schools tried to instill courage. "Teaching men

manhood" was the phrase in use at Harvard. Speaking for the age, Charles William Elliot, the president of Harvard, declared that "effeminacy and luxury are even worse evils than brutality." Sports, he went on, could transform a "stooping, weak and sickly youth into a well-formed robust one." Football games were so bloody, and so frequently produced fatal injuries, that President Theodore Roosevelt—who was not averse to machismo—tried to instill some restraint.

John Hibben was the president of Princeton in the teens and 1920s, in many ways a conventional elite-university president of his time. His sermons to the student body would not have seemed unusual to anyone then. But they sound odd to us because of his explicit formula for character building. He rarely gave a student address without mentioning the devil. Like many others on campus, Hibben spoke of the cataclysmic battle that takes place in every human soul. There is good and evil in each of us. We are half angel and half beast. And it is necessary to build the strength of the noble side of our character so that when the ultimate test comes, the muscles and the resources will be there to fight off temptation.

Here is an excerpt from Hibben's address to the Princeton graduating students of 1913, the generation that would soon be going off to war:

> You, enlightened, self-sufficient, self-governed, endowed with gifts above your fellows, the world expects you to produce as well as to consume, to add to and not to subtract from its store of good, to build up and not to tear down, to ennoble and not degrade. It commands you to take your place

and to fight in the name of honor and of chivalry, against the powers of organized evil and of commercialized vice, against poverty, disease, and death which follow fast in the wake of sin and ignorance, against all the unnumerable forces which are working to destroy the image of God in man, and unleash the passions of the beast. There comes to you from many quarters, from many voices, the call of your own kind. It is the human cry of spirits in bondage, of souls in despair, of lives debased and doomed. It is the call of man to his brother . . . such is your vocation: follow the voice that calls you in the name of God and of man. The time is short, the opportunity is great; therefore crowd the hours with the best that it is in you.

No doubt many of the young men in the audience that day were stuck-up country-house toffs for whom this kind of talk merely delayed a trip in their roadsters to a New York nightclub. But many of those students would go off to the trenches in France, and students from that social class died in that world war, as in the next one, in disproportionate numbers. Furthermore, many of the students raised on similar exhortations—including Teddy Roosevelt and John Reed at Harvard, Allen Dulles and Adlai Stevenson at Princeton—seem to have absorbed the idea that life is a noble mission and a perpetual battle against sin, that the choices we make have consequences not just in getting a job or a law-school admission but in a war between lightness and dark.

Today the days of the blue bloods are gone, and nobody wants them to return. We live in a much fairer society—one in which education is spread more broadly, so that the numbers of students at Ohio State and the University of Texas dwarf the numbers in the Ivy League schools. Still, the Hibbenses of the old aristocracy did take the system they were born into and articulate a public moral language, the language of chivalry and noblesse oblige. They did create activities and institutions designed to instill character.

Today's schools, unless they are religious schools, do not transmit a concrete and articulated moral system—a set of precepts instructing men and women on how to live, how to see their duties, how to call upon their highest efforts. Today's schools rarely even analyze the specific sorts of virtues this achieving culture requires, and the peculiar sorts of vices it rewards. The best members of the WASP aristocracy knew that privilege corrodes virtue in certain ways. They worked up a moral language to fight that. We have only the dimmest idea of how the achievement ethos corrodes virtue in certain other ways. And we have not begun to come up with a way to counter it.

The Obstacle Course

The achievement machine encourages some virtues. The young people who thrive in it are industrious, energetic, bright, flexible, responsible, tolerant, broad-minded, nice, compassionate, considerate, and lively.

These practices and virtues are not to be sneezed at. Moreover, the ethos presents a distinct set of challenges. Today's young people live mostly amid peace and prosperity, it is true, but has there ever been a generation compelled to accomplish so much—to establish an identity, succeed in school, cope with technological change, maneuver through the world of group dating and fluid sexual orientations, and make daily decisions about everything from multiple careers to cell-phone plans, all the while coping with a blinding diversity of friends, neighbors, and social patterns?

Meritocrats acquire accumulating personalities. They accumulate not only knowledge and skills, money and things, but also ideas, experiences, beliefs, and precious moments. But—and here's the key question—how do you organize your accumulations so that life does not become just one damn merit badge after another, a series of résumé notches without a point?

The life built around self-fulfillment and capacity maximization is one of flexibility, change, improvement, and ascent. But where in that life is there room for character, which is stolid, heavy, immovable, and inconvenient? Throughout each day society reinforces the message "You must be an arrowshot moving ever upward into the stratosphere toward your best self." At rare moments in life, commencements and other high-minded occasions, society also adds, "You must also be an oak planted stubbornly into the bedrock of moral truth." How do you become an oak that is also an arrow? How do you do that in the cracks of your eighteen-hour day? College students search earnestly for the wise old head that will answer that question. They hunger for the solution. But that is the one subject on which the authorities are strangely silent.

True Ambition

When America's young strivers do seek out moral instruction, they're confronted with people who offer them impossibilities. On the one hand, there are moralists, mostly but not entirely on the left, who tell them to renounce commercialism, materialism, and vulgar endeavoring. Live simply. Be content. Slow down, make boysenberry preserves, and read romantic poetry. These are modern progressive stoics. Then there are those, mostly but not entirely on the right, who tell young people to become Augustinians. Develop a consciousness of the permanent nature of humanity and of original sin. Be aware and confront the tragic nature of existence. Commit yourself to the fixed truth of natural law, and submit to the traditions of orthodox faith.

Both these moral traditions are noble. The only problem is that they are both so antithetical to the optimistic, climbing, burbling nature of American life as to be almost irrelevant. The hopeful young products of the achievement machine are not, in the full bloom of youth, going to renounce success, striving, and material things. They may buy some country furniture as a token homage to their well-intentioned desire to live simply and reject material things, but they will use the farmer's table as a computer stand, and they'll be back surfing the Net.

The hopeful American dreamers, who have their heads filled with visions of their own future glories, are never going to develop the tragic view of life that is supposedly the prerequisite for the probing and profound soul. They are not going to cultivate moral depths by contemplating the permanence of sin. They may go to a church, even a conservative one, but their faith will be optimistic and sunny, filled with good news, not a battle against depravity. They will have imbibed the centuries-old American assumption, born out of abundance and experience, that everybody, except maybe Hitler, is well intentioned in his heart; everybody wants to do what is right.

It is unrealistic to think that American dreamers are going to embrace moral philosophies that are incompatible with American life as it is actually lived. If there are to be character-building philosophies, and a moral vocabulary suited to real-life American students, they will have to grow out of the ascent-assuming nature of real life.

We can make the climb meaningful by lengthening the horizon of ambition, by reminding our students and ourselves that the goal is not the big house, the happy retirement, or even the noble reputation—though those things are fine—but knowing that each ascent is connected to a larger historical mission, and that mission will be realized only across generations and by institutions that transcend an individual lifetime.

The chief temptation these students face is not evil, it is nearsightedness. Parents, teachers, and coaches hone them for the future but not the distant future. As a result, students know there are hoops to jump through: school, tests, graduation. But the terrain beyond is fuzzy. They are rarely asked to apply their imagination to the far-off horizon—to envision some glorious errand for themselves, then to think backward from that goal.

During my time on campuses, I have met many students who accepted the system's definition of success. The system encouraged them to get into college, and they did that. The system said that Stanford, Duke, Northwestern, and a handful of other schools were the definition of success. So they achieved that. Then the system encouraged them to get into law, medical, or business school, so they were headed for that. I've met students who took the

LSATs, the MCATs, and the business-school admissions tests, figuring they'd see what sort of test they did best in, then head for that line of work.

I meet students who have a secret passion for philosophy but major in economics under the mistaken impression that economics represents a higher step up the meritocratic ladder. I meet students who apply for the special competitive majors and programs not because they have any interest in the curriculum, but because if something is hard to get into, then it must be good, so it is a prize they must grasp. I meet students who feel compelled to do summer internships at investment banks and consulting groups because the system encourages that kind of ascent-oriented summer job. These students know that all spring, people will be asking them how they're going to spend their summer. They don't want to answer, "Lifeguarding," because that will make them sound like losers in the climb up the ziggurat of success. They are engaged in objectless striving, working furiously at one level, so they can be admitted into the next and more exclusive arena of striving.

If I were a magazine entrepreneur, I would start a magazine called "CareerPaths." Each issue would describe how various successful people got where they are. Many bright college students don't have a clue about the incredible variety of career paths. They don't have the vaguest notion as to how real people move from post to post. Some students believe they are facing a sharp fork in the road. They can either sell their souls for money and work eighty hours a week at an investment bank, or they can live in spiritually satisfied poverty as an urban nursery school teacher. In reality, of course, the choices between wallet and soul are rarely that stark. Other students operate under the assump-

tion that there are only six professions in the world: doctors, lawyers, corporate executives, and so on. They
haven't been introduced to the massive array of unusual
jobs that exist; as a result, they fall into the familiar ruts. In
a weird way, the meritocratic system is both too professional and not career-oriented enough. It encourages a professional mind-set in areas where serendipity and curiosity
should rule, but it does not give students, even the brilliant
ones at top schools, an accurate picture of the real world of
work. And if these students are myopic about career
prospects, you can imagine how unprepared they are to
imagine what a human life should amount to in its totality.

If you go to college alumni offices, especially at smaller
schools, you will sometimes find the alumni books. At the
fifth- or tenth- or twenty-fifth-year markers, alums are asked
to write one-paragraph summaries of how they have spent
their time since graduation. These entries make for sobering
reading. Some people—the ones we would all regard as successful—who have made partner or president have written
paragraphs so mind-numbingly boring that they make your
mouth hang open and your eyes dry up. They know their
paragraphs are boring, and they apologize for it in the text,
but there is nothing they can do about it. Within the lines of
their little essays, one finds this retroactive question: What
imaginary future did I hope to achieve beyond jumping
through the next hoop placed in front of me?

Nobody expects twenty-year-olds to have life figured
out. But the Achievatron rarely forces students to step back
and contemplate the long term. It rarely forces students to
think in terms of how a complete life should be lived. When
they get together and talk about their futures, it is always
in that semiknowing tone that they are involved in a game,

and they have to figure out the rules to get to the next level.

And if you do push students in this way, it is startling how modest they tend to be, especially if they sense that someone other than they might someday read their mission statement and laugh at them. "I will start a business," one may declare, or "I will retire at age fifty and sail the world." What would be wrong with imagining something truly big? "I have a mission to help create a world in which all nations are democratic"; or "I have a mission to help create a world in which there is no cancer"; or "I have a mission to help create a world in which there is no starvation"; or "I have a mission to devote my life to God's word." These are all callings to which one could valuably surrender oneself. They all demand impossibilities and in this way are fit objects of hope. Each is an incorruptible dream that would redeem the normal material efforts that inevitably occupy many of our everyday hours. None can be achieved within a single lifetime, so each connects its bearer with the flow of history and the lives of those yet to be born.

Yet envisioning such a mission—thinking creatively about what you should devote your life to, exploring the range of missions that are out there, measuring which mission is highest, and which is best suited to your talents—is an ambitious and unrealistic activity virtually ignored by the vast achievement machine. They are too grand and pretentious and unprofessional. The paradox of modern American life, especially in regard to the young, is that while it seems driven by ambition, its citizens are not ambitious enough.

CHAPTER SEVEN

Shopping

LET US NOW MOVE from the ordeals of youth to a few pastimes of adulthood. The quest for perfection doesn't stop when we hit the age of majority. In fact, it never stops.

We adults look around, for example, and observe that while brain surgeons and Nobel laureates probably have their good points, surely glossy-magazine editors are the most impressive people in America. Every month, in the front of their magazines, many of them have to write those six-hundred-word columns with titles like "From the Editor's Desk" or "Welcome" that are supposed to establish rapport with readers. There's usually a signature on the bottom of the page to make it seem personalized, and a photo of the editor herself looking sensational yet casual.

Since nobody wants to read a lifestyle magazine edited by a shlump, the editor has to use the text to establish that she is perfect yet not stuck-up about it. She drops little hints about how she pays infinite attention to all the things we're too disorganized to master; she spends her morning sorting truffles at farmers' markets, her lunch hour hand-painting scenery so her gifted children can perform back-yard puppet shows in French and Italian, and her evenings jetting off to obscure ski resorts in Iran that use ponies instead of ski lifts. Yet while she is creating the impression of flawless accomplishment in all facets of the art of living, she also has to show that she is fetchingly modest and neighborly. She's just like us. She gets annoyed by the foibles of life—say, over-air-conditioned villas in Andalusia—just as we do. And if she bumped into us in the super-market, she'd really, really like us, and she'd want to share intimacies over extremely well-selected coffee.

Donna Warner, editor of *Metropolitan Home,* mentioned in one editor's letter that she'd been searching for a pocketbook for months. But her problem, darn it, was that she was too discerning. "My problem is that I know exactly what I want (and I do mean *exactly*)." And before you can say Ritz-Carlton, she has us jet-setting around the world in search of the right shoulder strap. "I pursued my purse in Paris and went on a satchel search in San Francisco. Naturally, I've been all over Manhattan at length."

Naturally!

"Every time I get on a plane my heart races," writes Dana Cowin of *Food & Wine* in the tone of obligatory enthusiasm that is essential to this genre. "No, it's not fear of flying—it's the anticipation of adventure. When I toured Burgundy on a bicycle trip organized by Butterfield & Robinson, I spent my days pedaling along vineyard roads and my nights learning about wine from local vintners. In

San Francisco, I walked every inch of the Italian enclave of North Beach, in search of divine espresso and homemade focaccia." Amazing. We have done the same thing while touring our local strip malls on a trip organized by the $14.95 Airport Service Van Company.

Jane Pratt, the editor of *Jane,* looks cryogenically youthful in her funky but fun editor's picture. "Kate White, who's the editor of *Cosmo* and one of the genuinely nicest people, had heard that I'd just gotten engaged and ran up to congratulate me after the Tommy Hilfiger show this morning," Jane gushes. But that doesn't mean she's uptight about the coming event. "The wedding day is still not something I'm just living for. Actually, last night I suggested putting it off for another year and Andrew said, 'Whatever you want, honey.' See, isn't he the greatest?"

You'd think spending month after month, year after year, churning out page after page on lip-gloss trends, armoire placement, or powerboat design would get you down, but these editors have, to use their favorite word, *passion.* They spend their lives in perpetual bouts of rapture and delight, finding new product lines they just have to show us. "We have a passion for our families, for our pets; we love to be surrounded by wonderful things to look at and listen to, or we live in anticipation of the next great meal. We love our homes and the way our homes look," writes Dominique Browning of *House & Garden,* speaking for all of us who join her in the magic circle of subscribers.

And these editors get to share it all with us. The other theme of these letters is that the issue you hold in your hand contains unimagined riches—glorious prose, fascinating features, original and useful ideas—and that the editors happen to be so fortunate (read, brilliant) as to have it all come together under their direction. Few other professions require such regular self-puffery. But these glossmasters pull it off—and with such falsely modest charm—because it's not about them. It's not about the advertisements. It's not about the products. It's not even about the self. It's about something much wider and more profound. "Fitness is about living a balanced life, one with physical, mental, emotional and spiritual growth and change," writes Barbara Harris, the editor of *Shape* magazine.

It's about the highest aspirations, the noblest causes. Dominique Browning, who is the Goethe of this field, enlisted us one month in her crusade against bad pruning. "I detest the amputated limbs, branches lopped off abruptly at midsection. . . . Such practices leave stumps that aim heavenward and yet are hopelessly thwarted in their yearning. . . . I can almost hear the torment and accusation in those stumps—testimony to the cruel cancellation of life." We are marching in solidarity with the great-souled editor.

Similarly, Michael Molenda, editor of *Guitar Player* magazine, laments the decline of culture: "Sound bites and media 'Cliffs Notes' are the opiate of the short-attention-span masses. We don't read. We don't question. We don't honor—or even have much knowledge—of the past. We're living in the 'whatever' years, where avoiding responsibility is a national pastime." Food for thought for amp enthusiasts.

By the time you get to Martha Stewart's magazines, you're almost impressed that whatever little disagreement she might have had with the Securities and Exchange Commission, she hasn't bought in to the falsely-modest etiquette. She doesn't even pretend to be just like us. In

Martha Stewart Living, she prints a monthly calendar mapping out her schedule over the coming days: March 27—take down and clean storm windows; March 28—appear on *The Early Show* on CBS; March 29—accept the Iphigene Ochs Sulzberger Award at the Waldorf-Astoria; March 30—prune raspberry canes. You're lucky the woman lets you buy her magazine.

And that's really the purpose of America's magazines: to help you get better, deeper, in fact, perfect. If you don't feel you are leading the perfect life, all you have to do is go over to the nearest magazine stand, and you're confronted by a buzzing hive of self-improvement. At every angle and for every taste, there are magazines to tell you how to make one little niche of your life better. In the health section, there are more "Buns of Steel in 20 Minutes a Day" cover stories than can be imagined. The magazine *Malt Advocate* fills you in on the merits and demerits of oak bourbon casts. *Murder Dog,* the magazine on rap artistry, contains stray hints on how to keep your pants up while the waistband is floating magically around your thighs. *Robb Report* has advice on how you can improve the atmosphere of your wet bar by selecting just the right whale-foreskin bar stool. For lovers of small cylindrical carnivores, there's a publication called *Ferrets USA,* which discourses on the pros and cons of four-story ferret bungalows, the charms of ferret-motif personal checks, and the virtues of Totally Ferret snack treats. This journal offers its readers, who apparently have high saccharine tolerances, examples of adorable ferret names, such as Popcorn, Poochins, and Cutems.

You look around the magazine racks, and there is no aspect of human existence that doesn't have some periodical offering advice on how it can be made better. You wouldn't be surprised to come across *ToughGums: The Magazine for Frequent Flossers* or *Inhale! The Bellysucking Monthly for the Embarrassingly Overweight* or *Pluckings: The Magazine of Tweezer Enthusiasts.* If you page through these magazines, you find that the devotees of each obsession are contemptuous of people who haven't taken the time to master their pathetically small sphere of expertise. Foodies can read *Chile Pepper* magazine, in which the editors seem to disdain pepper poseurs who can't tell the difference between a habanero and a cayenne. The adventure magazines are contemptuous of overequipped nature pseuds who couldn't even tell you if their parka is made from microfibril with left-hand-coiled strands or not. I recently read a bitter attack in *Field and Stream* on "torque dorks," idiots who haven't taken the time to perfect their torque-wrench techniques and so go through life with improperly mounted tires on their boat trailers.

But no matter how accomplished you are in your own little niche world, you can never rest. Each month brings a new issue with new trends, new products, and new info. Suppose you are a reader of a shelter magazine called *Victorian Home.* That probably means you were voted Least Likely to Show Cleavage in high school. Aside from that, it should mean that you don't have to keep up with the trends. Your whole design motif is based on reclaiming something from the past. But it doesn't work that way, because with every issue, subscribers learn that as we go through the twenty-first-century, there will be new and better ways to live more Victorian. You can be more Victorian than the Victorians.

The readers want it. Somewhere in the furnace of their bellies, there is a little voice telling them to be better Victorian decorators, better ferret equippers, better outdoor-adventure trekkers. There is some impulse to autopyg-malianism—the urge to transform oneself from the humdrum drone you used to be into the perfect God of the Rugged Adrenaline (if you read the adventure magazines) or the Goddess of Popularity (if you read *Cosmo*). We are so surrounded by the gospel of self-improvement that we might forget how overpowering it is. But all around us, from every magazine on the rack, there is the same cry: Go Ahead, Get Better, Go Ahead, Get Better. Work harder. Learn more. Catch the trends. Buy the latest gadgets. Build the right environment. Master the right activities. Inside you is the Ideal You waiting to be born. Life can be perfect.

It doesn't come easy. Glossy magazines have found they can't draw readers with long feature stories alone. They need curricula. They need "Fifty Ways to Drive Him Wild in Bed." They need "How to Fertilize Your Garden with Shredded Credit Card Come-ons." They need "The Six Things You Need to Know Before You Attempt a Do-It-Yourself Nose Job."

Nothing is left unimproved. *O*, the magazine dedicated to the first letter of Oprah Winfrey's name, recently had a feature called "Walk Like a Goddess." Most *O* readers, even those without historically significant first initials, know how to walk—but good is never good enough. "A goddess is both graceful and grounded," the magazine informs us. How to achieve that? "Hold your head so that your chin is horizontal to the floor. . . . Fully extend your front leg with each step. . . . To lengthen the neck and spine, imagine your head is floating above your shoulders. . . . Rotate [your] thumbs forward to open up [your] shoulders." It all works. Get up now, start rolling your thumbs and floating your head. Pretty soon your shoulders will open like 7–Eleven, your chin will be horizontal as a patient etherized upon a table, your spine stretched out like toffee on a spool. With one exercise, you will have taken a small but fully extended step for humanity and a giant leap toward fulfilling your life mission of releasing your inner goddess.

Here we begin to see the feature that we observe so often in American life—the ability to slather endless amounts of missionary zeal on apparently trivial subjects and thereby transform them into harbingers of some larger transcendence. The glossy magazines don't exactly tackle the big subjects. Passing on those articles that must come over the transom on the Problem of Evil and the Nature and Destiny of Man, the editors of, say, *Pen World* nonetheless devote such religious fervor on the subject of stylus design that you almost get the impression something sacred is going on here. "Fasten Your Seatbelts—New Spring Pen Introductions Soar!" was the cover line on a recent issue.

Similarly, the contributors to *Fly Rod &Reel* don't get cynical because, instead of writing the great American novel, they have to spend their lives pouring out four-thousand-word essays on this year's fishing-gear innovations. On the contrary, they are genuine reel enthusiasts who seem to start butt-bouncing in their chairs when the new shipments arrive with the latest Super Speed Shaft spool, which provides total freespool, Magforce magnetic control, a take-down sideplate feature, and hard-anodized construction to resist saltwater corrosion. There's an emotion here, accoutremania, that resembles love; getting the right gear seems like a path to par, the suburban version of Zen harmony and inner peace.

For many people, the pathway to perfection is achieved through connoisseurship of extremely narrow product lines. Most of us have hobbies and interests that are completely ridiculous to many of the people around us (including and especially our loved ones). Yet our mastery of some little sphere of life, our expertise in a tiny corner of human existence, is important, part of our life's journey and part of our identity.

For example, I have a watch that only tells time. But on the racks, one finds several magazines serving the watch-nut population, for people whose self-worth depends largely on their wrists. These publications are printed on paper so rich and glossy that it might be made from butterscotch. Each issue features a few new watches that transcend mere watchdom to become manifestations of the horologically sublime. *American Time* recently ran a cover story about Patek Philippe's Star Caliber 2000, which has 1,118 moving parts, a nocturnal sky chart, a perpetual calendar, and a chime system that exactly replicates the tone and rhythm of the bells of Big Ben at Westminster Palace. Only twenty of those watches were made, and they were to be sold in five sets of four, priced at $7.5 million per set.

In the watch magazines, there are ads for Italian display cabinets that will "exercise" the watches you never get around to wearing. There are features reassuring readers that people who have a life, such as Jay Leno, also care a lot about watches. There are profiles of watchmakers, who of course are not just engineers in a factory somewhere. They are portrayed as Watch Whisperers—profound, thoughtful men and women with European names and bad teeth who channel the ancient watch mysteries into the wristwear you see on these pages. Finally, there are instruction articles reminding you that every month brings new and better watches, new challenges for the watch aspirant, new trends to master and excellences to achieve, for why on earth would you want a grade-5 titanium case that is only 90 percent titanium, when you could have a grade-1 case (99 percent titanium) and live confident in the knowledge that if your arm is ever run over by a Boeing 747, your timepiece at least would emerge unscathed.

Sacramental Longing

Many people have commented on the luxification of American life. It's not enough to have a twenty-two-foot powerboat; a forty-six-foot inboard cruiser with sleeping cabins and bathrooms is better. The explanation for the trend is the one Thorstein Veblen sketched out in *The Theory of the Leisure Class:* People want to show off. But consider a boat nut, a person who subscribes to boating magazines, cares about boats, and gets a glow of self-validation from the knowledge that he has achieved boating excellence. Of course, such a person is going to spend his decades realizing his ever higher boating capacities. He can't buy the same boat he bought last time. He has to move up, move forward, progress to higher levels of deck superbness. This is the central fact of perpetual improvement. No hobby or passion can ever stop at its logical conclusion. It has to reach some level of otherworldly excellence that is at once completely ridiculous and somehow transcendent.

Freud thought he could get to the essence of people by analyzing their sleeping dreams. But individuals reveal more about themselves in their waking dreams. It is in the things they want, in the way they envision their blissful tomorrows, and, in particular, in the things they use to realize their perfect selves that individuals distinguish and reveal themselves. What people are doing as they page through these magazines is this: They are enjoying the longing. They are constructing fantasies of what their lives might be like, using the goods and images they see in these magazines. They are not there yet, and in truth they may never get there, but they get pleasure from bathing in the possibility of what might be, of sloshing about in the golden waters of some future happiness. They achieve a transubstantiation of goods, using products and gear to create a magical realm in which all is harmony, happiness, and contentment, in which they can finally relax, in which their best and most admirable self will emerge at last.

As a few of our most perceptive writers have noted, there is some sacred intent entwined in all the material yearning that characterizes middle- and upper-middle-class American life. In a review of a biography of John Updike, the writer Jay Tolson points out that Updike is a great American novelist precisely because he is able to capture the mystical element contained in consumer longing:

> What makes Updike a particularly shrewd analyst of civilization, particularly as it is played out on the North American continent . . . is that he perceives—really sees, with that remarkable Dutch painter's eye of his—the sacramental residue, in both the scientific and acquisitive habits of our culture. He portrays it, among other ways, in the desperate affairs and couplings of his characters, in their desire for ultimacy through the possession of

others, and in the elaborate savorings of that possession. He depicts it, too, in the fine regard his characters have for things—their appreciation of the subtle distinctions between, for instance, a Toyota Camry and a Toyota Corolla.

This mystical transubstantiation takes place in the venues of everyday life—at the magazine stand or on the train or in the doctor's office. Paging through ads is not a lofty or highly charged experience. Yet in these ordinary moments of life, the imagination is going about its business: measuring different futures, cooking up semiconscious fantasies, stoking the fires of anticipation, longing for different goods, homes, and lives, savoring the pleasures of fantasy.

The key aspect to understand is that the imagination never rests. As cognitive scientists are discovering, the imagination is not some rarefied gift that artists use to paint pictures. It's the brain at work every second of every day, blending one set of perceptions with others.

When we pick up a cup of coffee, we experience many sensations: the smell, the color, the feel of the cup in our hand, the weight. These perceptions register in different parts of the brain. Somehow the brain blends them together. We have no idea how. This is imagination in its most rudimentary form: blending disparate sensations. At higher levels, the imagination blends what is with what could be. Without our permission, and without our ability to control it, our imagination takes physical sensations— me looking at a perfect kitchen in a glossy magazine—and it blends a fantasy landscape, me with my perfect family in the perfect kitchen and the dishes are clean and the meal was relaxed yet perfect.

Imagination is slippery. It lives halfway in the world of physical reality and half in the realm of what isn't, what could be or never could be. In the realm of the imagination, it is very hard to draw a sensible distinction between the material and the nonmaterial. When we confront a new house, or a new car, or a new blouse, we see the physical object, but our imagination is racing ahead, concocting future pleasures and possibilities.

Each of us has little templates in our minds, cognitive scientists have found, influenced by culture, genetics, and individual will, so certain products or goods set off those light shows in the imagination, while other products leave us cold. You may be aroused by the aroma of a certain wine or perhaps the sight of a certain powerboat, depending on your background and tastes. But when a product or an image in a magazine hits the right ignition button, it is like July Fourth in the brain. The imagination goes wild. The longing begins.

Fantasy Snacks

These glossy magazines are nutrition for the imagination. It's common to say that they're like pornography. *Food & Wine* is pornography for food. *AutoWeek* is pornography for cars. *Condé Nast Traveler* is pornography for beaches, and *House Beautiful* is pornography for Italian-made truffle shavers. *Playboy* and *Penthouse* have the same kind of lavish photo spreads, the same glistening perfections, the same fantasies and lusts, just for different things.

For millions of people, the ridiculously perfect images—

the worlds in which every breast is round and firm, every house is immaculate, every vacation destination is uncrowded, and every thigh is firm—are the images that arouse the imagination most powerfully. Why else would so many men spend billions of dollars a year looking at pictures of women who are nothing like real women, let alone the women they are likely to sleep with? Why else would so many people subscribe to *Architectural Digest* and pore over flawless interiors that no human beings could actually live in and that few could ever afford? Why is it that the magazines that sell best off the racks are the ones with bright photos of smiling celebrities on the cover—stunning movie stars, rock stars, royalty, and athletes who are far better-looking than the people we know, far richer than anybody around us, and are depicted living in a social stratosphere far removed from the realm most of us inhabit?

In short, why do we torture ourselves with things we don't have and aren't likely to get? Why do we eagerly seek out images of lives we are unlikely to lead?

It is precisely because fantasy, imagination, and dreaming play a far more significant role in our psychological makeup than we are accustomed to acknowledging. We are influenced, far more than most of us admit, by some longing for completion, some impulse to heaven. The magazine images are not really about hedonism, about enjoying some pleasure that fits into our life here and now. They're not even mainly about conspicuous consumption, finding the right item that will help us show off and look richer and more sophisticated than our friends and neighbors. These magazines are about aspiration.

What they offer is the possibility of a magical conversion process. By mastering the skills described in the magazines, cultivating the tastes, building the sorts of environment, wearing the right fashions, adopting this or that diet, I will be able to transform my present caterpillar self into the shimmering butterfly that is the future me. The magazines show us the avenue to this infinity, and they fill in, in concrete detail, the substance of our vague longings for contentment.

As Jackson Lears writes in his history of the advertising industry, *Fables of Abundance,* "Gradually I began to realize that modern advertising could be seen less as an agent of materialism than as one of the cultural forces working to disconnect human beings from the material world." Lears argues that advertisements focus private fantasy. They detail a vision of the good life. They validate a way of being in the world. They are, he emphasizes, a way of reanimating material existence. They create playgrounds in the mind. They are one of the places adults can play, can enter into the realm of enchantment, anticipation, and ecstasy.

Lears is not entirely sanguine on the subject of ads. Dubious at best about capitalism and the marketplace, he is disturbed that they implicitly construct an image of "a striving self in a world of fascinating but forgettable goods." Imagination is not only more important than we tend to admit, it is more double-edged. It tricks us into doing things that we probably shouldn't do, into wanting things that we probably don't need. It is never content with the here and now. It is often the enemy, not the friend, of sober contemplation and quiet reflection. It's no accident that it is often the most imaginative people who lead the most disorganized lives.

Stairways to Paradise

Some people see advertisers as devious manipulators who manufacture wants and create dissatisfactions. That's not quite right. The people who look at advertisements *want* to want. They are not passive victims in these fantasies.

Turn the pages of any magazine, and what is there on offer but a yearning for ultimacy? Every magazine has its own vision of heaven and its own way to get there. For example, *Architectural Digest* offers a heaven for those whose ideal of perfection revolves around recently renovated horse farms decorated in tastefully muted color palettes. In the paradise of this magazine, the homes are inevitably rustic yet elegant. The rooms are intimate while generously proportioned (stretching as they do through several zip codes). Clients and interior designers work in perfect accord, much as the lion lies down with the lamb, delighting in the Italian carved giltwood half-urns for the master bedroom, exulting in the early-American quilts that set off the Japanese lanterns on the George II mahogany side tables, expiring with satisfaction in the perfectly shaded bed of lavender that lines the hillside adjacent to the vineyard.

In the promised land revealed in *Architectural Digest,* everything is immaculate. The Han Dynasty sideboards are unscuffed, the Flemish throw pillows don't bear so much as a crease. The homes look like they are lived in by people who vacuum the inside of their toasters and floss their Oriental carpets to stand all the little hairs up straight. In fact, in this heaven, there are no people. The rooms are almost always shown deserted. The sheets on the beds look virginal, and while the dining rooms are sometimes shown already set, with soup poured in the china, it is clear that no actual human could ever be permitted to exhale amid such pristine perfection. It's as if the houses are so wonderful, the owners and their design professionals spontaneously combusted with joy while taking a final savoring gaze at the Bauhaus motifs in the pigeonierre.

There is another set of magazines for people whose idea of heaven is a little more populated and close at hand. These are the women's lifestyle magazines, such as *Real Simple, Ladies' Home Journal,* and the alphabetically challenged *O.* These are magazines for women who have learned the hard way that they will have to provide for themselves all the things they once thought they were going to get from men: steady support, soft reassurance, patient pleasure, creative inspiration, open-hearted emotion. Still, they can dream.

In these magazines, claw-foot bathtubs are always placed lusciously in the center of vaulted-ceilinged bath-spas. Though the children can be heard working on their college applications in the family room, and the faint aromas wafting from below suggest that the husband is whipping up his special pasta primavera while doing his pec-flexing exercises in the kitchen, the wife is left alone to luxuriate in her neutrally colored bathtub, sloshing about lazily with her exfoliating sea sponge, and savoring the lemongrass aromas of her decaffeinated Persian tub tea.

The heaven of these magazines is an unharried sanctuary. Children bid for their mother's attention only when they are adorable. Oversize comfy sweaters and tube socks are considered the height of sexiness. Maya Angelou lives next door and drops by to offer marmalade, warmth, and validation. Every husband is James Taylor, and his main longing is for nights of soft cuddling. In this realm, women delight themselves by creating whimsical yo-yo designs, which they share during the legendary birthday parties they organize for their kids. Evenings are spent in pajamas eating popcorn while watching old movies and giggling with extremely unsulky teenage daughters. Not only are the husbands James Taylors, they also leave love notes on the pillows, read Barbara Kingsolver novels in the Jacuzzi, and make perfect snow angels come wintertime.

There are, of course, other heavens envisioned in the panoply of American niche magazines. For example, if you decide at some point in your life to become an outlaw biker, there are publications like *Easyriders* to help you become the best outlaw biker you can possibly be. In the biker heaven revealed on page after page, all the men and women have kick-ass, crotch-quaking hogs—perhaps with six-inch 44-magnum risers, an Andrews B grind cam, a set of Wiseco .030-over pistons, Axtell cylinders, and an S&S carb all packed into a Big Twin Chrome Horse frame. In this heaven, all the righteous bikers live up to the highest codes of outlaw connoisseurship, which essentially consists of taking everything approved of by readers of *The New York Review of Books* and doing the opposite.

Biker badasses roar through this promised land with their flaming-skull tattoos, their Dixie bandannas, their ZZ Top hair-explosion beards, their POW/MIA flags, and their "I Do Drunk Chicks" T-shirts stretched across their fuck-you bellies. In biker heaven, all the men are masters of witty repartee—"Show us your tits!" All the women chug beer from the pitcher and dream of becoming strippers. Anybody who would wear pastels is in hell.

Biker heaven is a garrulous place. The magazines are

filled with photos of delirious masses of black leather-clad biker dudes gathered at rallies. It's like the blessed union of the conspicuously nonhygienic. There are pictures of people smokin' and cruisin' and flashin' and chuggin' and mud-wrestlin' and huggin' and practically fornicatin', and everybody looks absolutely ecstatic to be joined in the brotherhood of the bike.

Stogie Utopia

Finally, and impressively, cigar lovers have their own paradise dreams. Their magazine, *Cigar Aficionado,* is a huge caramel slab of a magazine, and each month it features a celebrity on the cover with a humongous phallic symbol in his or her mouth.

Like all niche consumer magazines, *Cigar Aficionado* is built upon a series of pointless discriminations. There can't be just one or two cigar shapes; there have to be four hundred. Some of the cigars reviewed in the magazine are thick and rounded and look like nuclear submarines, others are fat and bulbous and look like the Hindenburg, others are menacing, like a railroad spike. Some scientist should do a study to see if cigar owners experience a phenomenon similar to what happens to dog owners: Do their penises come to resemble the rods they stick in their mouths?

Of course, the magazine also provides all manner of self-improvement advice for people who aspire to a cigar-centered lifestyle. Some of the articles seem superfluous— "Swearing Is Fun"—but many must be useful: shopping routes in Havana; fine points in the art of cigar rolling; price trends in the cigar auction markets (where prices can top $1,400 per cigar); how to use knives, piercers, and single- and double-blade guillotines to cut your stogie.

The perfect *Cigar Aficionado* reader pulls his Lamborghini up to his oceanfront home, which has one of those humongous built-in aquariums that look so good in casinos and your better class of Chinese restaurants. His cell phone is smaller than his fingernail and doubles as a sex toy for one-night stands. His exquisitely cut Anderson & Sheppard suit whispers as he walks, and his custommade John Lobb Ltd. shoes are so soft they barely leave an imprint in his shag carpets. As he sips his four-hundred-year-old port and slips one of his platinum-edition James Bond DVDs into the stadium-sized high-definition diamond-vision media center, he contemplates whether it is really worth it to travel to Russia just so he can break the sound barrier in a rented MiG, or whether his time would be better spent at the Dean Martin fantasy camp for frustrated crooners.

The remarkable thing about *Cigar Aficionado* is that it allows readers to demonstrate how effectively they, too, have lived up to the magazine's beau ideal of perfect living. In the back of most issues is a section in which readers send in photographs of themselves and their friends enjoying cigars, and the magazine publishes them page upon page. Now, it should be said that all photograph albums are partly propaganda efforts. None of our lives are one-tenth as happy and successful as the ones depicted in our albums. We enlarge the good and edit out the bad or unflattering. We do it because we want to trick our future selves—and our neighbors, if we can get them to look—into believing that compared to the drab gray lives of other people, our own existence has been an endless string of multiple-climax fulfillments. We like to live imaginatively in the ideal of the past as well as the future.

But the photo albums in the back of *Cigar Aficionado,* even measured against the normal distortions of the genre, are quite remarkable. The cigar is never the point. These are trophy photos meant to display some awesome level of personal achievement or magnetism, pictures of already achieved heaven. The shots generally were taken during some moment of testosterone-rich wonderfulness. There will be a bunch of guys in extra-extra-large golf shirts with tobacco logs sticking out of their grinning teeth on the eighteenth green at Pebble Beach. There will be a bunch of guys with tobacco logs sticking out of their grinning teeth on some Vegas pool deck. There will be a bunch of women at a bachelorette party, who, upon seeing themselves in this magazine, will realize that no matter how virtuous a woman may be in real life, it is impossible to look chaste in a cocktail dress with an eight-inch rod sticking out from between your lips.

Many of the people who submit shots look like normal, unobjectionable, and marginally tasteful human beings. But the best photographs do not come from the dignified Winston Churchill wing of the cigar-loving community. They come from the "You da' man!" Joey Buttafuoco wing of the cigar-loving community. So some of the shots of cavorting males imply their own captions: "A Big Night at Hooters" or "When We Wear These Shades, We Think We Look Like the Blues Brothers" or "Five Seconds After This Picture Was Taken, We All Started Air-Guitaring."

The photographs tend to fall into three genres. There is first the Men and Their Toys genre. There will be a shot of a guy with a big cigar in his mouth, posing in front of a gleaming Lincoln Navigator with vanity CIGR LOVR license plates, looking so proud of himself you'd think he'd just given birth to the thing. The best shot I ever saw in this genre featured a cigar smoker crouching in front of his Corvette, with his three-car garage and two rider mowers visible in the background—a masterpiece of compressing all of one's penis-augmentation devices into one small photograph.

Then there is the Expense Account Living genre, of people gathered in luxury boxes at college football games, at resort hotels for sales conferences, and best of all, at casino cigar bars. These latter shots, presumably taken at Sylvester Stallone film festivals, tend to picture men whose fashion sense is a delightful blend of George Hamilton and the Russian mafia. They appear uninhibited by their planetarium-sized bellies. They are outfitted with the full array of male hand jewelry—pinkie rings, bracelets, and multiple-warhead Rolexes—bravely willing to risk getting their gold chains painfully entangled in their chest-hair toupees.

Finally, there is the I'm As Obnoxious As I Want to Be genre. In the normal life cycle of the working male, there are many moments when one must be obsequious. But there comes a butterfly moment around middle age when it is no longer necessary to be deferential to bosses, solicitous toward clients, on eggshells with teenage children. During this stage, a man can let his inner Wart Hog out for a romp.

Men who have not yet achieved this level of freedom tend to venerate their Wart Hog–liberated peers. The extremely arrogant fifty-five-year-old male has always been a venerated figure in our culture—Howard Cosell, Bobby

Knight, Bill O'Reilly, etc.; men so free that they can tell the whole world to go to hell.

The extremely grand Robusto is to the obnoxious middle-aged male what the sword was to the chivalrous knight—his shaft, his weapon, his symbol of honor. The photographs these men submit are often to smugness what paintings by Rubens are to chubbiness. They don't care if you think menopausal men should have outgrown their fascination with assault rifles. They don't care if you think it's inappropriate for sixty-year-old men to hang around with cosmetically enhanced women who wear gold lamé E-Z Off party dresses. These men pose with their chests puffed, their hair ambitiously combed over, surrounded by bevies of women who look like they have double-platinum frequent-buyer cards from Wonderbra, and whose own handling of their own cigars can only be described as extremely fellatian.

It is impossible to imagine a British magazine running a feature like this, or a French magazine or a Lebanese magazine or a Chinese magazine. (Actually, the French invented the guillotine because they hoped to get rid of people like this.) If you glimpse the photographs quickly, they do seem to confirm the stereotype of modern Americans as crass vulgarians. But if you study the impulse behind these shots with a kinder eye—which admittedly takes Gandhian forbearance—you do see the quintessential American impulse: to depict some perfect world in which money, friendship, comfort, pleasure, and success all roll into one to create perfect bliss. These cigar aficionados have merely created images of their personal paradise and captured them in photographic form. As we see again and again in suburban life, this paradise drive, this longing to realize blissful tomorrows, can take both the highest and lowest forms, involve the most noble and the most crass qualities, sometimes in the same person or in the same hour.

Like their somewhat more reflective peers, these cigar aficionados have constructed images of what their world is like when all the work, all the self-improvement comes to fruition. Even here, in its most elemental form, the impulse to utopia is recognizable. We fancy ourselves a practical, hardheaded people. But the fact is, utopian fervor animates American life. We don't only dream of these paradises. Deep down, we expect to achieve them, and we know they are there in the future, calling to us. We are oriented toward the ideal the way a moth is oriented toward light.

Anticipatory Hedonism

If you study people as they shop, you quickly perceive that the economists' model of human behavior—in which rational actors calculate costs and benefits—doesn't explain the crucial choices. (Why do some people fall in love with Jaguars but not Corvettes?) Nor does Thorstein Veblen's model, in which consumers are involved in a status race to keep up with the Joneses. (Do you really think that's how you select your purchases? And if you don't, what makes you think everyone else is more shallow and status-crazed than you are? Furthermore, in a decentralizing world, which Joneses are you supposed to keep up with, anyway?)

The key to consumption is not calculation or emulation, it's aspiration. Shopping, at least for non-necessities, is a form of daydreaming. People wander through stores browsing for dream kindling. They are looking for things that inspire them to tell fantasy tales about themselves. That apple corer at Crate and Barrel can help you make those pies you've always savored; you can imagine the aromas and the smiles when you bring them out for dessert. That drill from Sears can help you build a utility closet; you can imagine the organized garage and the satisfaction of having everything in its place. That necklace is just what your wife would love; you can imagine the joy she will feel when you give it to her.

Often the pleasure that shoppers get from anticipating an object is greater than the pleasure they get from owning it. Once an item ceases to fire their imagination—when it no longer inspires a story about some brighter future—then they lose interest in it, and their imagination goes off in search of new and exciting things to dream about and buy. (Kids can go through this process with dispiriting speed, as anybody can tell you on a Christmas afternoon.)

People might browse through things they cannot possibly afford, simply because the pleasure they get from daydreaming in a luxury showroom compensates for the frustration of not being able to buy anything. The shoppers may play a distinctly modern game: They know that Gatorade won't make them jocks, that Nike sneakers won't make them jump like Mike. At the same time, they enjoy the fantasies and are happy to play along.

Sometimes shopping sets off a dream or a sensation that is actually revealing and true. In Virginia Woolf's short story "The New Dress," a woman tries on a dress:

> Suffused with light, she sprang into existence. Rid of
> cares and wrinkles, what she had dreamed of herself

was there—a beautiful woman. Just for a second . . .
there looked at her, framed in the scrolloping
mahogany, a gray-white, mysteriously smiling,
charming girl, the core of herself, the soul of herself;
and it was not true vanity only, not only self-love
that made her think it good, tender and true.

Woolf beautifully captured the way the woman's vision has
both the quality of hallucination—it exists for a moment,
the woman's cares and wrinkles vanish—but also the quality of truth, because in this moment, the woman sees her
truest and best self, which does exist deep down.

People tend to buy things that set off light shows in
their imaginations, which fit into the daydreams. For many
people, shopping is its own joy, a way of envisioning a better life to come.

In his book *The Romantic Ethic and the Spirit of
Modern Consumerism*, Colin Campbell calls this desiring/
consuming/daydreaming state "modern autonomous imaginative hedonism." He is describing the hedonism of the not
there yet. This is an imaginative hedonism rather than a
sensual hedonism: When a person is deciding what to buy,
she is not experiencing the good by merely fantasizing
about what the experience of the good will be like. This is
not an aristocratic Marie Antoinette–style hedonism practiced by people who already have access to everything.
Rather, it's a middle-class Walter Mitty hedonism practiced
by people—regardless of their current economic situation—who hope to fulfill their ideals someday.

Nor is it entirely benign. Campbell says that shoppers
suffer from a "pleasurable discomfort"—pleasurable
because they enjoy living in their daydreams, discomforting

because shoppers are aware that they remain, in real life, unfulfilled. Still, shoppers are bathed in hope. The products they confront might be trivial baubles or shams, but shoppers get caught up in the romance and spend optimistically if not always wisely. Campbell argues that shopping is not the opposite of working. Shopping is not about instant gratification while work is about deferred gratification. Both activities are part of the same process of pursuing satisfaction.

The magazine stand, the department store, and the mall are all arenas for fantasy. The more upscale you go, the more imaginatively evocative the stores become. Cartier is less utilitarian than Dollar General. Lamborghini is more fantasy-oriented than Ford. People with money flock toward things that don't only serve a purpose but stir the heart. They are drawn by their imagination to move and improve and chase their fantasy visions of their own private heaven. The cash register is a gateway to paradise.

CHAPTER EIGHT

Working

WHEN I WAS A TEENAGER, I stumbled across a small paperback autobiography by Ray Kroc, called *Grinding It Out,* in which he recounted his first visit to the little McDonald's hamburger stand in Illinois. Amazed by the quality of the food and service, he told Dick McDonald, one of the owners, that they should expand the company. But McDonald was content with his life and wasn't interested in growth. "His approach was utterly foreign to my thinking," Kroc wrote, so he decided to expand McDonald's himself. He soon realized that the key to the restaurant's success was not the hamburgers, it was the fries. "The french fry would become almost sacrosanct to me, its preparation a ritual to be followed religiously."

Naturally, I was impressed by this statement of faith. If, at twelve or thirteen, I had been blessed with the same sort of entrepreneurial fervor that fired Kroc, I would have had a life-transforming moment. I would have had myself grow up to be about six-five, with a monumental head of hair and enormous teeth, and I would have become a motivational speaker. My message would be: "Find Your Fry! Follow Your Fry!" If I had done this, books like *Who Moved My Cheese?* and *What Color Is Your Parachute?*, currently in their third or fourth centuries on the bestseller lists, would be mere footnotes in publishing history. I'd be the one with the line of motivational videos, my own adrenaline-pumping Caribbean-cruise seminars, and a string of $2 million a throw pep rallies for midlevel corporate dreamers in minor-league hockey arenas.

"Find Your Fry! Follow Your Fry!" would suggest the key to success in this world is having the ability to focus an entire lifetime's worth of zealotry onto one small thing, product line, or concept. Religious people spread their zealotry around on a vast theology. Political zealots spread theirs across a huge vision of society. But Ray Kroc's fanaticism lasered down on that one thing, the fry. For him, the fry was the alpha and the omega, the burning center under his magnifying-glass-concentrated beam of energy and ambition.

So you must Find Your Fry! (In motivational speaking, you cannot be stingy with upper-case letters and exclamation points.) You must find the insight or product wrinkle that will become your own personal key to paradise. Once you encounter that life-altering moment when you and your Fry! become one, every waking hour is devoted to your Fry! Every thought, when you are twenty and when you are sixty, is devoted to the ultimate realization of your Fry! And you come to believe that your Fry!, if you can only perfect it, will change the world. If you can make the perfect Fry!, then peoples will unite, enmities will fade, history will come to a glorious completion, and you, not coincidentally, will become enormously rich and successful. You will not only be revered and emulated, you will join the other Fry! followers in the stratosphere of success. The secret to American economic success is that we have millions of people in this country capable of devoting intensity to infinitesimally narrow product niches.

This is the country, after all, where it wasn't good enough to have liquid highlighters. Somebody dreamed up the exciting possibility of nonliquid highlighters. This is a country that offers consumers an infinite variety of change sorters (none of which work) and more designer-water options than the mind can comprehend. In America we have space-saving pop-up dish racks, prewaxed home dusters, turkey- and bacon-flavored dog biscuits, and self-propelled vacuums. If you open up the SkyMall catalog from the airplane seat pocket during your next flight, you can browse for wristwatch-style motion-sickness sensors, illuminated-shaft safety umbrellas, rechargeable candles, the extra-slim Martin backpack guitar, automatic rotating blackjack card dealers, built-in compass cuff links, and antibacterial toothbrush purifiers. Behind each of these ingenious and highly unnecessary items there is some inventor, some tinkerer, some junior Thomas Edison dreaming of his patent-protected millions, and of his contribution to humanity. And for every product and innovation there is a larger army of sales reps hawking it, production managers building it, senior executives managing it, and IT professionals organizing data about it.

"Would anyone but an American," a nineteenth-century

visitor asked, "have ever invented a milking machine? or a machine to beat eggs? or machines to black boots, scour knives, pare apples, and do a hundred things that all other peoples have done with their ten fingers from time immemorial?" Maybe, maybe not. But it is true that in this land of two hundred iced-tea flavors and four hundred shower-head designs that people get ahead by finding their Fry!

And it is not only gadgets. It is management procedures, consulting schemes, best practices notions, Six Sigma philosophies. Sales conferences across the land are filled with slightly deranged enthusiasts earnestly pushing their own conceptual breakthrough that will build teams, enhance customer loyalty, revolutionize corporate governance, ensure profitability, unify mankind, assure eternal peace and global understanding, and trim flabby thighs all in thirty days! At a business conference for food executives in Miami, I saw the world's fourth best yo-yoer give a motivational talk. The yo-yo was this man's Fry! He did amazing tricks and told the executives that they should approach their work with a sense of play. Yes! They wrote it down. A sense of play! Maybe one of them was having a Fry! moment.

You can see the Fry! followers every day in the magazines, or in the course of your daily life. They are obsessed, they are passionate, they are driven, and they are totally nuts. They could even be accused of being slightly narrow. "People ask me, 'What do you do? Golf? Tennis?' I say, 'I do ice, I just do ice,'" the ice merchant James Stuart told *The New Yorker*. Here are some samples from a single day's edition of *The Wall Street Journal*:

When Helen Greiner was eleven, she went to see *Star Wars,* and saw R2D2 and thought, Robots! She devoted her life to small robots. She went off to MIT, interned at NASA's Jet Propulsion Lab, and now she runs iRobot Corp., which is going to build little robots. Within ten years, she insists, every U.S. home with a computer will have a robot, too. "If we don't take robotics to the next level," she told the *Journal* reporter, "we'll have a lot of explaining to do to our grandchildren."

Charles Lieber dedicates himself to growing nanowires only a few atoms thick, which will conduct electricity. "It's really an amazing time. . . . My students are working day and night, and . . . I've never worked so hard in my life," he exclaims.

Mary-Dell Chilton is working on a technique to place new genes at specific spots on plant chromosomes. "I am in the lab day, night, Sundays, and holidays," says the woman who has been labeled the Queen of Agrobacterium.

Some people spend their lives flitting from occupation to occupation, imagining that if they could only find the product or dream that would ignite their passion, then all fulfillment would be theirs. But of course it's not the product that supplies the fulfillment but the obsession with excellence in whatever niche you stumble into. Many of these Fry! followers didn't grow up thinking they would devote their professional lives to the cause of idiot-proofing electric can openers. Many of them didn't dream of becoming water choreographers for casino fountains, or of imposing account-sharing and cross-selling information systems across a range of autonomous business units at a major corporation. But then they found themselves in a job, and after a while they were absorbed. Gradually, they came to feel they had found their place in the cosmos. Or perhaps it happened all at once. Perhaps there was that magic day when they read in a magazine some little datum—say, that in 1961, 90 percent of American children were potty-trained by age two and a half; by 1997, only 22 percent were, and it hit them: Pull-Ups diapers! Millions of parents will need pull-up diapers for their unpotty-trained three-year-olds. A Fry! was born.

Confronted with some specialized task that seems at first glance to be a certain formula for brain death, many people find a challenge, a hope, and an opportunity to transform their lives.

The Quiet Zealots

It is not brains that are most closely correlated with business success, it is persistence and intensity. Thomas J. Stanley surveyed hundreds of millionaires for his book, *The Millionaire Mind,* and according to his research, millionaires are not exactly Einsteins. The average millionaire in the U.S. had a collegiate GPA of about 2.92, a B– average. The average SAT score for the millionaires is 1190, good but not nearly good enough to get you into an Ivy League college—and that average was pulled up by the doctors and lawyers in the group, who had much higher scores than the entrepreneurs.

What matters is energy, discipline, and focus—the components of Fry! fanaticism. Stanley noticed that many millionaires have undergone a shaming experience. Somebody told them they were too stupid or too disorganized to succeed. They resolved to prove the asshole wrong.

The odd thing is that these obsessed people often look bland and uninteresting from the outside. If you wandered around some suburban American workplace, some typical cubicle farm, you'd never guess what sort of fervor burns inside certain individuals as they stand around trying to remember which is their favorite flavor packet for the company coffee machine.

I don't know if the human mind can truly grasp the tediousness of pod after pod of the highway-side office parks where many Americans now pursue their passions. I don't know if the brain, which functions on electrical impulses, after all, can measure the sheer existential nothingness of an office-park lobby in the middle of the afternoon: the empty or comatosely manned security desk; the whisper of labor-unintensive lobby vegetation, which is a grouping of sturdy houseplants and the sort of small, not very attractive trees that kill poetry on the lips. If you try to read the building directory, you fall asleep. It's a list of vacuous company names of either the three-initial-abstraction type (DRG Technologies, MLF Solutions) or the compound-word/spare-capital-letter type (SignWave, MedTech, MerchanDesign).

The buildings themselves are five-to-eight-floor layer cakes of tinted glass and composite stone. They have takeout cafés near the atrium, FedEx drop-off boxes just beside the main driveway, huddles of smokers near the outdoor fountains, airport shuttles cruising by throughout the day, and rows and rows of open parking.

You join a bunch of the cubicle-farm people in, say, a retail company upstairs in one of the conference rooms, which has views that would be considered glorious by entrance-ramp connoisseurs. If it is a working lunch, perhaps they have Southeast Asia–inspired sandwich wraps and potato chips that nobody eats because their crunch is so embarrassingly loud. The men look like the sort of daring fashionistas who, when they come home from a two-piece-suit shopping spree at Today's Man, their wives look up from the paper and call out, "What shade of gray did you buy this time?" The women do not mind that neither their company ID badges nor their navy blue work suits were identified as the height of fashion during fall shows in Milan this year.

These cubicle-farm folk spend their pre-meeting chatter time complaining about coworkers, or which personnel moves were listed in the latest issue of *POP,* the trade journal for people in the point-of-purchase industry. Yet deep inside one or two of them is this obsession, this Fry! fantasy. Perhaps one of the people at this table dreams of revolutionizing supermarket razor displays and has exactly the concept to do it. Perhaps another is contemplating breaking off to start a company that markets the little concrete bumps that prevent you from pulling too far into your parking space at the mall. Perhaps one of them has figured out how to build cardboard display signage that is hollow inside, and thus 30 percent cheaper to produce. Maybe others spend their days thinking about how to reduce glare on cash-register display screens so that older employees can read them better; or perhaps they obsess over how to speed up the receipt printer so the checkout lines can move a tiny bit faster.

These are the drivers of the American economy. The press concentrates its attention on the remarkable figures, the dot-com geniuses, the zillionaire investment bankers, or the paradigm-shifting, over-the-horizon-peering, outside-the-box-thinking corporate rebels who let their wacky but brilliant employees scooter down the company hallways while squirting each other with Super Soaker water cannons. But the real engines of American capitalism are the people you see in the most unremarkable locales—sitting around in the bland office parks or checking in to the suite hotels.

In the late 1990s, business writer Jim Collins and his research team went out to find the companies that beat the market year after year, decade after decade. He found that the real growth leaders were the sort of dowdy companies that worry about the speed of cash-register-receipt printers and send their budget-conscious middle managers on the road to Residence Inns: Walgreens, Kroger, Wells Fargo, Circuit City, and Pitney Bowes. These companies outperformed the overall stock market during the 1980s and 1990s by anywhere from 400 percent to 1,800 percent. They are led by quiet executives in flavorless work environments, and the book Collins wrote about them, *Good to Great,* became a huge bestseller and was devoured by a million similar executives who, on the outside, don't look any spicier.

How do they build great companies? According to Collins, they didn't capitalize on any technological revolution. They are not in fast-growing industries—Walgreens builds drugstores, Kroger is a supermarket chain. They were not aggressive in mergers and acquisitions. They did not have innovative compensation schemes (in fact, their executives earned slightly less than their competitors). They did not spend more time than their competitors on strategic planning. They did not hire superstar CEOs from outside. Instead, Collins argues, they found one small thing, or a few things, they could do better than anyone else in the world, and they did that thing over and over, and they got better and better at it. They found their Fry!

One of the advantages these companies had was that they did not suffer from what Collins calls the liability of charisma. The corporate culture at these places encouraged simplicity and humility. In these places, it would have been socially unacceptable for an executive to portray himself as a flamboyant genius, a countercultural maverick, or an intellectual pioneer. The social standards encouraged self-effacing behavior, modesty, and reserve. "Throughout our research," Collins continues, "we were struck by the continual use of words like disciplined, rigorous, dogged, determined, diligent, precise, fastidious, systematic, methodical, workmanlike, demanding, consistent, focused, accountable, and responsible."

Many of these companies had been trudging along fine for several decades, but there came a point when their stock began to take off, when they moved from good to great, in Collins's terminology. Oddly, though, none of the employees knew at the time that they were involved in some dramatic transformation. They had no name for the new phase their company was going through. There was no key innovation, launch event, strategic decision, or breakthrough that correlated with the takeoff in performance. Each company had spent the prior few years attracting and promoting excellent employees, and the accumulation of small improvements built up over time and eventually cohered into rapidly accelerating growth, sustained decade after decade.

These companies are staffed by quiet zealots. One employee at Wells Fargo described its former CEO, Carl Reichardt, this way: "If Carl were an Olympic diver, he would not do a five-flip twisting thing. He would do the best swan dive in the world, and do it perfectly over and over again."

In the past few years, dozens of books have reinforced Collins's basic message. *Leading Quietly* hit the *New York Times* bestseller list. *Searching for a Corporate Savior: The Irrational Quest for Charismatic CEOs,* by Harvard professor Rakesh Khurana, argued a similar line. *Execution* hit the top of the *Wall Street Journal* bestseller list, with its message of executing and finishing your strategies rather than simply thinking outside the box and developing a revolutionary mind-set.

The world of American business is not really one of swashbuckling executives who learn the leadership secrets of Attila the Hun. In reality, it is a world of outwardly genial but inwardly intense Fry! followers. Many of them are so interested in doing their job well that they don't have the time to be flamboyant or interesting. Their self-expression often comes out in their work, not in their lifestyle. Many of them love making money and have amazingly little competence for spending it. Seventy percent of the millionaires Thomas Stanley surveyed for his books *The Millionaire Mind* and *The Millionaire Next Door* have their shoes resoled and repaired rather than replaced, and the average millionaire spends about $140 on a pair of shoes. After Visa and MasterCard, the most common credit cards in the millionaire's wallets are charge cards for Sears and JC Penney. Ford is the most popular automaker among the group. In the 1996 study, Stanley reported that the typical millionaire paid $399 for his most expensive suit and $24,800 for his or her most recent car or truck, which is only $3,000 more than the average American spent.

If you filmed a TV show accurately depicting the lifestyles of these rich and not famous, it would be hopeless. These people have incredibly low divorce rates. They still clip supermarket coupons, if only to demonstrate the value of thrift to their children. They are far less likely to gamble than other Americans. They shop at price clubs. They spend a significant amount of time with their tax consultants, trying to trim their annual bill.

You'd call them misers, but that suggests a level of devious venality they generally do not have. They simply are lifestyle-fabulousness vacuums. They live very much like regular middle-class Americans—visiting the kids, going to soccer games—it's just that they work harder, started successful companies, and have a lot more money in the bank; and somewhere inside, they've got the little burn, the little engine that, as Abraham Lincoln's law partner once said of him, knows no rest.

If a novelist or an academic sociologist set out to capture their ethos, he would probably get them wrong. He might describe them, Sinclair Lewis–style, as narrow-minded Babbitts. Or he might describe them, William Whyte–style, as Organization Men, the soulless corporate cogs who lose their identity within the company machine. However, that doesn't come even close to describing what these people are like and what motivates them. American writers are famously ignorant of American business, but they are especially ignorant about success. Even Tom Wolfe, our finest contemporary writer on these subjects, usually describes businesspeople who are in the process of failing. It is nearly impossible (discounting Ayn Rand, who is off in her own world) to find a convincing portrayal of success.

That's because it is so hard to answer the mystery of motivation. What propels the quiet zealot to work so hard?

What explains his or her hunger to go from good to great? While the ranks of corporate America are dotted with midlevel managers who are terrified of change and who just want to show up in the morning and go home placidly at night, others do have that focus and need to be significant at work, even to be the best in the world. Collins hints at this trait in his description of Colman Mockler, the former CEO of Gillette: "His placid persona hid an inner intensity, a dedication to making anything he touched the best it could possibly be—not just because of what he would get, but because he simply couldn't imagine doing it any other way."

Two Work Ethics

When you start probing for the roots of this intense drive to work and rise, you realize that history is a stubborn thing. Cultural trends crest and burst, but there are some deep features of national life that are unchanging. And one of the deep features of American life is a dogged, and many would say insane, commitment to work.

A German proverb holds that in America, an hour is only forty minutes long. Indeed, it has always been this way. Benjamin Franklin called America the "land of labor." "Everybody works," Alexis de Tocqueville observed during his journey though America, "and work opens a way to everything; this has changed the point of honor quite around." George Santayana later declared that the "gospel of work and the belief in progress" constituted the two American faiths. "Works and days were offered to us," Emerson admitted in 1857, "and we chose work."

The nineteenth-century Viennese immigrant Francis Grund came to the same conclusion, in a more rueful tone, after living in Boston for a decade:

> There is, probably, no people on earth with whom business constitutes pleasure, and industry amusement, in an equal degree with the inhabitants of the United States of America. Active occupation is not only the principal source of their happiness, and the foundation of their national greatness, but they are absolutely wretched without it, and instead of the "dolce far niente," know but the *horrors* of idleness. Business is the very soul of an American: he pursues it, not as a means of procuring for himself and his family the necessary comforts of life, but as the fountain of all human felicity. . . . It is as if all America were but one gigantic workshop, over the entrance of which there is the blazing inscription, "No admission here, except on business."

Grund may have been overstating things a bit, but his tone of mixed respect, fear, and horror exactly captures the mood in which most visitors have regarded the American work ethic.

The standard historical explanation for this mentality is that it goes back to the Puritans. Every person has two callings, Cotton Mather preached, "and is a man in a boat rowing for heaven." With one oar he pulls for salvation and serves the church; with the other he pulls for usefulness, for success, for material increase. These two callings merge, uncomfortably, in the national mind, so that success is often taken as a sign of virtue.

The central thrust of this approach to life—absorbed even by those who never heard a Puritan sermon or heard of Cotton Mather—is that salvation is earned through strenuous action. Virtue is cultivated through industriousness and will. Filtered through the secularizing pen of Benjamin Franklin and a thousand eighteenth- and nineteenth-century moralists, this gospel of work came to shape American culture.

According to this ethic, it is through work, and our contribution to society, that we define ourselves. Far from being solely a thing you do, work is a way of justifying one's existence, of fulfilling one's purpose on earth, and of creating one's identity. "But do your work, and I shall know you," Emerson declared in *Self-Reliance*. "Do your work, and you shall reinforce yourself."

The lingering power of that work ethic, especially in rural America, is impressive to behold. It is not limited to farmers and well-paid executives. Sometimes you go into a Food Lion or a rural drugstore, and you notice that the aisles are meticulous and the cans are stacked on the shelf with millimeter-width precision. Someone cares about doing a good job; it is his or her source of honor. He or she may work in an apparently dead-end job, but being a good worker is what he or she is about.

Early on in American history, a different work ethic layered itself on top of the Puritan sense of calling, and character building through diligence. This later work ethic is sweeter, more optimistic, and yet more frenzied. It was born of abundance. In America, it was immediately obvious that opportunity was plentiful. The frontier beckoned, offering an open field for development, plentiful land, and the possibilities of rewards beyond all imagining. After the physical frontier closed, new frontiers were perpetually opening up—scientific and technological frontiers, new markets, new products, and new ways of doing business.

Abundance created a distinctive mentality. People came to assume that wonders must be available here, some ultimate happiness must be realizable here, if only one could go out and seize it. The abundance mentality starts with the unconscious premise that there exists, at all times, close by, a happy hunting ground, a valley where the acre of diamonds is there for the picking. In the land of abundance, fanatical work is worth it, because it can be lavishly rewarded. In the land of abundance, a person's class status is always temporary, because nearby, a complete idiot has managed to pull himself up to the realm of Lexus drivers, so someday you will, too.

The land of abundance is the land of hope. It is true that some people hang around waiting for the future to land in their laps. In *You Can't Go Home Again,* Thomas Wolfe observed:

> It is also true, and this is a curious paradox about America—that these same men who stand upon the corner and wait around on Sunday afternoons for nothing are filled at the same time with an almost quenchless hope, an almost boundless optimism, an almost indestructible belief that something is bound to turn up, something is sure to happen.

But for many others, abundance electrifies. Work is not an obligation or a duty but a fantastic chance. It's like one of those old contests—you get to keep anything you pull down from the toy store's shelves in the next two minutes. So get going!

In the land of abundance, people work feverishly hard, and cram their lives insanely full, because the candies are all around, looking up and pleading, "Taste me, taste me, taste me." People in such a realm live in a perpetual aspirational trance. They are bombarded from first waking till nighttime's last thought by advertisements, images, messages, novelties, improvements, and tales of wonder. It takes a force of willpower beyond that of most ordinary people to renounce all this glorious possibility. It's easier to work phenomenally long hours and grasp at all the candies than it is to say no. It takes incredible dedication to renounce opportunity, get off the conveyor, and be content with what one is.

Dreams of future advancement dance around one's head. "Americans are born drunk," the English sage G. K. Chesterton wrote; "they have a sort of permanent intoxication from within, a sort of invisible champagne." Accordingly, they take amazing risks, for that is the paradox of the business types. They seem dull, selfish, and sober. But inside, they are naive, childlike, and hungry. They believe everything! There is no management fad so stupid that you can't get some senior executives to buy in to it. You get these engineers who have spent their whole lives studying metallurgy, and then you feed them some dumbed-down version of Jungian psychology, and it is all brand-new to them. They think you are unlocking the mysteries of the human soul. This is the insight, they fervently believe, that will enable them to climb to the promised land. They pay you hundreds of thousands of dollars to probe the unconscious mind of the consumers of micro-wave ovens and discover the magical source of their mysterious tastes. These executives believe—desperately want to believe—that the answer to all the mysteries, the secret to market dominance, the key to their glowing transformation and earthshaking success, is just out there, just out of reach, just beyond the next door, if they could only seize it. At a builders' conference not long ago, I saw a man standing at the podium, practically screaming at the audience of five hundred people to "Be the Purple Cow!" He had been sent a copy of an article in *Fast Company* magazine called "In Praise of the Purple Cow." Brown cows are boring, the author had pointed out. But if you saw a purple cow in a field, you would notice it. So in your job, you should be the purple cow. This insight was amazing! the speaker declared. A colleague had sent him the piece with the commandment: Drop everything! Before you do anything else, read this article! It will change your life!

He'd been converted. It was fantastic! He was delirious! Now he wanted to share the secret with everyone! Be the Purple Cow! Two years before, he was probably wanting everyone to move their cheese. But that was old. *This* was the key! The Purple Cow! The secret to success and eternal happiness! The Purple Cow! was his Fry! The guy was practically beside himself with excitement. He was shouting into the microphone, and his words were infectious. People were writing them down. I found myself wanting to be the Purple Cow! too. Nobody could possibly claim that this atmosphere was simply the product of the Protestant work ethic; something far more intoxicating, as Chesterton said, was going on.

We have been blessed and plagued for centuries by

these cycles of hope and experience. Some group of supposedly sober investors and outwardly dull businesspeople
fall into a sort of trance in which they come to believe they
stand on the precipice of a radically glorious future, a
transforming technology or business practice, whether it is
the railways, nuclear power, or the Internet. They lose their
heads. They throw money from the mountaintops into the
valley of the future, hoping to raise a new utopia. Most of
them end up going broke, whereupon the cycle of disillu-
sion sets in, but they do usually lay the infrastructure—the
railways or the miles of fiber-optic cable—that leads to real
progress.

"Nothing remarkable was ever accomplished in a prosaic mood," Thoreau wrote. And he would probably deny
it, but his maxim applies as much to the supposedly prudential world of business as to anything else. These boring,
obsessed business types dream of corporate greatness. They
long to be famous through the ages as the one who refash-
ioned the oral-hygiene industry, who became the Bill Gates
of frozen bagels. They start companies knowing that most
new enterprises fail. They contemplate massive schemes at
night, then spend their days seeing if they can make the
numbers work out. The hope and poetry are as vital to
their success as the number crunching, narrowness, and
restraint. The secret of success is being visionary and practical at the same time. The American work ethic grows
both out of the old-fashioned work ethic—creating oneself
through labor—and out of the intoxication induced by
plenty, the availability, all around, of opportunities to
punch through and surpass one's fondest dreams.

The Consuming Challenge

Americans have always switched jobs with amazing speed. As historian Daniel T. Rodgers notes in his book, *The Work Ethic in Industrial America, 1850–1920,* the majority of industrial workers between 1905 and 1917 changed jobs at least every three years. A Bureau of Labor Statistics study using data from 1913–1914 found that a "normal" factory had turnover of about 113 percent. This was during depressed economic conditions, and it probably understated the amount of turnover. Very few of the workers who left work had better jobs in hand. They were just dissatisfied, hoping something better would turn up around the next bend.

Today, as we have noted, Americans remain the hardest-working people on the face of the earth. We work the longest hours and take the shortest vacations of any affluent people. Polls indicate that it is not all forced; far more than people in other lands, Americans choose to live this way. Nearly half of all Americans take the initiative to check in with work while they're supposedly on vacation: Six in ten people earning over $85,000 a year do so, according to a survey done for *American Demographics.* As the sociologist Seymour Martin Lipset observed in his book *American Exceptionalism,* "The recent comparative studies of work behavior indicate that Americans are more inclined to be workaholics than other industrialized populations."

Those Americans with the most discretion over how hard to work are precisely the ones who have chosen the longest hours. For most of human history, people at the bottom of the income ladder worked longer than people at the top. But that's no longer true. According to former labor secretary Robert Reich, over the past two decades, the percentage of American executives and professionals who work over fifty hours a week has grown by a third; their number now includes nearly 40 percent of male and nearly 20 percent of female college graduates. In a hothouse environment like Manhattan, 75 percent of the college-educated twenty-five- to thirty-two-year-olds work over a forty-hour week, whereas in 1975, only 55 percent did.

That doesn't measure the emotional intensity many Americans invest in their work lives. Many of these genial but intense workers are up in the middle of the night, scribbling down ideas. They know they need some sleep for the next day, but their brain just will not shut down. People seem to like the stress, or at least fear boring work more than stressful work. Decade after decade, in poll after poll, 80 or 90 percent of respondents say they are satisfied with their jobs. In a 1997 survey done for the Department of Labor, 69 percent of Americans told researchers they would take the same job again "without hesitation." Just 6 percent of the respondents said they would definitely not accept the same job. Yet these people still switch jobs with amazing frequency, in search of something better.

Today a phenomenal 8 percent of Americans have started their own businesses. There's a vast literature on entrepreneurship, and most of it displays an admirable grasp of the obvious (people who want to be their own boss are more likely to become entrepreneurs than people who don't). A study published in 2000 by Anisya S. Thomas and Stephen L. Mueller, in the *Journal of Interna-*

tional Business Studies, compared entrepreneurialism across cultures. They found that innovative people are spread fairly evenly over the globe. But they also found that people in the United States are more likely to feel they can control their own destinies than people in Britain, Australia, Venezuela, Colombia, and elsewhere. Entrepreneurs in America also felt more comfortable with risk than those in any of the twelve nations studied. Most of all, and most puzzling to the researchers, the study found "the likelihood of high energy level decreases with cultural distance from the United States." In other words, the farther one gets from the culture of the U.S., the less likely people are to live at the same thyroidally charged pace.

Far from wanting a comfortable, easy life, as bourgeois humans are supposed to do, the Fry! followers want a consuming challenge. They want a task that will occupy all of their faculties, temporarily blotting out everything else. According to Thomas J. Stanley's research for *The Millionaire Mind,* only 55 percent of millionaires went into their profession because of some intrinsic love of the product line, but about 80 percent went into it because they felt they would be able to realize the full potential of their abilities in this sphere.

In this way, the pursuit of gain is etherealized into a pursuit of something larger and holy, the pursuit of the fully completed self.

The Dark Side of the Fry!

You see the modern workaholics coming down the airplane aisles during boarding. They've got hands-free wires clipped to their shirt; they're trying to shimmy out of their suit coat and get their carry-on bag into the overhead rack without interrupting their cell-phone conversation. And they're talking faster and faster, because they know that in just a few minutes, the door of that plane is going to close, and they'll be ordered to turn off their phones and it'll be like someone ripped out their trachea. Cut off! Severed from the information superhighway! Restricted to the tiny capsule of their own immediate experience!

As the plane fills up, and the order to turn off the phones approaches, you can hear the tone of rising panic, like drowning people trying to get those last few gulps of life. What is it they'll miss so much? It can't be the substance of their conversations, because when you overhear them you realize this is not exactly dialogue on the order of Plato's *Republic*. Much of the time they are just narrating their own lives: "Yeah, I'm boarding a plane to Atlanta. Hold on. I'm just putting my stuff in the overhead rack . . ." You imagine that the person on the other end of the conversation is doing the same thing: "Uh-huh. I'm driving by the hardware store. I'm turning left onto Maple."

But they need it. They need the stimulation, the rhythm, the connection to the world of work, productivity, the hive of information. Somewhere in this world of roughly six billion people, there might be someone trying to reach them, with some vital bit of data that only they—indispensable as they are—can handle. And what if that person can't get through!

A few hours later, you can watch the infoholics as the plane begins its final descent. They slide their cell phones surreptitiously out of their pockets. They finger the buttons. You can see them wrestling with a moral quandary.

At five hundred feet, they are tempted to turn on the phones, because they are pretty sure they can get coverage at that altitude. On the other hand, the pilots say cellphone use disrupts the plane's navigational system.

Usually, exercising the sort of willpower that would make a Prussian officer proud, they wait until the wheels hit the tarmac and then, all up and down the plane, you can hear the trilling of the message-alert chimes, and seconds later, all the wireless men and women are restored to life: "Yeah, I've just landed. I'm unbuckling my seat belt, and I'm going to get my travel bag from the rack . . ."

If you opened up their rolling luggage, you'd be amazed by how close these business Bedouins have come to achieving perfect wirelessness, that magical state of total freedom in which all of human experience can be replicated without once resorting to a landline. The Wireless Woman's phone has voice-dial-recognition capabilities, because who has time to press the buttons? She has an Internet-access PDA, the Web clipping service, a RIM pager (whatever that is), a stowaway keyboard, and a thong clip, in case she wants to do business by the hotel pool. Her portable DVD screen allows her to watch videos and sales presentations in the van to the car-rental lot, which was formerly unproductive time, and if she swallowed all the lithium batteries in her accessories bag, that would be enough to cure depression for life.

The Wireless Man has a ruggedized Panasonic Toughbook 27 with a magnesium case, a TreePad 2.8 Freebyte Software personal organizer, a Rage Mobility AGP video controller, and full hibernation and standby modes. If it came with special helium cavities, it would be lighter than air, and if it had a disk drive that could turn into an inflatable sex doll, he wouldn't ever have to return home. He could stay out there on the road his whole life, communing with his fellow IT junkies about the CRM solutions on his mobile and how many WAP gateways he can access from his ISP. (The tragedy of his life is that while he can talk to anybody, anytime, almost nobody understands what he is saying.)

In a decentralized business age, the wireless wanderers realize, you have to be fully gadgetized. You must be at one with the huge swirling loop of communication, the living, breathing life force of digitally harmonized human interfaces. As a result, you have so many electronics on your person that if they went off all at once, with all the beepers, buzzers, vibrators, and lights, you would look like the inside of a pinball arcade.

It is this constant sense of being connected, of novelty, of relentless if low-level stimulation—this is what the infoholic can't live without. He needs to be connected to his all-consuming challenge. His brain has adapted to rhythms of wireless life. He's become an eating, breathing network server. He knows it's given him attention-deficit disorder. He acknowledges that he has a little rhythm machine in his brain; like a nursery school teacher, he's used to having his attention ripped over to something new every forty-five seconds. He can't read ten pages of a book without stopping to do something else; part of his attention is always distracted. He answers his e-mails fast and sloppy. Even as he's working on a document on his computer, he can't help himself, the new-mail alert beeps, and he toggles over just in case it's something important. His patience is totally shot. Waiting for something feels like a moral affront. His brain has shifted to handle the incessant demands of the time-maximization ethic.

He knows that it's not healthy to live so entangled in the thicket of communication, so absorbed in the bombardment of the trivial. There are too many messages, too many websites, too many reports, too many bytes screaming for his attention. He knows there's something dehumanizing about the way he has become a deft machete wielder in the jungle of communications, ruthlessly cutting away at all the extraneous but potentially interesting data forever encroaching upon him. He never allows himself to explore some curiosity. He's never at peace. Never lost in a creative fog, never mentally at play.

Occasionally, he fantasizes about life beyond the network, a life in which his mind can wander and reflect, in which he can stop for days on end to gaze at the mountains. But that is just a dream, because the Wireless Man and the Wireless Woman are headed somewhere. They are in the grip of these twin work ethics, the Puritan obligation to justify one's existence through productivity, and the abundance-induced fever to seize all the goodies. This work ethic is not without its costs and temptations. It is relentless, and it has made the Fry! follower relentless.

On the Road

Indeed, the Fry! follower is not merely on the road, he is master of the road. Every American considers him- or herself an unusually gifted driver, a masterly commuting route strategist. Go back 150 years, and there were probably streams of Conestoga wagon drivers volubly proud of their steering capacities, amazed by how many idiots there were out on the trails that day. Today air travel is the field of competition where the wireless wonder can demonstrate his or her mastery of pointless but ego-inflating life skills. The Wireless Man has his seven frequent-flier numbers memorized. He is careful to drop a bit of knowledge on 767 design so the ticket agent will be aware he is a member of the Important People Who Fly Places club. He is insanely impressed by his own ability to almost never set off the metal detectors, and he knows which shoes will keep his winning streak going. He never stands still on the moving conveyor belts, because he feels like an airport superhero to be walking at double the normal speed. He knows never to board the plane first or second, because that person often gets pulled aside for an extra bag check. He knows that on red-eye flights, you want a window seat if you have a strong bladder and an aisle seat if you don't. He knows that on morning flights, his reading material can tax 80 percent of his IQ capacity, but on evening flights, the recirculated air is fortified with special moron enzymes, and his spy thriller had better reflect that.

If Wireless Man had an orgasm every time he was reminded the luggage may have shifted in the overhead bins during flight, he would be the happiest man on the face of the earth. He is proud of his discerning taste in rental-car companies. He is pleased with his ability to reset all the car's rearview mirrors and radio station buttons by the time he's on the access road to the highway. He can find his way in every city, even though he has never once rented a luxury car in which the OnStar navigation system actually worked.

Because of his prowess, he is recognized as something of a deity by the corporations who move people. Every piece of plastic in his wallet affirms his elevated place on the Olympus of capitalism. His American Express Card is Platinum. His American Airlines Advantage card is Double Diamond. With United he is Premier Plus. His Avis Wizard is Oriental Despot, and with Hilton Honors he is Sun God. There is no arena of modern life more subtly stratified than the world of travel.

He has access to all the thick-carpeted airport clubs with sliding doors, pretty hostesses, and plentiful mimosas, a drink he would never touch off airport property. He knows that in the world of the travel lords, you never say you are flying first class. You say you are flying up front, which sounds casual and assumed. He knows that when he settles into his wide seat, 2C, he should never make eye contact with the proles trudging back to 17F. There are more of them, and if incited, they could revolt. He knows how to slide the little mini ledge out of the first-class arm-rest, which is the perfect place to put his pre-takeoff nut bowl. He knows the ultimate secret of the frequent traveler, which is that all the luxuries and amenities going to the top rung of corporate fliers—the airport clubs, the first-class cabins, the express security lanes—are actually shabby and disappointing, but you must never let the folks back in coach suspect this. All that matters is that you have access—testimony to the vital role you play in the turbo of American capitalism—and others do not.

Enrichment

Off they go in the relentless pursuit of their Fry! They go to sales meetings, industry conferences, and learning seminars in sanctified pursuit of perpetual advancement. A few times a year, they find themselves at a golf resort hotel in a place like Scottsdale, Arizona, or Monterey, California, at some trade-association learning conference with a name like Leading Edge or the Leadership Seminar. They check in at the registration desk, get a canvas bag with corporate tchochkes—a company-logo baseball cap, a simulated-leather binder, complimentary popcorn—as well as an ID badge that has little ribbons down the front denoting the person's importance, so that the really big shots look like Guatemalan generals with their multicolor Speaker, Sponsor, Seminar Leader, Board of Directors, and Hall of Fame ribbons stretching down their tummy.

Such is their genuine commitment to learning that in between the closest-to-the-pin contests, the spousal spa sessions, and the Range Rover driving lessons, they will force themselves to confront the greatest evil of modern times: PowerPoint presentations.

Like the soldiers in Pickett's charge, they will march straight into the hail of bullet points. They will endure hour upon hour of jargonics, the unique sales-conference language, receiving valuable advice on how they can prioritize their cost-effective operational performance and increase network functionality while magnifying their brand power through strategic B-to-B partnering in ways that will leverage their competitive-advantage matrixes without sacrificing any of their core-competency components or their multiple-vendor, mission-critical supply-chain service-provider solution resources.

The slides flow by on the screen like one of those May Day Soviet missile parades, so that after forty-five minutes of Leadership, Quality, Change, and Excellence, the speaker could have his girlfriend's sex diary up on the screen and nobody would even notice.

Business leaders *do* go to these conferences, and they sit there hoping to learn. They don't go just for the golf and the schmoozing and the chance to wear Four Seasons terry-cloth robes down to the massage center. They go to absorb, with high hopes of having their minds expanded and their optimism refurbished. While they have been pursuing their Fry!, the whole world has been going on outside, and a speaker might let them know what they've been missing. Sometimes a speaker, if his hair is historically significant enough, and if his teeth are cosmically bright, and if his tales of winning Olympic gold are sufficiently inspiring, will cause the adrenaline to pump, the old intensity to get recharged.

A speaker may offer one of those precious takeaways, a snippet of data: a consumer trend, a quotation from Marcus Aurelius or Jack Welch, that they can clasp to their chests. Hope for the future will be reinflamed. A new tool! A new concept! A new understanding or a new opportunity! The fire will flicker a little higher in the furnace of the belly. They begin to feel again that power, that drive. They begin to feel the joy of discovery, the pleasure of creating something new, the thrill of embarking on some new project, which is the most delicious sensation in professional life.

Business learning isn't mainly about knowledge and the wisdom of the past. It's not like university lecture-hall learning. Business learning is about offering glimpses of the future and getting everybody excited enough to lunge toward the horizon again.

The Soul of the Fry!

"I hail with joy the oceanic, variegated, intense practical energy, the demand for facts, even the business materialism of the current age," Walt Whitman wrote in "Democratic Vistas." "The one thing in the world of value," Emerson echoed, "is an active soul."

The redeeming fact about American business life is that it is a stimulant. It calls forth boundless energy. Even in those boring office parks, even among those narrow workaholics who have never had a philosophical self-reflection in their lives, the successful ones are driven by some inner intensity. They must relentlessly improve, perpetually grow.

In this way, the American business class has reversed the conventional moral formulae. In classical morality, money enervates and corrupts. The Roman empire illustrated the life cycle of great nations. As the historian John Anthony Froude put it: "Virtue and truth produced strength, strength dominion, dominion riches, riches luxury, and luxury weakness and collapse." It's as inevitable as death. Nations, and individuals, grow to adulthood by virtue of their simplicity, and fall to decay because they get spoiled by comfort and ease.

But in the land of abundance, money and wealth do not enervate, spoil, and corrupt. Success is never good enough. No matter how rich you are, no matter how comfortably you live, those opportunities are still out there beckoning, calling forth more work and industry. The competition never stops.

Of course, the tragedy of the Fry! followers is that the

virtues cultivated are means, and there is a near-vacuum when it comes to ends. Many successful Fry! followers work hard, aim skyward, and treat people fairly, yet ultimately, all this effort and cultivation are still dedicated to nothing more than a fast-food item. The quest may be epic, but the goal is trivial.

The endemic temptation in the Fry! life is to become so obsessed with the process of producing a better fry or a better widget that you may stop thinking about the ultimate purpose of your life. You become enmeshed in the arduous pursuit of the unimportant. You develop a furrow mentality, driving to push the plow farther down the furrow to achieve your goal and your excellence. Eventually, you become oblivious to the fact that your whole life is lived down in the furrow. Your horizon is far but narrow.

In that furrow, your personality becomes a mere selling device. Friendships become contacts. The urge to improve deteriorates to mere acquisitiveness. Money becomes the measure of accomplishment. So much intellectual energy is devoted to outward market research that there is none left for inner observation. The language of commerce obliterates the vocabulary of morality. The imagination becomes professionalized, so you find yourself budgeting your thoughts on the useful tasks at hand, rather than letting your mind roam over the landscape and into the unexpected gullies. You live by the clock, so when you pull up to the gas station, you are impatient over the three minutes you'll have to waste while the pump slowly fills up the tank.

Throughout American history, there have always been writers who looked at the vulgarities of business life and urged their readers to renounce commerce, material striving, and that bitch goddess success. But most Americans rejected that advice, concluding that commerce, for all its obvious flaws, is the instigator that electrifies and propels. A business culture is a dynamic culture. Enterprise calls forth a vitality that is the antidote to stagnation, enervation, and mediocrity. It demands certain skills and disciplines, it forces people to pay attention to others' needs, to face reality, and to avoid retreating into the realm of self-indulgence.

Many of the best people have embraced commerce while knowing it is insufficient. They adopt a gradational ethic that begins with material striving and is meant to lead to higher aims. They start with the fry, the sincere passion for taking one little corner of the universe and making it excellent. Some take the talents, skills, and virtues that have been cultivated while pursuing their fry, and they dedicate them to things loftier even than really fine fast food.

CHAPTER NINE

A History of Imagination

SO NOW WE'VE completed our hopscotch drive around middle- and upper-middle-class America, touching down in the exurbs, among the Ubermoms, on college campuses, in the office parks, into the inner-ring suburbs, the big-box malls, and the magazine racks. What we've seen at each stop is this distinctive American energy expressed in different ways: highly programmed kids being churned through the Achievatron; ambitious college students hooking up because they don't have time for real relationships; shoppers in the thrall of advertising-inspired heavens; Fry!-following businesspeople looking for that all-consuming challenge; suburbanites moving and sprawling across the landscape.

In my travels reporting for this book, I've continually been struck by how much of American life is an attempt to live out a dream. Albert Einstein famously said that imagination is more important than knowledge, and anybody can see that Americans have a talent for fantasy. The suburbs themselves were built as conservative utopias. Children are raised with visions of ideal lives. This is the nation of Hollywood, Las Vegas, professional wrestling, and Disney, not to mention all the other fantasy factories. This is the land of Elvis impersonators, jazz improvisationalists, *Penthouse* letters, computer gamers, grown men in Michael Jordan basketball jerseys, faith healers with bouffant hair, and the whole range of ampersand magazines (*Town & Country, Travel & Leisure, Food & Wine*) that display perfect parties, perfect vacations, and perfect meals—ways of living that couldn't possibly exist in real life. This is the land of Rainforest Café theme restaurants, comic-book superheroes, Shangri-La resort hotels, Ralph Lauren WASP-fantasy fashions, Civil War reenactors, gated communities with names like Sherwood Forest Grove, and vehicles with such names as Yukon, Durango, Expedition, and Mustang, as if their accountant-owners were going to chase down some cattle rustlers on the way to the Piggly Wiggly. This is the land in which people dream of the most radical Walter Mitty–esque personal transformations, in which one in three women *admits* to changing her hair color, amid all the other lifestyle alterations and fabrications that are a normal part of daily life.

This is a country in which every suburban high school has its collection of goths and chaperoned gangsta rappers and the boardrooms are filled with men and women who go to work in cowboy boots and then return home to Tudor estates, dreaming of software solutions that will revolutionize their industry and make them Sun Gods of the corporate-accounting universe. This is a land conceived in advertising, in which sneakers have personalities, and hamburgers and pizza chains have mascots. This is the land that perfected the celebrity culture, far above the realities of everyday mortal life. America is a land rife with make-believe.

Americans—seemingly bland, ordinary Americans— often have a remarkably tenuous grip on reality. I have come to think that the human longing for transcendence, spiritual depth, and moral cohesion has not perished in the sprawls of suburbia, it has just taken a different form, because Americans live so much of their lives in the imagined land of the future.

I suspect that to really understand America and the American suburb, you have to take seriously that central cliché of American life: the American Dream. You have to see that beneath the seeming flatness of American life, there is an imaginative fire that animates us and propels us to work so hard, move so much, invent so much, and leap into so much that is new and different—not always to our benefit.

The historian Sacvan Bercovitch observed that the United States is the example par excellence of a nation formed by collective fantasy. Despite all the claims that American culture is secular, pragmatic, and materialist, what is truly striking about this country is how material things are shot through with enchantment.

A History of Imagination

America, after all, was born in a frenzy of imagination. A newly discovered continent begs to be fantasized about, and from the moment they stumbled upon it, Europeans projected their hopes, utopian dreams, and paradisiacal visions onto this place. It was the biblical Eden, the Israelite's land of milk and honey, the Fortunate Islands of the Romans, the Elysium, the wish-image utopia of the medieval mind. In America, Europeans imagined, they could find Eldorado, the City of Gold, and the Fountain of Youth. The America they imagined was the virgin continent that would redeem the corruptions of the Old World.

These dreams of perfectibility had powerful effects on people from the first. During his voyage of 1497, Columbus perceived that the water grew sweeter as one approached the New World. The elevation seemed to grow higher. He concluded that the world was not in fact round, but was in "the form of a pear, which is very round except where the stalk grows, at which part it is most prominent; or like a round ball, upon which is a prominence like a woman's nipple, this protrusion being the highest and nearest the sky."

Soon Europeans were seeking this nipple of the earth for bounty, salvation, and utopia. In a letter home, Amerigo Vespucci described a communal paradise in which the natives existed naked, healthy, and free: "They live amongst themselves without a king or ruler, each man being his own master, and having as many wives as they please." All property was shared, he continued. The women were "libidinous, but comely." The natives often lived 150 years.

Almost immediately, America was established as the richest neighborhood in the world's imagination. By 1605, Europeans were already satirizing these lavish descriptions of American wealth and grandeur. A character in the English play *Eastward Ho!* declares:

> I tell thee, gold is more plentiful there than copper
> is with us. . . . Why, man, all their dripping pans are
> pure gold; and all their chains with which they
> chain up their streets are massy gold . . . and for
> rubies and diamonds they go forth on holidays and
> gather 'em by the seashore to hang on their chil-
> dren's coats.

The early settlers were aware of, and must have been oppressed by, the obvious potential of this land. They saw the possibility of plenty everywhere, yet at the start, they lived in harsh and primitive conditions. They knew and felt that heaven would be realized in this place that was God's greatest gift, but at that moment, they faced starvation. Their lives took on a slingshot shape—they had to pull back in order to someday shoot forward. Through the hardship of their present life, they dwelt imaginatively in the grandeur that would inevitably mark their future, that would make their sufferings and daring sacrifices worthwhile.

The American continent itself encouraged this dreaming by making the glorious future seem inevitable. The land stretched on infinitely, so paradise surely would be realized here. The abundance aroused the visitors' capacity for wonder.

As John Harmon McElroy has noted, the early settlers saw flocks of geese so large that it would take a half hour from when the leader bird took off to when the last bird was aflight. The settlers would shoot cannons into these clouds of birds just to see if they could change the flock's direction, but they could not. They saw untouched forests, thick vines of wild grapes, valleys of oaks, walnuts, pines, beds of oysters and clams bigger than any they had ever seen, and the abundance stretched on for miles and miles. They saw new crops, new animals, and above all, endless mountains and valleys terrifying but promising.

There were, of course, about a quarter million or more Native Americans living on the continent, but what the Europeans perceived was emptiness—vast room for them to move and move again, create a home, and then create another. John Smith's manual for colonists declared that in America, every family could "plant freely without limitation so much as he can," and that for every acre he planted, his heirs—the future generations—would realize "twenty, thirty, forty, or an hundred" additional acres.

This pattern recurred decade after decade. Each time pioneers pushed west, they found virgin land and perceived it as paradise. Indeed, their writings begin to run together, whether the new land is Virginia, Massachusetts, Wisconsin, Oregon, or California. The mood is exalted wonder. The joy is always the same, the potential is always limitless. "Let us speak of Elkhorn Creek," one farmer wrote about a spot in Kentucky. "The lands that it waters are so fertile and so beautiful, the air there is so pure, so serene almost all the year, that this country is veritably a second terrestrial paradise."

Many of these writers were marketing their discoveries; there was a bit of a sales job going on. Still, the mood of ecstasy was genuine, and the promises were not implausible. Progress in America really was incredible. Even in the seventeenth century, New England enjoyed a low infant-mortality rate that was not matched in Britain until the 1890s. In that century, over 90 percent of those who came to America as indentured servants—sacrificing their present for some free but distant future—eventually became land-owners. Hundreds of new towns were created. Despite a widening gap between rich and poor, farm laborers enjoyed wages that were far higher than those in Europe, and they ate food, including meat, that was cheaper and more nutritious. Americans in the eighteenth century were on average three inches taller than their European counterparts, owing to their superior diet.

And they were well aware of their good fortune. As the Reverend Francis Higginson of Salem, Massachusetts, exulted in 1629:

> It is scarce to be believed how our [cows] and goats, horses and hogs do thrive and prosper here and like well of this country. In our plantation we have already a quart of milk for a penny; but the abundant increase of corn proves this country to be a wonderment. Thirty, forty, fifty, sixty are ordinary here. Yea, Joseph's increase in Egypt is outstripped here with us.

By 1740 the American population as a whole enjoyed a higher standard of living than the population of any European country, a lead that has never been surrendered. By 1770, the historian Jon Butler argues, America had become "the first modern society," with its own commercial farmers, multicultural trading centers, and a distinct secular-material culture producing its own furniture, clothing, and housing styles. Land speculation was feverish. Ministers complained that they could not keep their congregations together; families would spy some distant sixty acres available for tillage and pick up and move. Enveloping it all was a tremendous sense of opportunity. "We have been prospered in a most wonderful manner," exalted the Reverend Samuel West.

In his 1954 book, *People of Plenty*, historian David Potter argued that the mentality fostered by abundance is at the core of the American character. Indeed, the American example forces us to reverse our conventional notions of the psychological and spiritual effects of wealth. Classical thinkers tended to believe that abundance inevitably led to decadence and decline. The course of empires was clear: Nations grew because they were poor and hungry. Their ambition produced wealth. Wealth produced ease. Ease produced softness, and softness produced collapse.

But in America, abundance led to a different set of responses. It produced an ethos of availability. Risk-taking was rational because it so often paid off. Restlessness was natural because you knew that somewhere over the next horizon, there was a richer destiny waiting. Individualism was the norm because each person or family had the space to carve out a distinct mode of life. Progress was inevitable because each year saw an increase. Education was sacred because each generation could learn new skills to surpass the one before. An aristocracy and its habits of social deference were obsolete because you never needed to live under someone else's thumb; you could just move away. The universe was benevolent because it offered such bounty, and all present problems could be solved plausibly in the ever more abundant future. In short, abundance didn't seem to produce corruption and decline. It produced work, mobility, self-reliance, energy, and liberation.

Hector St. John de Crèvecoeur was a Norman cartographer who fought with the French in the French and

Indian War. He married an Anglo-American wife, settled on a farm twenty-five miles west of the Hudson River in New York, and soon became one of the most appreciative chroniclers of how American conditions altered the European mind. Distances mattered less, Crèvecoeur famously observed:

> A European, when he first arrives, seems limited in his intentions as well as in his views; but he very suddenly alters his scale; two hundred miles formerly appeared a very great distance, it is now but a trifle. He no sooner breathes our air than he forms schemes and embarks on designs he never would have thought of in his own country.

In his middle age, Crèvecoeur recalled a journey he took around 1767 along the upper Ohio River: "I never before felt myself so much disposed for meditation: my imagination leaped into futurity. I consider the settling of these lands, which are watered by this river, as one of the finest conquests that could ever be presented to man. . . . It is destined to become the source of force, riches, and the future glory of the United States."

It didn't take a Crèvecoeur to see that America's present good fortune was nothing compared to what lay ahead. The present was pleasant, but from the start, Americans, and many around the globe, realized that the future was dazzling. "It requires but a small portion of the gift of discernment for anyone to foresee," Samuel Adams wrote in 1775, "that providence will erect a mighty empire in America." Adam Smith predicted that the British Parliament would someday move to the New World, since the economic and political weight of the colonies would obviously overwhelm the motherland. At a time when the United States was a scraggly stretch of colonies along the Atlantic seaboard, Alexander Hamilton declared that the country would soon become a mighty empire, "in many respects the most interesting in the world," and would be stronger than all the great empires of the day, "able to dictate the terms of the connection between the old and the new world!"

Noah Webster, who began work on his dictionary of American English just after 1800, observed a need for a standard guide to a language that he predicted would one day be spoken by three hundred million people. America is today closing in on that mark, but when Webster made the forecast—as John Harmon McElroy has also noted—the United States possessed only 4 percent of that total.

America's future greatness was a large glimmering fact hanging over the heads of each American, every hour of each day. From the start, Americans were accustomed to thinking in the future tense. They were used to living in a world of dreams, plans, innovations, improvements, and visions of things to come.

Their situation aroused their spiritual aspirations as well. To give meaning to their lives, early Americans had to place their bounty in some larger historical and moral narrative. It couldn't be that they had won the lottery; that they'd stumbled upon a rich land; that they were merely the recipients of its natural resources. It couldn't be so meaningless and random. Other nations might see the New World as an Eldorado to be looted, but as Arthur K. Moore writes in *The Frontier Mind*, the English pioneers saw it as an Eden to be occupied. These new Americans saw God's hand at work. They interpreted their abundance as part of a Divine Plan, as the latest and last in a series of God's dispensations. This meant that Americans had a specific destiny, a specific role to play in the history and culmination of the universe.

They looked around and concluded that they must be God's chosen people. Colonial sermons on America were studded with references to the colonies as the New Israel, the New Jerusalem, and the New Canaan, and to Americans as the Israelites of the age. They had recreated the Exodus story and settled in the land of milk and honey.

Their minds instantaneously leaped from their charmed if difficult present life in the blessed isle to their destiny as the culmination of the human race. It is striking how many thinkers and writers at the time of America's founding believed that they were not only the chosen people, they were the *final* people, the children of prophecy. History would end with them. God had sent them on this sacred errand into the wilderness; His plan would be fulfilled through them. Paradise would be realized on this new continent, and the redemption of all mankind would spread outward from here.

As Sacvan Bercovitch has remarked, many people in Europe interpreted Bishop George Berkeley's maxim "Westward the course of empire takes its way" as an example of the vanity of human wishes, because it showed how all glory was temporary—it passed on to other nations in due course. But the American colonists interpreted it as an assignment. There had been other phases in human history, other dispensations. But this American phase was the last, the completion of God's designs.

"There are many arguments to persuade us that our Glorious Lord will have an Holy City in America; a City, the street whereof shall be pure gold," Cotton Mather preached in his 1709 sermon "God's City: America." "This new world," Jonathan Edwards later wrote, "is probably now discovered that the new and most glorious state of God's church on earth might commence there." For "When God is about to turn the earth into a Paradise he does not begin his work where there is some good growth already, but in a wilderness." Other times and other places, Edwards continued, "are only forerunners and preparatories to this." America had been discovered to prepare "the way for the future, glorious times." It would welcome the arrival of "the new heavens and the new earth." And so, Edwards concluded, "we can't reasonably think otherwise, than that this great work of God . . . will begin in America."

By the time of the Revolution, this idea had passed from pulpit prophecy into the realm of public cliché. "From their birth," Thomas Yarrow of New York argued, "the American states were designed to be the political redeemers of mankind." John Adams wrote, "I always consider the settlement of America with reverence and wonder, as the opening of a grand scene and design in providence, for the illumination of the ignorant and the emancipation of the slavish part of the earth." In 1797 the Reverend James Smith, a Methodist minister in Ohio, exclaimed:

O, what a country will this be at a future day! What a field of delights! What a garden of spices! What a paradise of pleasures! When these forests shall be cultivated and the gospel of Christ spread through this rising republic, unshackled by the power of kings and religious oppression on the one hand,

and slavery, that bane of true Godliness, on the other.

Americans considered themselves a covenanted people. Like the ancient Israelites, their faith was promise-centered. The corruptions of Europe, of the past, would be left behind, and this new nation would be responsible for building the City on the Hill. Something original, new, and glorious would happen here. History would end with us. Humanity would be redeemed by us. The evils of the world would be purged by us. The whole train of thinking was soon summarized in the phrase quoted from on the seal of the United States: *"Annuit Coeptis, Novus Ordo Seclorum"*—God prospered this undertaking; it shall be the new order of the ages.

Last Best Hope

This sense of high mission has reverberated through the centuries, and the imaginative visions were made to seem plausible by the awareness of material abundance. The Louisiana Purchase in 1803 gave the United States a landmass over three times the size of modern France, Germany, and the United Kingdom combined. Everything seemed to be growing and expanding. Between 1830 and 1880, the population of the United States skyrocketed by 400 percent (at a time when the French population rose by only 17 percent). In the three decades after 1850, factory output in the United States rose by 600 percent (while Britain, then at the height of the industrial revolution, saw its output double). By the early 1880s, there were more miles of railway track and telegraph wire in the U.S. than in all the European nations combined. Between 1899 and 1905, America's food output grew by 40 percent. In 1890, Americans produced 32,000 pianos; ten years later, the nation produced 374,000 pianos. During the nineteenth century, in other words, the United States became a consumer wonderland. Magical baubles, mass-produced luxuries, limitless possibilities dangled before the eye.

Like a teenager becoming aware of his own muscles, each American was awestruck by his vitality and strength. "Our national birth," the *Democratic Review* editorialized in 1839, "was the beginning of a new history . . . which separates us from the past and connects us with the future." At the same time, the country was approaching its most serious crisis, the Civil War. It's not surprising that many interpreted the war as yet another opportunity to realize the nation's potential, to purge all that was corrupt and backward from the land.

"The time will surely come—the holy millennium of liberty—when the 'Victory of endurance born' shall lift the masses," the young Walt Whitman wrote a few decades before the war in the *Brooklyn Daily Eagle*, "and make them achieve something of that destiny which we may suppose God intends eligible for mankind. And this problem is to be worked out through the people, territory, and government of the United States."

Daniel Webster gave voice to this sentiment in his famous eulogy to the martyrs of Bunker Hill: "In our day there has been as it were a new creation. . . . The last hopes of mankind . . . rest with us." During the war, Abraham Lincoln summarized the strain of thought when he called the United States "the last best hope of earth."

The important word in these speeches is "last." This is the final nation, Lincoln was saying. No better system of government would ever emerge to supplant it. America would be the place where mankind's dreams were tested and possibly realized, and from here, they would radiate across the globe. Lincoln's phrase has resonated through history, and its promise is invoked in just about every presidential inauguration, in every July Fourth speech, in all the political slogans that promise a Great Society or a New Deal or a New Frontier or a New Beginning (because in America an old beginning is never good enough).

The Popular Imagination

Lincoln and Whitman had deep souls. But what is fascinating about American history is that it is the deprived and the ordinary who most often seem gripped by the fire of imagination. It is often the hungriest, the uncultivated, the most grasping people who lead the way into the future. They are the desperadoes who strike out to the West, the gold-crazed adventurers who lunge for California, the crass vaudevillians who create Hollywood, the highly educated but socially awkward computer geeks who build Silicon Valley. Time and again in American history, the pioneers have been the people who rank low on the scales of grace, manners, and cultivation. Time and again the spiritual revivals start on the frontier, among those on the margins.

We may like to think that it is the most noble and heroic who are seized by grand visions. But in America the people with the broadest perspectives and the most cultivated manners are rarely the most imagination-frenzied.

Why should they be? They already have fulfilling low-risk opportunities in front of them. They can go to law school, med school, or a prestigious investment bank. Here, it is the fantastical visions of the vulgarians that constantly amaze. It's the dreams of the uncultivated—the Donald Trumps, the Don Kings, the Henry Fords. As Ralph Waldo Emerson taught, in America everyone is average and extraordinary at the same time, a democrat and also a king, a regular schmo and also a new Adam, ready to strike out.

When raw immigrants come to the United States, it is their fantasies about the future that have lured them. New York, the city of dreams, inspired wonder for generations of semiliterate immigrants. Sometimes they had visions of streets paved with gold, or of glorious business empires and limitless wealth. Others imagined simply owning a house, a car, a life.

In true American fashion, immigrants live in the future, undergoing that slingshot life course, pulling back so that someday they and their children can shoot off into the richer future. In true American fashion, they live pragmatically and materialistically, clawing around to get money and position and a foothold in society, and their practicality is constructed on a foundation of fantasy and imagination.

When the pioneers went west, it was speculation about the future that pulled them. Guides who led (and sometimes exploited) nineteenth-century pioneers were shocked by how little the trekkers knew about the surroundings they had thrown themselves into, or what would be involved in their new lives. As so often happens in American history, masses of people leaped before they looked.

In many cases, their behavior cannot be explained by the calculus of rational self-interest. The act of moving into the wilderness meant miserable homesickness; you were essentially dead to the parents and brothers and sisters and friends you had left behind. There was a very high probability that you would lose a child or a spouse or other family member en route. The settlers endured years of grinding poverty, crippling loneliness, and uncertainty. Insane asylums quickly popped up in the West because so many people were driven mad by their ordeals (or else it was a tint of madness that propelled them westward). In short, the pioneers faced risk-reward ratios, as the economists would say, that didn't make sense from any rational perspective.

In most cases, people launched on these journeys because they felt in their bones that some set of unbelievable opportunities was out there. They could not tolerate passing out their years without a sense of movement and anticipation, even if their chances were minuscule.

Whether in 1704 or 1904 or 2004, Americans have moved to new places because they've felt, sometimes semiconsciously, that they could build some piece of heaven there. They live in that heaven of their imagination long before they ever get around to constructing it in real life.

In his novel *The Pioneers*, James Fenimore Cooper's hero, a land developer, takes his cousin on a tour of the city he is building. He describes the broad streets, the rows of houses, the bubbling metropolis. His cousin looks around bewildered. All she sees is a stubby forest. "Where are the beauties and improvements which you were to show me?" she asks. He's astonished that she can't see them. "Where! Why, everywhere," he replies. Though they are not yet built on earth, he has built them in his mind, and they are as concrete to him as if they were already complete.

Cooper was illustrating one of the features of a distinctly American cast of mind, a Paradise Spell: the capacity to see the *present* from the vantage point of the *future*. It starts with imagination—the ability to see a vision with detail and vividness, as if it already existed. Then the future-minded person is able to think backward from that vision; to ask, "What must I do to take the future that is in my head and make it exist in the world?" That person is more emotionally attached to the glorious future than to the temporary and unsatisfactory present. Time isn't pushed from the remembered past to the felt present to the mysterious future. It is pulled by the vivid future from the unsatisfactory present and away from the dim past.

Future-mindedness is a trait that repeats in the biographies of inventors, entrepreneurs, and political leaders, and it is a prominent feature in the literature of the pioneers. As John Harmon McElroy notes in *American Beliefs*, there's a particularly vivid description of the mentality in Ole Edvart Rölvaag's classic 1927 novel, *Giants in the Earth: A Saga of the Prairie*. The protagonist, Per Hansa, is a Norwegian immigrant who settles in the Dakota prairies in the 1870s. His circumstances are harsh, but in his imagination, he has already moved into the future:

> But dearest to him of all, and most delectable, was the thought of the royal mansion which he had already erected in his mind. There would be houses for both chickens and pigs, roomy stables, a magnificent storehouse and barn . . . and then the splendid palace itself! The royal mansion would shine in the sun—it would stand out far and wide! The palace itself would be white, with green cornices; but the big barn would be red as blood, with cor-

nices of driven snow. Wouldn't it be beautiful—
wasn't it going to be great fun! . . . And he and his
boys would build it all!

Like the actual pioneers he depicts, Rölvaag's characters
are, he writes, "more interested in visualizing how things
were going to turn out than in making a bare statement of
how they actually were." The novel's tragic element concerns Per Hansa's wife, who longs for her old traditions
and the family she has left behind. Per Hansa finally con-
fesses his guilt over the misery he has caused her: "She has
never felt at home here in America. . . . There are some people, I know now, who never should emigrate, because, you
see, they can't take pleasure in that which is to come—they
simply can't see it."

In both Cooper's and Rolvaag's stories, it is the man
who is future-minded. But in real life, both men and
women were propelled onward by imaginative future
worlds. In *The Land Before Her: Fantasy and Experience
of the American Frontiers, 1630–1860,* the historian
Annette Kolodny plumbs the diaries of female pioneers and
finds them rife with fantastical visions. Female fantasies
tended to have a different character than male fantasies,
Kolodny writes, owing to the expectations that young
women were raised with.

Both men and women fantasized a paradise, she notes,
but "As a result, 'paradise' implied radically different
places when used by men and women. For men the term
(with all its concomitant psychosexual associations)
echoed an invitation for mastery and possession of the vast
new continent. For women, by contrast, it denoted domes-

ticity." While the men dreamed of conquering the forest, often as solitary adventurers, the women dreamed of establishing homes and neighborhoods, of building communities in which every new family was part of an extended circle of love. They dreamed of pine-tree quilts, little gardens around their pioneer cabins, and appliquéd counterpanes with brightly colored designs. The male fantasies dominated the adventure stories and the movie westerns. But the female fantasies had more influence on real life, for ultimately, settling the West was more a matter of building homes, neighborhoods, and communities than Daniel Boone adventures.

The pioneer experience and the cowboy mythology have played such an important role in the American identity because they embodied the dream-culture character that is at the core of who we are.

This really is a deep and mystical longing. In the early nineteenth century, the writer Edwin James noted "a manifest propensity, particularly in the males, to remove westward, for which it is not easy to account." The esteemed historian Francis Parkman remembered that he, too, was gripped by this mystical longing for the horizon. Writing of his youthful self, Parkman noted, "His thoughts were always in the forest, whose features possessed his waking and sleeping dreams, filling him with vague cravings impossible to satisfy."

Timothy Flint, the nineteenth-century biographer of Daniel Boone who was himself an itinerant preacher and writer and spent most of his life in the Mississippi Valley, wrote about the forces that motivated the people he met there:

There is more of the material of poetry than we imagine, diffused through all the classes of the community. . . . I am ready to believe, from my own experience, and from what I have seen in the case of others, that this influence of imagination has no inconsiderable agency in producing emigration. Indeed, the saturnine and illiterate emigrant may not be conscious that such motives had any agency in fixing him in his purpose. But I need not observe, that those who examine most earnestly what passes in their own minds, are not always aware of all the elements of motive that determine their actions.

As Arthur K. Moore concluded in his 1957 book, *The Frontier Mind*:

Common sense dictates a coming to terms with present circumstances, for change dissipates whatever goods labor has produced; but the imagination tricks people into emigration through creating a distant life in which laws of wild and human nature are miraculously suspended. More or less consciously, they seek a lost garden, where, as Horace represented the Fortunate Islands, "yearly the earth unploughed brings forth grain, and the unpruned vine flowers continuously and buds the branch of the never-failing olive." Ironically, emigrants very often flourished because the new situation is in fact no Eden and, far from affording ease and abundance, compels extraordinary energetic responses.

Future-Mindedness Today

Our minds are still with Parkman's in the forest. Our imagination still tricks us into undertaking grand projects—starting a business, writing a book, raising a family—by enchanting us with visions of future joys. When these tasks turn out to be more difficult than we dreamed, the necessary exertions, as Moore observed, bring out our finest excellencies.

Of course, in normal times, and especially these days, few would claim that Americans are the chosen people of God. Few live strictly according to their fantasies. But the past survives in the present. The cognitive strands established early in American history and through its period of explosive growth—the sense that some ultimate fulfillment will be realized here, that happiness can be created here, that the United States has a unique mission to redeem the world—are still woven into the country's fabric. The old impulses, fevers, and fantasies still play themselves out amid the Palms, the Hummers, the closet organizers, and the travel-team softball leagues. We Americans have not abandoned the horizon mentality of our forebears.

We are a bourgeois nation, but unlike some other bourgeois nations, we are also a transcendent nation infused with everyday utopianism. This utopianism lures us beyond the prosaic world. It gives us a distinct conception of time, so we often find ourselves on some technological frontier, dreaming of this innovation or that management technique that will elevate the world—and half the time, our enthusiasms, crazes, and fads seem ludicrous to others and even to us, in retrospect. We still find ourselves venturing off into world crises, roaring into battle with visions of virtue on our side and evil on the other, waging moralistic crusades that others do not understand, pushing our movie, TV, and musical fantasies onto an ambivalent and sometimes horrified world.

Mentality matters, and in the end, perhaps mentality is all that matters. The tacit assumptions, intuitive judgments, unconscious mental categories, and inherited perceptions of time and space form what John Dewey called the shared "sense of an extensive underlying whole" that binds a people. If somehow America were conquered and its institutions erased, there would still be some future-minded group of people related to a certain way of being in the world. As James Russell Lowell commented, "Our ancestors sought a new continent. What they found was a new condition of mind."

This doesn't mean all Americans think alike, simply that there is a prevailing current to national life that one feels when one comes here from other places with other currents. Some nations are bound, in all their diversity, by a common creation myth, a tale of how they came into being. Americans are bound, in all our diversity, by a fruition myth.

Born in abundance, inspired by opportunity, nurtured in imagination, spiritualized by a sense of God's blessing and call, and realized in ordinary life day by day, this Paradise Spell is the controlling ideology of American life. Just out of reach, just beyond the next ridge, just with the next home or entrepreneurial scheme or diet plan; just with the next political hero, the next credit-card purchase, or the next true love; just with the right all-terrain vehicle, the right summer home, the right meditation technique, or the right motivational seminar; just with the right schools, the right community values, and the proper morality; just with the right beer and a good set of buddies; just with the next technology or after the next shopping spree, there is this spot you can get to where all tensions will melt, all time pressures are relieved, and all contentment can be realized. Prosperity will be joined with virtue, materialism with idealism, achievement with equality, success with love, the Cosmic Blonde's dream of gleaming happiness with the Cosmic Brunette's dream of self-fulfillment and understanding, thereby producing a new Eden.

This Paradise Spell is at the root of our tendency to work so hard, to consume so feverishly, to move so much. It inspires our illimitable faith in education, our frequent born-again experiences. It explains why, alone among developed nations, we have shaped our welfare system to encourage opportunity at the expense of security; and why, more than comparable nations, we wreck our families and move on. It is the call making us heedless of the past, disrespectful toward traditions, short on contemplation, wasteful in our use of the things around us, impious toward restraints, but consumed by hope, driven ineluctably to improve, fervently optimistic, relentlessly aspiring, spiritually alert, and, in this period of human history, and maybe for all time, the locomotive of the world.

Most of the time, we are not even aware of how this mentality shapes us. The worldview is so ingrained in our culture that it doesn't even need to be passed down consciously from parent to child. Yet when you go to a place where people do not live with a mood of radical hopefulness, where people's lives are not infused with a sense of perpetual anticipation, where people do not assume that they have the power to remake their own destinies and radically transform their own lives, you do feel the difference. When you go to a country where the past is more real than the future, and then you return to America, it becomes clear how distinct the American imagination really is, and how each of us in this culture is molded by our horizon dreams. It becomes clear that the eschatological impulse really does influence ordinary life, that we remain lured by the promise of total happiness. We still live under the spell of paradise.

Hope Is a Trickster

This hopeful frame of mind does not mean everything is hunky-dory, for hope is not entirely a good thing. This is what the critics of middle-American life never understand. They see the treacly optimism of Disney, the sugary comfort of Hallmark, the upbeat maxims of Successories, the burbly chirpiness of the morning talk shows, the power of positive thinking, the cheery banter of the evening newsreaders, and the whole warm bath of obligatory optimism and 24/7 good cheer, and they think, America is this bland, optimistic, and fundamentally complacent place. They don't see that hope is a trickster and a seducer and a torturer. American culture is more complicated than it seems.

The German theologian Jürgen Moltmann wrote a brilliant book, *Theology of Hope*, ostensibly about Christianity, but because he was dissecting the hopeful frame of mind, he illuminated the American experience. One of his central points was that a hopeful person lives in tension with reality. He is always ahead of himself. He "finds himself a riddle and an open question." He "does not stand harmoniously and concentrically in himself, but stands excentrically to himself." He has dreams, but they do "not yet bring him to the haven of identity." He has goals, but he has a hard time experiencing pleasure and a sense of harmony with the moment. He is constantly disturbed.

Hope induces a sort of salvation panic. Though America is the land of optimism, it is also the land of lacerating self-scrutiny, of dark foreboding, of fevered pleas for reform. From the very start, Americans have felt that the same God who selected them for their sacred mission might repudiate them if they failed to live up to their side of the covenant.

The cry is always the same. Some great possibility is realizable here, so if we as a nation and as individuals are not on the right path, then we are committing some exceptional sin. Every decade, every year, every day, new jeremiads have risen with urgent cries that we get back on track and fulfill our possibilities. The American press has always had a more earnest and moralizing tone than, say, the British press, because there is a national solemn duty to make sure the national errand is scrutinized and kept on track.

The shelves of American bookstores are stacked with descriptions of our moral, material, or spiritual decline, with hysterical attacks at the supposed enemies within who are sapping our true national virtue. As we saw in Chapter 4, the most influential social critics of the past fifty years have been relentlessly pessimistic. This pessimism grows from the deep and fundamental sense of possibility. The writers see in their mind's eye how much is out there for us to accomplish, and they despair that we aren't achieving it, or aren't on the right route toward achieving it.

The historian Perry Miller argued that it was by this very process of self-improvement and self-correction that Americans forged themselves into a people: "I suggest that under the guise of this mounting wail of sinfulness, this incessant and never successful cry for repentance, the Puritans launched themselves upon the process of Americanization."

Furthermore, hope is the breeding ground for anxiety. Americans often feel, as Tocqueville remarked, a manic need to seize their opportunities before they slip away. "It is strange to see with what feverish ardor the Americans pursue their own welfare," he wrote, "and to watch the vague dread that constantly torments them lest they should not have chosen the shortest path that leads to it."

In *People of Plenty*, David Potter also noticed that everything in America turns into an arena for advancement. He pointed out that in the United States, the word "liberty" really means the freedom to grasp opportunity, and the word "equality" also means the freedom to grasp opportunity. He needn't have stopped there. In the United States, education means opportunity, welfare means opportunity, happiness means opportunity, fairness means opportunity, morality means opportunity, and civil rights mean opportunity.

Fired by hope, Americans have built a society that opens up opportunity and undermines security. We have relatively low tax rates to encourage entrepreneurialism and the accumulation of riches, but relatively little job protection, making it easier to fire workers and close companies. We encourage venture capital but discourage—compared to most other countries—regulation that might soften the blows of the marketplace. Compared to say, Germany, we

favor the desires of the consumers over the safety of the pro-
ducers. There are relatively few protected industries,
because the old companies must be allowed to die or move
away so new growths can emerge and cheap goods can
flow. It is easier to get rich here, but more miserable to be
poor here.

The hopeful person is always chasing the grapes of
Tantalus, which remain always out of reach. The hopeful
person has trouble living in the present and savoring the
moment, for she is imprudently distracted by the mirages
of the future. She doesn't appreciate what she has, because
she is consumed by the thought of what she might have.

The hopeful person dreams of being liberated from the
future. She dreams of experiencing, just once, a world in
which the future is not always right over the horizon, beckoning and luring. She dreams of arriving at that resting
spot where time does not exist and all striving ceases. In
fact, the American Dream is the dream of finding a place
where one will feel liberated from the burden of the future,
though that place is always in the future. The American
Dream devours its own flesh.

Throughout history, Americans have worried about
their own rat-race existence. Certain countercultures have
erected systems meant to serve as antidote to the ever
upward nature of mainstream commercial life. In the
pre–Civil War South, cavaliers tried to build a semifeudal
aristocracy in which one's identity would be determined by
birth, honor, race, and a chivalric code. The agrarians tried
to build changeless pastoral communities rooted in the soil,
immune to industrial progress. In the North, artists and
intellectuals tried to create little bohemias, enclaves where
people could reject the bitch goddess success and serve

beauty and truth. Around the country, socialists and other utopians tried to build communities where harmony would replace competition and communal solidarity would replace climbing. In the 1960s, hippies and yippies tried to build a civilization in which we could be free to drop out and just be. At West Point and Annapolis, some tried to create a warrior code in which duty, courage, and honor would be more important than success, riches, and ascent.

All of these countercultures were eventually devoured by the voracious hunger of hope. The southern cavaliers were crushed by northern commerce. Almost all the bohemians have been co-opted. The hippies wound up founding organic salad dressing companies. The military has turned into a profession as much as a calling. In the United States, it is very hard to maintain a creed based on the renunciation of advancement. The dazzling lights of opportunity lure the young; the ethos of achievement undermines stasis and simplicity. There is virtually no escape.

By and large, Americans are utter failures when it comes to leading the simple life, which we profess to desire. You may start the day with noble intentions in your heart and one of those simplicity magazines by your side. You may tell yourself that today you are going to renounce material things. You're going to slow down and savor the moment. So you break out the seaside-scent candles, fill up the claw-foot tub with fluoridated water and tub tea, and soak with a volume of Robert Frost in your hand and some almond-scented body wash on the shelf. But then the bathroom-renovation fantasies start crowding into your brain, and along come the second-home longings.

To clear your mind, you realize, you need a country

place in the mountains where you can get away from it all, and just a couple more big financial scores so you can carry that soul-saving second mortgage. And before long, you are back in the land of desire. You've been sucked in by the alluring availability of increased earnings and the narcotic of potential capital gains. You have returned to the realm of buying and selling and earning and investing. The sheer wealthiness of American life has swallowed you back up. You turn back to the Simplicity Bible in one last desperate effort to escape from the whole chorus of buying and getting, the world of goods whispering, "Taste me . . . taste me . . . taste me." But you find that the magazine is nothing but a series of tips on how you can be a better simplifier. It has merely taken the achievement ethos and applied it to the goal of simplification. And that is no respite at all.

Even if you win the race, there is no rest. There is no position you can be awarded that will guarantee you status and respect regardless of your behavior. There is no title you can pass down to your children. Even if your own future is secure, there are still your children's futures and grandchildren's futures looming. The mentality of ascent still has you in its grip. The universe, as they say, is still pursuing its adventures, and you must work to keep your place. We must all, as the Puritans said, continue rowing for heaven.

The Provisional Life

Hope tortures and incites in other ways. In the land of the future, one's relationship to a place, to a job, to a lifestyle is provisional, because at any juncture, you might move on in pursuit of the horizon. But more fundamentally, a relationship to beliefs is provisional, because they are always being renovated and improved. George Santayana observed that Americans tend not to believe in eternal and absolute truth. Instead, ideas are always in motion, and people are always progressing on to new opinions and beliefs.

Under the influence of pragmatism, truth does not inhere absolutely in an idea; truth happens to an idea. An idea is held to be true when it turns out to be useful and good, when it serves its purpose in making life better at that moment and for that individual.

One saw this phenomenon in the nineteenth-century age of the transcendentalists, and one sees it today in the age of Oprah. What is most absolute is not truth and falsehood, virtue and vice; what matters most absolutely is the advancing self. The individual is perpetually moving toward wholeness and completion, and ideas are adopted as they suit that mission. Individual betterment is the center around which the entire universe revolves.

This is a brutal form of narcissism. The weight of the universe is placed on the shoulders of the individual. Accordingly, in modern American culture, the self becomes semidivinized. People feel free to pick and choose their own religious beliefs, because whatever serves the self-journey toward happiness must be godly and true.

This means that each individual must be the locus of values. It means that the central question of life is not "What does God command and love?" but rather "What is my destiny and fulfillment?" It is not our duty to humbly obey God's law and submit to the universal order. It is our duty to create and explore our self, to realize our own inner light. It is up to each of us to justify our own existence.

The obligation of life, in this vein, is not to hew to the straight-and-narrow course. It is to lead the richest, fullest, and broadest possible life, so as to realize as many potentialities as possible. As Oliver Wendell Holmes put it, "The chief worth of civilization is just that it makes the means of living more complex. Because more complex and intense intellectual efforts mean a fuller and richer life. That means more life. Life is an end in itself, and the only question as to whether it is worth living is whether you have enough of it."

Only a radically hopeful nation would pile so much complexity and richness onto individuals, or would believe that individuals are capable of bearing such a weight. There are, of course, many orthodox believers in America, people as rooted in absolute truth as a mountain is rooted in earth. But most Americans know very little for certain except that whatever works for me is valid, and whatever works for you probably is, too. There are few rules, this mentality holds, that apply at all times in all situations. What may be true for you may not be true for me. What may be true for me now might not be true for me later. Therefore, it is important not to judge others too harshly, because we are all pursuing our own horizons. Americans are inclined, as Henry Adams observed, to relax severity.

The sociologist Alan Wolfe has called this nonjudgmental state of mind moral freedom, because we are each free to choose our own ideas and virtues as we see fit, and we hope to be tolerant toward those who have chosen differently. Others have been alarmed by this state of belief and its radical openness.

Such a mentality puts incredible pressure on the individual. All belief is challenged by ambiguity and impermanence. Everything is provisional and instrumental. The future-minded person must perpetually be advancing, because the bridge under his or her feet evaporates as the phases of life and the needs of the moment come to an end. It is necessary to move on to the next stage or lose the presence of hope, which is life itself.

Moreover, the future-minded person is discouraged from crashing his progress on the rocks of principle. On the contrary, he is encouraged to be a little fuzzy in his principles for the sake of perpetual advancement. He is not likely to be unprincipled, exactly, just flexible. Hope is a lawyer, not a martyr.

America Is the Solution

So hope instigates, but it also lures. It arouses the most amazing energies, but it produces its own set of awful temptations. More than in most places, American life is an obstacle course demanding relentless energy and work. Whitman was right when he wrote in "Democratic Vistas" that political democracy, as it exists in America, and "with all its threatening evils," nonetheless "supplies a training school for making first class men. It is life's gymnasium, not of good only, but of all." Life in the United States is so demanding and so full of possibility that the best Americans—and by this he meant regular middle-class Americans—become "freedom's athletes." They attain "the experiences of the fight, the hardening of the long campaign," and they come to throb with the currents of their expectations. America strives to be a powerful nation so that it can bring about the full flowering of individuals.

Writing after the Civil War, Whitman lamented the materialism and crassness all about him. "Never was there, perhaps, more hollowness at heart than at present, and here in the United States. Genuine belief seems to have left us," he wrote in one dark mood. Yet no matter how disgusting his neighbors appeared superficially, he always saw down to their nobility. "Shams, etc., will always be the show, like ocean's scum," but the American people are "the peaceablest and most good-natured race in the world, and the most personally independent and intelligent."

Americans are reliable in emergencies, he continued, and possess "a certain breadth of historic grandeur, of peace and war" surpassing the citizenry of any other great nation. The behavior of the average American during the Civil War, he added, proved beyond all doubt "that popular democracy, whatever its faults and dangers, practically justifies itself beyond the proudest claims and wildest hopes of its enthusiasts."

Whitman understood that whatever the nation's problems, America, and the idealism present in that word, are the solution. America is the solution to bourgeois flatness, to materialistic complacency, to mass-media shallowness, because America, with all its utopian possibilities, arouses the energies and the most strenuous efforts. America is the answer to insularity, to balkanization, to complacency, to timidity, because America is a set of compulsions pulling people out of their narrow and trivial concerns and lifting their sights to the distant hopes.

For the past century, radicals, intellectuals, artists, revolutionaries, and dissidents have assumed that the way to see truth, to realize their highest selves, and to promote social change is to rebel against the supposed complacency of middle-American life. But those rebels only managed to send themselves off into a cul-de-sac of alienation, and they find themselves repeating the same stale gestures as their fathers and grandmothers and great-grandfathers and great-great-grandmothers. They failed to see what Whitman saw, that America is the permanent revolution, that deep in middle-American life, even in the most placid-seeming suburb, there is an unquenchable longing and hope, and it is in committing to far-off dreams that we fight the insularity and the trivialization that threaten to swallow us up every day.

Whitman, too, was gripped by the possibility before him, and before his nation. "It seems as if the Almighty had spread before this nation charts of imperial destinies, dazzling as the sun," he wrote. America will someday, he forecast, be "the empire of empires . . . making a new history, a history of democracy, making old history a dwarf . . . inaugurating largeness, culminating time."

Even in his darkest mood, Whitman radiated a spirit of radical optimism and inspired hopefulness. "Far far indeed, stretch, in distance, our Vistas," he sang. "Thus we presume to write, as it were, upon things that exist not, and travel by maps yet unmade, and a blank. But the throes of birth are upon us."

Today we wear different clothing. We live in different sorts of houses. We work at different sorts of jobs and buy different sorts of appliances. In these pages, I have described aspects of everyday American life that are tawdry, inspiring, and comic. But I think for all his overblown rhetoric, Whitman was still essentially right. America is not a perfect country. It is often an embarrassing country. But it is a great country, and it is greatly different from other countries. It is infused with a utopian fire that redeems its people, despite the crass and cynical realities.

At the start of this book, I asked, What motivates Americans to work so hard and move about so feverishly? We are motivated by the Paradise Spell, by the feeling that there is some glorious destiny just ahead. Then I asked if we are as shallow as we look. No, we are not. We are an imaginative people, a dreaming people. Middle Americans may not be contemplative or dark and brooding. We may not be rooted in a deep and mysterious past. But we do have our heads in a vast and complicated future, and that gives the American mind a dimension that is not easily understood or dismissed. In Saul Bellow's novel *The Adventures of Augie March,* one of the characters says to Augie, "You have a nobility syndrome. You can't adjust to the reality situation."

That's a pretty good description of life as we see it around us today. Americans have a nobility syndrome. We have trouble adjusting to the reality situation.

Bibliographical Essay

I really should dedicate this book to CVS, Walgreens, and Eckerd. In the stationery sections of those drugstores, they always sell these three-by-five-inch memo pads, often produced by the Mead Company in Dayton, Ohio, or the Carolina Pad Company of Charlotte, North Carolina. I would fly somewhere, stop in at a drugstore, buy a dozen of these pads, and then go out and take notes on how people live.

I spent many days in big-box malls, in housing developments, and on college campuses, watching ordinary behavior. When I conducted interviews, I found that people are really good at describing certain things about their lives, but they are generally not good at seeing broad patterns. They do not think sociologically, because they don't walk around with notepads in their hands. The pads are like little barriers that force you to see everyday life from the outside. They encourage a certain sort of observation.

Of course, observation has to be backed up by data, so that you know your impressions are not wildly unrepresentative. I've benefited enormously from the work of demographers such as William Frey and Robert Lang. I've become a fanatical devotee of the magazine *American Demographics,* which packs its pages with reliable statistics about everyday American life. I make weekly visits to the website of the University of Michigan's Institute of Social Research. I've learned a lot at conferences sponsored by the Urban Land Institute and the International Council of Shopping Centers. I've tried to use the data supplied by such individuals, magazines, and organizations to buttress my firsthand reporting. In many cases, data from different sources conflict—for example, on how much homework the average student actually does. In those cases I've tried to use the safest, least controversial findings, but there is no way to please everybody.

For broader historical perspective, I dove in to the vast literature on the American character. As always, I found that some of the most provocative books were written during the 1950s and 1960s, the golden age of American nonfiction. If I were teaching a course on this subject, I would assign David M. Potter's *People of Plenty,* R.W.B. Lewis's *The American Adam,* Arthur K. Moore's *The Frontier Mind,* Louis Hartz's *The Liberal Tradition in America,* William R. Taylor's *Cavalier & Yankee,* and Henry Steele Commager's *The American Mind.*

There are other, more recent authors I would put on my reading list. Seymour Martin Lipset has explored American exceptionalism as exhaustively as anyone. Sacvan Bercovitch has commented brilliantly on the ideas that animate this country, especially in *The Puritan Origins of the American Self.* Alan Wolfe has contributed a series of superb books on American moral belief. Michael Kammen has written beautifully on the texture of American life, especially in *People of Paradox*. John Harmon McElroy's *American Beliefs* accomplishes the impossible task of capturing the entire national mind-set without dissolving into vague generalities. I have done very little primary historical research. I have relied upon the quotations and observations found in these and other similar books to guide me as I tried to make sense of contemporary culture.

Finally, I'd like to take the opportunity to recommend a few more books that I enjoyed reading while working on this one: Jürgen Moltmann's *Theology of Hope*, Reinhold Niebuhr's *The Irony of American History*, Wilfred M. McClay's *The Masterless*, Luigi Barzini's *The Europeans*, Gregg Easterbrook's *The Progress Paradox*, Leszek Kolakowski's *The Presence of Myth*, and Colin Campbell's *The Romantic Ethic and the Spirit of Modern Consumerism*. Put all those books together, and you've got a great, if demanding, summer reading list.

Acknowledgments

Some parts of this book grew out of reporting I did for *The Atlantic Monthly, The Weekly Standard,* and *The New York Times Magazine.* Therefore, I'd like to thank David Bradley, Cullen Murphy, Amy Meeker, and the late Michael Kelly from the *Atlantic*; Bill Kristol, Fred Barnes, Richard Starr, and Claudia Winkler from the *Standard*; and Dean Robinson, Hugo Lindgren, and others from the *Times Magazine.*

I'd also like to thank my parents, Lois and Michael Brooks, for reading and commenting on the manuscript; Erich Eichman for his wise advice; Glen Hartley and Lynn Chu, my agents; Reihan Salam for his careful reading; and my editor, Alice Mayhew, for her thoughts and suggestions.

Finally, props go out to my wife, Jane, whose design for our new house made this book necessary. Just kidding.

Index

About the Author

DAVID BROOKS is a political journalist and "comic sociologist" who writes a biweekly Op-Ed column for *The New
York Times.* He appears regularly on PBS's *The NewsHour
with Jim Lehrer* and NPR's *All Things Considered.* Formerly
a senior editor at *The Weekly Standard,* he has also written
for *The Atlantic Monthly, Newsweek, Reader's Digest,
Men's Health,* and other publications. He lives in Bethesda,
Maryland.